The Theory of Price

THE THEORY OF PRICE

third edition

George J. Stigler

The University of Chicago

The Macmillan Company
Collier-Macmillan Limited, London

Ninth Printing, 1971

Earlier editions copyright 1942, 1946, 1952
by The Macmillan Company.

Library of Congress catalog card number: 66-19406

THE MACMILLAN COMPANY
866 THIRD AVENUE, NEW YORK, NEW YORK 10022
COLLIER-MACMILLAN CANADA, LTD., TORONTO, ONTARIO

Printed in the United States of America

Preface

Not only a man's ideas, but also his ways of expressing them, have a strong persistence over time, so it is possible for the statisticians to determine disputed authorship (as in the case of the *Federalist Papers*) by the pattern of words and the structure of sentences. I have rewritten the present edition almost completely, but I have no doubt that it is the same book, and by only a slightly different author. Its distinguishing feature continues to be its concentration upon the traditional central core of economic theory—the theory of value. I thank Sam Peltzman for helpful suggestions, Julius Schlotthauer and Richard West for doing much of the graphical work, and Claire Friedland for her assistance at every turn.

G. J. S.

Contents

viii

The Theory of Price

chapter one

Introduction to Economic Analysis

A THEORY

Suppose a person wishes to buy a new automobile, and has decided upon the make, the body style, and the accessories that he desires. If now, in an excess of diligence, the buyer higgled with every dealer in a large city, he would encounter a considerable array of prices. In one such experiment in Chicago, thirty dealers offered prices for an identical automobile ranging from $2,350 to $2,515, with an average price of $2,436. Obviously the buyer would purchase at the lowest price, if the services of dealers were identical.

But this buyer was atypical and foolish. That he was atypical is a statement of fact, easier to believe than to prove. That he was foolish is an economic-statistical proposition: if shopping for low prices is not a sheer pleasure, the buyer will soon find that the probable savings from searching further do not compensate for the cost. To visit only thirty dealers requires at least two or three days; if we had chosen a hardware staple the number of dealers would have been in the hundreds and a full canvass would have required several weeks.

So the costs of semiexhaustive search (what of the suburbs?) would be high. The returns would show "diminishing returns"—the lowest price the buyer found would fall more slowly as he expanded the number of dealers canvassed. This is the statistical proposition, which need not be proved here, and is in any case plausible: as one canvasses additional dealers, the lowest price he finds will on average fall but each additional dealer is more likely to quote a higher price than the lowest price already encountered.

1

This is simple common sense, which the economist translates into the language:

> To maximize his utility, the buyer searches for additional prices until the expected saving from the purchase equals the cost of visiting one more dealer. Then he stops searching, and buys from the dealer who quotes the lowest price he has encountered.

That this rule maximizes utility may be shown, the economist says, by considering its failure. If the canvass of an additional seller will save more (on average) than the cost of the canvass, the buyer gains by making the search. Contrariwise, if the cost of a search exceeds the prospective gain, the buyer would gain by searching less. And here the trouble begins—for the noneconomist.

For, first of all, where did maximizing utility come from? The answer, which is that it came from experience with similar problems, will not satisfy a noneconomist. He will say that people typically do not maximize anything—that the consumer is lazy or dominated by advertisers or poor at arithmetic. And indeed there are consumers who not only suffer from these disabilities but are also downright confused. Why attribute to them the cold-blooded, logical approach of a well-built modern computer?

Second, what precisely is the cost of canvassing one more seller? All one had to do is drive over to another dealer and talk to him for a few minutes. How can a monetary value be placed upon these actions—which are pleasant for some people and distasteful to others?

Finally, does not the economist merely say, in language that is rather pretentious (when he does not use formidable mathematical symbols), that the buyer will visit as many dealers as he visits—no more, no less? The rule does not say whether he visits one or every seller.

This is a wholly typical economic theory and a wholly typical reaction to it. Since economics is still taught, we economists must have replies to these criticisms which we think are adequate. What are they? The basic reply, which is directed chiefly to the third complaint (that the theory merely says people do what they do), is that that the theory does more than this: it enables us to predict how consumers (and markets) will behave. Consider again the proposition:

To maximize his utility, the buyer searches for additional prices until the expected saving from the purchase equals the cost of visiting one more dealer. Then he stops searching, and buys from the dealer who quotes the lowest price he has encountered.

The cost of searching out one more price varies—it will be more with higgling than without, for example. But it will vary much less among commodities than the gain from a 1 per cent saving in price varies among commodities. On an automobile, 1 per cent is perhaps $25; on a washing machine 1 per cent is perhaps $2. So any person, the theory predicts, will search more for low prices when buying an automobile than when buying a washing machine. A person who enjoys shopping may visit 10 automobile dealers and three appliance stores; one who does not may visit three automobile dealers and one appliance store—but in each case the consumer will search longer before buying the automobile. This is a testable implication, and if the facts contradict the prediction, the theory underlying the proposition is wrong.

Again, since buyers will search more for low prices on commodities which take more of their income, any seller who quotes a price that is high relative to other sellers' prices will sell little—most buyers will search on to find a lower price. So the theory predicts that the range of prices of washing machines quoted in a city's retail outlets will vary more (relative to their average) than the prices of automobiles. This too is testable—and much less obvious than the first prediction.

Suppose we make the tests and find that the predictions of the theory are right. Then clearly the other two objections which were raised also lose their force. The consumer has indeed been acting "rationally"—which is another way of saying that he has been maximizing utility. (The reasons for introducing utility will be discussed in Chapter 4.) No doubt some silly people have even paid the higher price after canvassing two sellers, but the dominant tendency must have been to search to a degree governed by costs and expected returns, and act sensibly on the information, or the tests would not have been passed. The consumer must have been able to attach a workable meaning to costs, or the predictions would have been contradicted: the dispersion among sellers on prices of commodities like washing machines would have been as small as for automobiles.

Let us now actually test the theory. The standard statistical measure of relative dispersion is the coefficient of variation: the standard deviation of a group of observations divided by the average of the observations. One illustrative but real set of data for the second test may be given:

COMMODITY	AVERAGE PRICE	COEFFICIENT OF VARIATION
Automobile	$2,436.00	1.72%
Automatic Washing Machine	223.45	3.42

One other objection to this theory, of the many that can be contrived, now deserves notice. It may be said, that the facts were already known and all the economist has done is make out a fancy explanation for them. The answers are various. This objection is not factually correct: the theory was contrived first and the facts then sought. But it is not necessary for the reader (economist or non-economist) to decide whether I am telling the truth.[1] The real reply is that there are infinitely many sets of data that can be used to test the predictions. The reader can go out in his city and collect prices of automobiles and washing machines or (since this general theory applies to all homogeneous goods) prices of refrigerators and paring knives. There are many other testable predictions of the theory. So a competent scientist need not, and should not, accept theories (whether economic or physical) on faith.

And anyway, although a fancy theory is not so good as a simple one (more things can go wrong with the fancy one), a fancy theory is better than none. Let the reader try to contrive an alternative explanation of the fact that prices of washing machines vary relatively more than prices of automobiles. He may come up with a rule such as: the more expensive the commodity, the less its price varies, that seems to fit our facts—in fact it makes the same prediction. But quite aside from the fact that it has no logical basis, it will be wrong: the price of sugar varies much less than that of tea, although sugar costs less per pound. This is *not* a contradiction of our theory, which in a fuller version says that the aggregate amount spent on a commodity governs the amount of search.[2]

---

[1] The data are from two articles by Allen F. Jung, *Journal of Business* (October 1958 and January 1960).

[2] And also, in this fuller version, tells us over what time period the purchases should be added. See my "The Economics of Information," *Journal of Political Economy* (June 1961).

SCIENCE AS FICTION

A useful general rule, which is all that a scientific theory is, has two properties. First, it ought to be more or less true. Second, it ought to apply to a fairly large number of possible events. Most of the anguish that people have with scientific theories arises because these two conditions are moderately incompatible.

It is easy to make up empirically valid rules: for example, the Dow-Jones average always falls on January 25, 1960. It is even easier for a trained person to make up broad rules: for example, business declines always begin in odd-numbered years.[3] The combination of the two characteristics is more difficult to achieve.

Indeed the combination is, on a strict view, impossible. Every event, every situation to which a theory can be applied, must differ in a thousand respects from every other. Consider our proposition that consumers canvass more sellers for a lower price when their expenditures on the commodity are larger. Does this apply literally to an invalid, or to a man who wishes to buy something the morning after a 30-in. snowfall? Does it apply literally to the man who gets things "wholesale" from his brother-in-law, or to the young man and young lady who urgently seek the services of a justice of the peace? Or does it apply *equally* to the millionaire and the pauper seeking a cup of coffee or to the same man whether buying a meal on his own or on an expense account? Or to postage stamps?

Clearly a general theory must ignore a thousand detailed variations or it cannot possibly be general. Yet only general theories are useful. In fact general theories are the only useful theories even if they are to be used only once. Suppose, to use a reprehensible example, I embezzle a fortune with which I shall (1) engage in a bold speculation and (2) prosper and reimburse the bank or (3) spend my declining years in custody. I wish a theory of capital gains, whether from horse racing or roulette or futures in soybeans. If the "theory" I act on says only that soybean futures rise next week, there is no possible way to test its reliability in advance. But if the theory says that a particular inventory level relative to sales leads to a price rise, I can test it against a dozen previous instances and get some idea of its reliability.

[3] Such as 1837, 1873, 1907, 1929, 1937, and 1960.

For the scientist seeking to construct or improve a theory, this fact that theories cannot be "realistic" in the sense of being descriptive, is a source of endless charm and frustration. It inevitably poses the question: what common trait in the phenomena should be incorporated in the theory? Should we, to revert to the search for low prices, emphasize the nationality of consumers, their possession of automobiles, their years of formal education or—as we did—the amount they spend on the commodity?

The user of a theory has a simpler task: his is not to reason why, his is but to sigh and try. If the right element in the diverse situations has been isolated, the theory will work: it will yield predictions better than those which can be reached with any alternative theory.

Suppose the alternative theory is very poor: it may be, for example, that the amount of search for lower prices is a random event, normally distributed, and that it yields predictions which have hardly any relevance to the facts?[4] The answer is that it takes a theory to beat a theory: if there is a theory that is right 51 per cent of the time, it will be used until a better one comes along. (Theories that are right only 50 per cent of the time are less economical than coin-flipping.)

When we assume that consumers, acting with mathematical consistency, maximize utility, therefore, it is not proper to complain that men are much more complicated and diverse than that. So they are, but if this assumption yields a theory of behavior which agrees tolerably well with the facts, it must be used until a better theory comes along.

Economic theories are infinitely diverse in their predictive power. Entirely too many have zero predictive power—they are statements of tautologies. Thus, the statement that to maximize profits one should operate a firm where marginal revenue equals marginal cost is a mere mathematical theorem. Some theories have negative power: they predict the opposite of what happens (and then become useful in the hands of a sophisticated user). Thus the statement of a chancellor of the exchequer that the nation will never devalue the currency is a traditional prelude to devaluation. At the other

---

[4] Such simple alternatives—another is that whatever happened last time will happen next time—are called "naive" models, a terminology due to Milton Friedman.

extreme, the simple rule that people buy more of a thing at a lower than at a higher price is (properly used) a completely universal truth. The essence of scientific progress is to edge up this ladder from ignorance to knowledge, and it is complicated by the fact that the ladder keeps getting longer!

SOME APOLOGIES

The goal of the economist is not merely to train a new generation in his arcane mystery: it is to understand this economic world in which we live and the other ones which a million reformers of every description are imploring and haranguing us to adopt. This is an important and honorable goal.

It is not an easy goal, however, nor one which is now or ever will be fully achieved. A modern economic system is of extraordinary complexity. Imagine a three dimensional jig-saw puzzle, consisting of roughly 100 million parts. Some parts touch against, let us say, 1,000 other parts. (That is, each family deals with that many employers, banks, retail stores, domestic servants, and so on.) Other parts touch, let us be conservative, 50,000 other parts. (Firms that sell to retailers and buy from other firms and hire laborers, and so on.) It would be enough of a task to fit these 100 million pieces together, but the real difficulties have yet to be mentioned. The pieces change shape quite often—a family has twins, a firm does the next best thing and invents a new product. The economist has the interesting task of predicting (in the aggregate) each of these movements. Meanwhile a busy set of people—congressmen, members of regulatory bodies, central bankers, and the like—are changing the rules on who the jig-saw pieces will be and how they are shaped. And of course there are other jig-saw puzzles of comparable complexity, and these other puzzles (foreign economies) are connected at literally a million points with our puzzle.

This analogy is imperfect in many ways—for example, it suggests the fitting together of units of economic life when in fact it is the working together of parts (some sort of gigantic set of gears) that would be more appropriate. Its biggest deficiency is that it does not portray the fact that a change in the relation between two pieces will affect other pieces which touch neither of them: thus a change in wage rates in the steel industry will affect (through a variety of economic relationships) the output of crude petroleum. Yet even with its deficiencies it may convey some sense of the complexity of a modern economic system.

The economist, and his brethern in the social sciences, have a second level of difficulty not shared by the physical sciences. Our main elements of analysis are people, and people who are influenced by the practices and policies we analyze. Imagine the problems of a chemist if he had to deal with molecules of oxygen, each of which was somewhat interested in whether it was joined in chemical bond to hydrogen. Some would hurry him along; others would cry shrilly for a federal program to drill wells for water instead; and several would blandly assure him that they were molecules of argon. And this chemist, who in analogy would also be a chemical element, could never be absolutely certain that he was treating other elements fairly. Several elements would hire their own chemists to protect their interests. We economists have always had the advantages and disadvantages of this lively participation by our "units of analysis."

It requires no special apologies, therefore, that many important economic phenomena cannot be explained, or explained only imperfectly. In this respect all sciences are alike. That some important and pervasive phenomena can be understood is sufficient justification for the set of theories and techniques which comprise modern economic analysis.

To a much greater degree than the other social sciences, economics has developed a formal and abstract and coherent·corpus of theory. The standards of both logical precision and empirical evidence are steadily rising. Splendid as this trend is, it makes life no easier for the writer of a textbook. Adam Smith, the founder of the science, could (in his *Wealth of Nations*) write in these words about the immense increase in output achieved through division of labor in Western societies:

if we examine, I say, all these things, and consider what a variety of labour is employed about each of them, we shall be sensible that without the assistance and co-operation of many thousands, the very meanest person in a civilized country could not be provided, even according to, what we very falsely imagine, the easy and simple manner in which he is commonly accommodated. Compared, indeed, with the more extravagant luxury of the great, his accommodation must no doubt appear extremely simple and easy; and yet it may be true, perhaps, that the accommodation of a European prince does not always so much exceed that of an industrious and frugal peasant, as the accommodation of the latter exceeds that of many an African king, the absolute master of the lives and liberties of ten thousand naked savages.

A modern economist who hopes to maintain the respect of his colleagues will rewrite this:

The difference between the mean income of Habsburg males (1871–1917), not counting uniforms, and the mean income (after taxes) of farmers owning an equity of at least 10 per cent in a farm with no more than 12 hectares (11 in Bavaria), excluding dairy farmers, in 1907–15 was $1,800 (in 1914 dollars). The income of African tribal leaders, using the mean of Paasche and Laspeyres indexes (which diverge enormously) fell short of that of the farmers (in 1904–10) by $2,400 (but only $1,400 if we use Kuznets' estimate of the value of a second wife) in 1914 prices. The difference between the means of $1,800 and $2,400 is significant at the 3 per cent level. Incidentally, a tribal leader had an average of 10,000 ($\pm$721) members of the tribe in 1908, and they were clothed only by an average of 6.2 sq. in. of cotton bagging. [14 footnotes omitted.]

I will not say, and you would not believe, that this change is an unmixed blessing. It is an advance from the scientific viewpoint, however, and the example itself will serve to show this. My own version is pure fiction, but as soon as one starts to think of numbers it is obvious that Smith's statement was wrong. The income of a peasant family in Europe in 1776 (when Smith wrote) was surely less than (say) $500 of present-day dollars, and that of an African king was surely not less than zero; so Smith is asserting that princes had incomes less than $1,000. Even nonstatistical evidence sheds lavish doubt on this.[5]

[5] The following quotations—from W. H. Bruford, *Germany in the Eighteenth Century* (Cambridge, England: The University Press, 1935)—may serve:
On peasants he quotes several contemporaries: "The fields and the livestock provided the necessary food and clothing. . . . Women spun wool into coarse cloth; men tanned their own leather. Wealth only existed in its simplest forms. . . . From morning till night [the peasant] must be digging the fields, whether scorched by the sun or numbed by the cold. . . . The traveller comes to villages where children run about half-naked and call to every passer-by for alms. Their parents have scarcely a rag on their backs. . . . Their barns are empty and their cottages threaten to collapse in a heap any moment." (pp. 118–21)
One noble will do: "Graf Flemming, for instance, Generalfeldmarschall under Augustus the Strong, the soldier and diplomat who secured for his master the throne of Poland, . . . had [in 1722] about a hundred domestics

The corresponding illustration of the need for formal analytical methods to ensure reaching correct conclusions will be illustrated at many points in subsequent chapters. Here let us give a century-old statement of a theory that is still very popular:

> For the most part, [employers] so far accept the principle of "live and let live" as to be willing that their labourers should have any wages that will not sensibly encroach on their own profit. In fact, it is of little consequence to them how high the wages of labour may be, provided the price of the produce of labour be proportionably high. But if among many liberal employers there be one single niggard, the niggardliness of that single one may suffice to neutralise the liberality of all the rest. If one single employer succeed in screwing down wages below the rate previously current, his fellow-employers may have no alternative but to follow suit, or to see themselves undersold in the produce market.[6]

The first sentence is merely cruel, the second sentence is wrong, and the third and fourth are grossly fallacious. Yet ask a person untrained in economics what the merits of these views are, and he will usually be unable to arrive at any persuasive judgment. At a later point we shall analyse the fallacy with the assistance of fairly elementary analytical techniques.

Some frequently-employed quantitative concepts and relationships in economic analysis are presented in Appendix A; mastery of this material is a wise investment.

---

of different grades. There were twenty-three 'superiores,' from an Oberhofmeister, secretaries and tutors down to an equerry responsible for ninety-two horses; and over seventy 'inferiores,' from the five pages and a 'Polish gentleman' who played the Bandor and waited at table, the eight musicians and their Italian leader, ... The count's salaries and wages bill came to 13,534 Thalers a year [say $60,000]. The appointments of the count's palaces were correspondingly magnificent; he lived on a scale that would make the life of a Hollywood millionaire look tawdry." (pp. 77–78)

[6] W. T. Thornton, *On Labour* (London: Macmillan, 1868), p. 81.

chapter two

The Tasks of an Economic System

The list of things that one can "demand" of an economic system is limited only by the human imagination, itself a fairly outrageous thing. Madmen and/or reformers have insisted that the economy must produce quite impossible things, such as more than the average amount of housing for everyone. Even calm men, well-acquainted with the laws of arithmetic, have assigned tasks which are adequately diverse. Some wish the economy to elevate the tastes of consumers—drawing them away from comic books toward conic sections, from gadgets (mechanical devices not worth their price to the speaker) toward symphony orchestras (which produce music worth less than its cost, and hence is almost everywhere subsidized). Others, again, wish the economy to foster political values: such estimable entities as Thomas Jefferson and modern Switzerland have believed that an independent agricultural class would be the mainstay of a stable democratic system.[1]

Ambitious views of the role of the economic system are based upon a sound, although often an exaggerated, instinct. An economic system assuredly influences much of what people call "non-economic" aspects of life. For example, the systems of reward for personal efforts will surely influence the kinds of education that the population desires and receives. When one pauses to realize that well over half the waking hours of mankind have been devoted to earning a livelihood—the fraction fell below a half in the United

[1] Karl Marx carried this approach to the extreme of asserting that an economic system had within it a set of forces which irresistibly transformed all society. His peculiar limitation on this view—that only one more transformation would take place (to communism)—changed the view from a hypothesis into propaganda.

States only in this century—it is obvious that the economic side of life cannot be separated cleanly from the political, cultural, and other sides of life.

And equally, almost every widely held view in "noneconomic" areas leaves its traces on economic life. In the United States the output of playing cards was reduced by a heavy federal excise tax, because card playing has been considered frivolous if not immoral. The output of newspapers on the other hand, is increased by heavily subsidized postal rates on the ground the newspapers are necessary to an informed citizenry. A study of activities which are tax exempt, or of occupations and industries which are given preferential treatment under wartime conscription, would reveal a whole range of such opinions and effects.

We shall not discuss the tasks of an economic system in terms so broad as these. These wider tasks vary greatly from time to time and place to place, but one, more narrowly defined set of tasks is intrinsic to any and every economic system. These intrinsic tasks are fundamentally four: (1) fixing the composition of output; (2) allocation of resources; (3) distribution of the product; and (4) growth.

FIXING THE COMPOSITION OF OUTPUT

An economic system has at its disposal a set of resources—labor, natural resources, and capital. These resources can always be used to produce a variety of products—even a primitive agricultural community can choose between more meat or more grain, more food or more lumber, more housing or more wars. In a modern society, the advances of technology have created an almost unlimited number of different commodities and services, and they can be produced in a literally unlimited number of proportions.

The first task of every economic system is therefore to establish the composition of output. A noneconomist often says, of such problems, that the "priorities" must be established, implying that the most important things be ascertained and produced, then the next most important things be produced, and so forth until either the resources are incapable of producing more, or—inconceivable state—everyone is sated. The language of priorities has the merit of emphasizing the fact that values (estimates of importance or desirability) have to be attached to various outputs, but it has the defect of grossly simplifying the task.

If I were to try to construct a scale of priorities of categories of consumer goods to which most of mankind (or at least my dearest friends) would subscribe, it might begin confidently something like this:

I. Food—to keep alive
II. Shelter and clothing (in cold climates)—to keep alive
III. Medical care—to keep alive
IV. Police protection—to keep alive
V. Education—to keep teachers alive

and then stop suddenly. Long before I had to face the problem of whether an air conditioner was more or less important than attractive furniture or an automobile, I would have to recognize the deep ambiguity in what I had already written. Food certainly has a primacy in survival under ordinary conditions, and most men esteem survival, but even the most gluttinous men would prefer some clothing and shelter, on a —10° F day, to a twentieth helping of potato dumplings. And so it goes through the list: medical care sounds very basic and important, but do men really think that a family with funds just sufficient to straighten a boy's teeth or send him to college should always choose the former alternative?

So the fixing of the composition of output amounts to much more than simply giving priority numbers to various categories of goods. It involves the much greater task of deciding how each increment of output should be composed. In effect one must approach the problem this way: assume that we can produce a total of outputs somewhere about $500 billion.[2] How should the first billion of output be composed, then the second, and so forth to the 500th. The first billion will be dominated by food; the 500th billion will—if we use numbers appropriate to the United States—contain less than $200 million of food.

Who fixed the composition of output? In our society, where men are relatively free to choose their own goods, and the productive system responds to these choices, it is done by the individual con-

---

[2] How diverse kinds of output are added together to obtain a single number is discussed much later.

sumer (household). A man indicates, by the price (amount of money) he offers for a good, the importance he attaches to another unit of the good. If he offers $15 for a pair of shoes, and $10 for a hat, he indicates that he believes a pair of shoes is 1.5 times as important as a hat. Obviously how much he will offer to pay for a unit of a commodity (a subject we investigate in Chapters 3 and 4) depends, among other things, on how many units of each commodity he already possesses. This system is usually described as one of consumer sovereignty, and if one does not read into the phrase the extreme view that the consumer is uninfluenced by tradition, social opinion, advertising, and the like, it is valid enough.

Our society does not rely exclusively on the preferences of individual consumers. In some areas the composition of output is fixed by political decisions: highways, schools, and police protection are examples. In still other areas the political system imposes limits on the choices of individuals, sometimes for reasons of public safety (guns), sometimes for reasons of distrust of the individual's competence to make wise decisions (the electrical wiring of houses, the sale of prescription drugs, and so on), sometimes to please important groups (the prohibition of certain activities on Sunday).

In other societies and other times this sort of political regulation of the composition of output has gone so much farther as to be almost a difference of kind. In a war economy there is much central direction of the composition of output: the production of automobiles and refrigerators is prohibited, and the outputs of many goods are limited and allocated by rationing. In a dictatorial society the extent of control over the composition of consumers' goods can be highly variable: it will always prohibit some commodities (for example, books highly critical of the regime) but often influence the composition of others by taxes, output quotas, and the like.

THE ALLOCATION OF RESOURCES

Once a set of values have been placed on various outputs, it is necessary to organize production so that proper proportions of these outputs, and not other goods or wrong amounts of the desired goods, will be produced. This might appear to be a task simple enough to be assigned to technicians: why not ascertain the quantities of each resource necessary to produce a unit of each kind of product, and then allocate enough of each resource to the making of each product?

This delegation to technicians would indeed be possible, but it would not be wise. The task of production also depends upon values: there are generally many ways in which to produce a commodity: one can vary the raw materials; use different qualities of labor; use different kinds and amounts of machinery; locate the plant in a thousand places; and so forth. The methods of production that an engineer might consider most "efficient" would probably leave large amounts of certain types of resources unemployed—and therefore lead to a smaller output of commodities than could otherwise be achieved. The choice of production methods must take account of the importance of the inputs as well as that of the finished goods.

In addition the task of production consists of more than simply producing an assigned schedule of goods. Outputs of agricultural products vary with the weather—how big an allowance for safety should be made by having extra stocks? Demands for goods fluctuate because of chance events—for example the replacement demands created by tornados and earthquakes are not easily predicted.

We have tacitly assumed that the desired outputs are highly stable, aside from chance fluctuations. But what if consumers may change their preferences next month?—then what should be produced? Or suppose the methods of production are changing rapidly under the impact of advancing technological knowledge—should we build the plant today or wait a year for a better one, or ten years for a still better one? The impact of uncertainty on production is not a matter of technology alone; it involves costs and returns.

Finally, production consists of much more than turning iron ore into automobile engines. It consists of retailing and servicing goods—together as large a part of our economy as production. It consists of supplying opera singers, and ski instructors and their staffs of orthopedic surgeons. It involves the sales of securities, the collection of debts, and the investigation of foreign markets.

All the resources cannot be treated as tools. Labor is much the most important resource in all economies, and men have preferences as workers as well as consumers. One may prefer regular hours of work, another may prefer irregular hours, one urban life, another rural life. If these preferences are to be taken into account, the allocation of resources is complicated further.

How can we get the task of production done efficiently? Since production involves judgments on innumerable details (should Joe or Henry become foreman?), and rests on many predictions of the future, it is not easy to contrive a good scale on which to judge the efficiency of a productive system. Yet such a scale is necessary: men are often lazy; stupid men are often unaware of this fact; nepotism is a not uncommon problem; and so on. So the task of getting production done efficiently is not an easy one.

In our society, the basic method of organizing production is through the price system. Just as prices register the desires of consumers, so they register the desires of workers. If men prefer to work in a small town, wages will be less there and employers will tend to move to small towns. If a given set of technologies leave some resources unemployed, their prices will fall and it will become cheaper to use production methods that use relatively more of these resources. If there is a chance, say 1 in 10, that a crop failure will drive up the price of oranges, some men will hold inventories of canned or frozen orange juice in hopes of realizing the higher prices. The incentives and penalties attaching to the direction of productive enterprises take the form chiefly of profits—both negative and positive—which are calculated to weed out the less efficient and increase the area of activity of the more efficient.

Our society does not rely exclusively on private efforts directed by prices to organize production. Quite aside from providing a legal framework (contract, property, methods of settling disputes), there are many social restraints on production processes. Since a monopoly is free of the restraints imposed by competitors, there are antitrust laws and public utility regulatory bodies. Some kinds of production processes are forbidden and others regulated for reasons of safety. A simple example is the examination of the health and competence of airline pilots; the reader may find it interesting to examine why the owner of the plane is not believed to have adequate incentive to look after pilots' abilities. Only licensed persons may enter many trades and occupations in an interesting mosaic that includes elementary school teachers (but not college teachers) and electricians (but not physicists).

THE DISTRIBUTION OF THE PRODUCT

If George Bernard Shaw, the well-known Irish economist, had read this far, he would complain bitterly at the discussion of how the composition of output is determined in a private enterprise economy. "Consumer sovereignty" would have raised his volatile spirits—the sovereignty of rich consumers, he would have said, and he might have quoted his favorite author:

A New York lady, for instance, having a nature of exquisite sensibility, orders an elegant rosewood and silver coffin, upholstered in pink satin, for her dead dog. It is made: and meanwhile a live child is prowling barefooted and hunger-stunted in the frozen gutter outside.[3]

(Here is another instance of the benefit of the quantification of economics: parables, and counter parables,[4] are a very poor way to describe the distribution of income.)

It is a trifle too early in our work to judge the merits of Shaw's complaints on the distribution of income, either in 1889 (when the passage was written) or today. Assuredly the distribution of income is a major task of any economic system, and almost every major economic reform movement rests on a proposal to change whatever distribution is in existence.

But, important as the distribution of income is, the importance is probably less from its influence on the composition of output than from its importance in production and in ethical judgments of an economy. This heretical view rests on the fact—for it is a fact—that as a very crude rule, if one family has twice the income of another, it spends twice as much on every category of consumption. This is obviously untrue in detail: the richer family will not double its purchases of salt and will more than double its travel abroad. But if the crude rule is not pressed to the finest classifica-

[3] From Shaw's essay in *Fabian Essays* (London, 1950), p. 24.

[4] A counter-parable:
Dr. John Upright, the young physician, devoted every energy of his being to the curing of the illnesses of his patients. No hours were too long, no demand on his skill or sympathies too great, if a man or child could be helped. He received £2,000 net each year, until he died at the age of 41 from over-work. Dr. Henry Leisure, on the contrary, insisted that even patients with broken legs be brought to his office only on Tuesdays, Thurdays, and Fridays, between 12:30 and 3:30 P.M. He preferred to take three patients simultaneously, so he could advise while playing bridge, at which he cheated. He received £2,000 net each year, until he retired at the age of 84.

tion of expenditures, it has ample support. The percentage distribution of expenditures of families with high, low, and average incomes in 1950 is given in Table 2–1. The effect of income on expenditures is exaggerated because other conditions also vary with income: for example high income families had 4 persons on average, low income families 2.7 persons. Even so the general agreement between the three distributions is very pronounced.

Table 2–1
Percentage Distribution of Current Expenditures of
Urban Families of 2 or More Persons, 1950

CATEGORY	ALL FAMILIES	FAMILIES WITH INCOMES OF	
		$1,000–2,000	$7,500–10,000
Food	29.6	35.9	26.9
Alcoholic beverages	1.6	1.1	2.0
Tobacco	1.8	2.2	1.4
Housing	11.0	13.8	9.8
Fuel, light, refrigeration	4.2	6.7	3.4
Household operation	4.6	4.2	5.4
Furnishings and equipment	7.0	5.4	6.4
Clothing	11.6	8.9	13.6
Transportation			
Automobile	11.9	6.3	13.6
Other	1.7	1.8	2.0
Medical care	5.2	5.9	5.3
Personal care	2.2	2.4	2.1
Recreation	4.5	2.4	5.1
Reading	0.9	1.0	0.8
Education, formal	0.6	0.2	1.0
Other	1.5	1.8	1.3
TOTAL	99.9	100.0	100.1

The relevance of distribution to production, on the other hand, may be suggested by the fact that no thoroughly egalitarian society has ever been able to construct or maintain an efficient and progressive economic system. It has been universal experience that some system of differential rewards is necessary to stimulate workers. Communistic economies have even found it expedient to stimulate savings by individuals through rewards. At a much later point we shall examine the relationship of income distribution to the functional structure of production.

ECONOMIC GROWTH

J. B. Bury tells us, in his excellent *The Idea of Progress,* that throughout most of recorded history the idea of continuous and cumulative progress of mankind, whether in science or in social or economic life, was absent, and that only in the sixteenth century (and chiefly in Western Europe) did the idea begin to gain authority. We who live in an age when the idea of economic progress has reached the economically most primitive and rigid economies must therefore be reminded that the task of providing growth does not really belong in our list of functions intrinsic to economic life, and that most societies known to history have had economically unprogressive economies.

But intrinsic or not, it has become a major task demanded of all economies: they are required (as sovereigns use this word) to provide technological advances, capital accumulations, improved labor forces, and larger incomes. So strong is this demand, that sometimes a method by which western nations become richer—industrialization—is confused with the growth itself, and inappropriate industries that reduce a nation's income are adopted to increase it. And nations with unbroken histories of secular growth, such as the United States and Canada, now strive through a host of public policies to foster what was once a completely decentralized process.

The constituents of growth are basically two: increases in productive resources, and increases in the efficiency with which they are used. Both types of increase can be directed by a price system. The rewards for increasing the stocks of resources vary with the type of resource: higher earnings for better trained labor; dividends, interest, and capital gains for capital accumulation; large incomes for the discovery of new natural resources. The rewards for innovations are profits from a head start in a new trade or exclusive control for 17 years of a process by means of a patent (and control for 56 years by an author, through copyright). Such private rewards are supplemented by preferential tax treatment of research expenditures, subsidized exploration for minerals, and so forth.

There are many social problems involved in economic progress. Huge changes (which those unpleasantly affected call disruptions) are imposed on particular economic areas: the labor force on farms in the United States has fallen by almost half since 1910; the number of engineers has increased almost ten-fold in the same period. There are large tasks of informing consumers of new products, laborers of new employments, entrepreneurs of new technologies. The impact of rapid economic growth is felt in every part of social life; family size, political attitudes, foreign relations.

It is established practice in economics to postpone the analysis of the problem of growth until the analysis of the performance of the first three tasks has been completed for an unchanging (stationary) economy. The reason is simple: the problems of growth are vastly more complex and in any event require an understanding of the working of a stationary economy. We follow this practice, and the final chapters of this book take us to the threshold of theories of growth.

And now, on to the analysis.

chapter three

Consumer Behavior

We wish to explain the behavior of consumers, and one approach to this explanation would be to view the consumer (or household) as an enterprise. This enterprise obtains income from the sale of labor services or from hiring out capital and uses the income to purchase commodities and services which will efficiently serve the desires of the household. It would of course be bizarre to look upon the typical family—that complex mixture of love, convenience, and frustration—as a business enterprise. Therefore economists have devoted much skill and ingenuity to elaborating this approach, and we shall sketch it in the next chapter.

There are other approaches to the study of consumer behavior, but before we choose one it will be wise to ask what questions we wish to answer with our theory of consumer behavior. As economists, our questions are chiefly of two types:

First, will consumers initiate important changes in the economy spontaneously? If so, will these changes be sudden or gradual? If the consumer is an important source of economic change, naturally we should seek to discover the factors that explain changes in consumer behavior, whether they be in religion, political life, changing technology, or other "noneconomic" areas.

Second, how will consumers *respond* to changes in their incomes or in the prices of goods and services? Will their responses be stable and consistent, or volatile and inconsistent?

The answers to these questions are far from complete, but this chapter will summarize the ruling views of economists. One may say that consumers are generally viewed as passive adapters to the economy rather than as agents who induce changes in the behavior of the economy, at least in the time periods ordinarily considered. Thus even the large decline in average family size (a decline, which is at least partly a *response* to economic forces), which has led to large changes in housing and other areas, has been a slow and steady change. Consumers are not revolutionaries like business innovators, on this view. One would have more confidence in this position if it were not so widely held that it has never been thoroughly tested.

In their responses to price and income changes, consumers behave in a tolerably reliable and predictable way. They invariably obey one law as universal as any in social life; they buy less of a thing when its price rises. Their buying propensities are a stable function of prices and income, and we shall discuss these variables in turn.[1]

THE PRICE OF THE COMMODITY

The price of a product is simply the terms on which it can be acquired. The oldest and most basic rule of demand theory is that

---

[1] The modern economist has an almost irresistible urge to write this demand function in the language of mathematics, as

$$x = f(p_x, p_y, p_z, \ldots, R),$$

where x is the rate of purchase of X, p_x is the price of X, p_y, p_z, . . . are the prices of other consumer goods, and R is the consumer's money income. This expression states that if prices and incomes are fixed, then some rate of purchase of X is determined and that x responds in a stable way to changes in prices or income.

The symbolic statement of the demand function serves two purposes:

1. It is a forcible reminder that one cannot treat the effects of these determinants of consumer purchases as independent of one another. Suppose the price of X rises by 1 per cent: then the resulting decrease in quantity may be 2 per cent if income is $4,000, but 3 per cent if income is $8,000.

2. The notation helps us to distinguish two things that are often confused: a change in consumer purchases due to a change in prices or income, and a change in purchases due to a change in the demand function. Suppose a consumer buys more of X because its price has fallen (other things not changing)—in this case the demand function is unchanged. Alternatively, suppose he buys more (even at the same price) because he likes the commodity more—here a new demand function has appeared. If, to take the simplest case, he now will buy 20 per cent more at given prices and income, the function becomes

$$x = 1.2f(p_x, p_y, p_z, \ldots, R),$$

a new function.

people will not buy less, and usually buy more, of a commodity when its price falls.

Since the purchases of a commodity depend upon other factors as well as its price, we must specify these other factors, and we must hold them constant when the price of the commodity changes if the effect due only to the price change is to be isolated. The factors we shall hold constant are:

1. The prices of other commodities.
2. The money income of the buyer.
3. The tastes or preferences of the buyer.

Each of these other factors will be discussed below.[2]

The rule was stated that no one reduces the consumption of a commodity when its price falls, and this formulation is designed to take account of the fact that some commodities are indivisible. A family may still take only one copy of the newspaper when its price falls. Such indivisibilities offer no interesting difficulties, but it should be emphasized that they are uncommon. Continuous variation in quantity can be approached even for a lumpy good by one of several devices:

1. By using it only part of the time, say by rental or joint ownership.
2. By buying the item (say a haircut) with varying frequency.
3. By choosing a larger or smaller, or a more or less durable specimen. Very few goods come in only one size or quality.[3]

For a market as a whole, demand curves are continuous even if every individual's demand curve is discontinuous, providing (as is surely certain) that not every individual varies his purchases at the same critical price.

---

[2] Note that this is only one possible specification of the factors we hold constant. We might hold real income (to be defined later, but roughly an income yielding a constant amount of satisfaction) instead of money income constant, to get a different demand curve. Or we might hold the quantities rather than the prices of other commodities constant, to get another demand curve. Any well-defined demand curve can be used but the one described in the text is much the most common.

[3] This variation in quality does not yield a continuous demand curve for a given quality, of course. One must then talk of (for example) a quantity of automobile, measured (by means of prices) in terms of, say, a specified two-year old four-door sedan.

How can we convince a sceptic that this "law of demand" is really true of all consumers, all times, all commodities? Not by a few (4 or 4,000) selected examples, surely. Not by a rigorous theoretical proof, for none exists—it *is* an empirical rule. Not by stating, what is true, that economists believe it, for we could be wrong. Perhaps as persuasive a proof as is readily summarized is this: if an economist were to *demonstrate* its failure in a particular market at a particular time, he would be assured of immortality, professionally speaking, and rapid promotion. Since most economists would not dislike either reward, we may assume that the total absence of exceptions is not from lack of trying to find them.[4] And this of course hints at the real proof: innumerable examples, ranging from the wife who cuts down on strawberries because they are out of season (= more expensive) to elaborate statistical investigations, display this result.

The "demand curve" is the geometrical expression of the relationship between quantity purchased and price, and our law of demand says that demand curves have a negative slope.[5] Three demand curves for the same commodity are shown in Figure 3-1, corresponding to each different value of other prices (Y is a substitute) and income.

The responsiveness of quantity to price changes is measured by the elasticity of demand—the relative change in quantity divided by the relative change in price (see Appendix A). The elasticity of demand with respect to price is necessarily negative if quantity and price vary inversely. Can we say any more than that it will differ among commodities for any individual? The only general rule is that the elasticity of demand will be (numerically) greater, the better the substitutes for the commodity. Suppose we divide a homogeneous commodity, let us say gallons of identical gasoline into two classes: those from pump A and those from pump B. The elasticity of demand for gasoline from pump B will be very high, holding the price of gasoline from pump A constant. On two days, an

---

[4] For the history of the one famous attempt, see "Notes on the History of the Giffen Paradox," *Journal of Political Economy,* **40** (1947).

[5] In terms of the full demand function, the demand "curve" is given by

$$x = f(p_x, \bar{p}_y, \bar{p}_z, \ldots, \bar{R}),$$

where the bar over each price and income means we are holding them constant.

individual's purchases will be

	PUMP A	PUMP B
Day 1		
Price	30¢	30.1¢
Quantity	10 gallons	0
Day 2		
Price	30¢	29.9¢
Quantity	0	10 gallons (at least)

The arc eleasticity of demand of the individual for gasoline from pump B will be

$$\frac{\dfrac{0 - 10}{0 + 10}}{\dfrac{30.1 - 29.9}{30.1 + 29.9}} = -300.$$

Here the substitution is obvious, but how can we measure the goodness of substitution between non-identical goods? There is an easy measure, the cross-elasticity of demand, which we shall soon discuss, but it is defined in terms of consumers' behavior and therefore offers no independent explanation of this behavior. There is no simple "technological" measure of substitution: not only is it diffi-

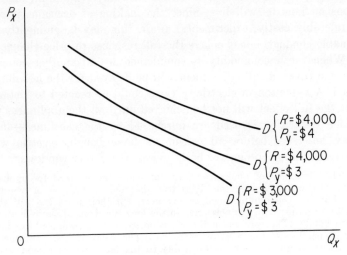

Figure 3-1

cult to compare heterogeneous things (is radio a better substitute
for television than for a theatre or a newspaper?) but substitutability varies with circumstances (a tractor is a substitute for a horse
to a farmer, less so to a riding academy).

This is only one of many places where economists have reached
a general position without formal evidence, or even a measurable
concept usable in a test. It is widely accepted that coal has good
substitutes (oil, natural gas, electricity) but insulin does not, and
that the former probably has a more elastic demand for this reason.
When the Antitrust Division asked that Dupont be compelled to
sell some 22 million shares of General Motors stock over a ten-year
period, most economists were convinced that the effect upon the
price of General Motors shares would be negligible, simply because
these shares were such good substitutes for other "blue chips." This
sort of intuitive estimate of substitutability will be encountered
often in economic literature; the only sound advice to give the student is to accept these estimates when they are correct.

The Effects of Time

A given change in price will usually lead to a larger change in
the quantity consumers buy, the longer the price change has been
in effect. One reason is simply habit—a shorthand expression for
the fact that the consumer does not each day remake all his decisions on how he will live. Since the making of decisions is often
a tolerably costly, experimental affair, this may be eminently reasonable conduct, but it delays the full response to price change.

Whenever a commodity is complementary to another commodity, moreover, a full adjustment will be delayed for the less durable
good. A reduction in electricity rates could be reacted to instantly,
but the full effect will not be achieved until all the appliances with
which electricity is used are purchased by the consumer—and it
may be years before all consumers have bought electric water
heaters or larger ranges, or built houses with larger windows.[6]

[6] The durability of appliances does not make the demand for appliances
more elastic in the long run. It is true that only a fraction of consumers
will buy a given durable good in any year, but their purchases will (habit
aside) be adjusted to the new price so the long-run demand curve is attained
immediately. (The appearance of new customers, however, will lead to a bunch-
ing of purchases after a price reduction.) The delay in the adjustment of
electricity consumption to price is due to the fact that it depends on the
stock of appliances, not the annual rate of purchase of appliances.

We may illustrate this effect by a simple example. Suppose consumers have the long-run demand curve (after full adjustment to price),

$$q = 100 - p,$$

illustrated by D_0 in Figure 3-2. The price has been \$40, the quantity 60. The price now falls to \$30, and only one-fourth of the con-

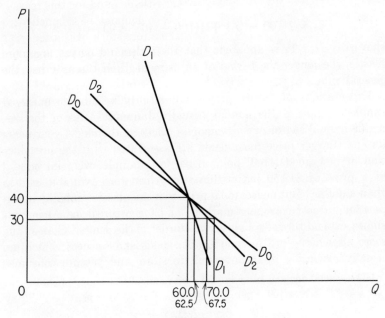

Figure 3-2

sumers, we shall assume, are able to adjust to this new price in the first year. The quantity demanded becomes

$$q_1 = \tfrac{1}{4}(100 - 30) + \tfrac{3}{4}(100 - 40) = 62.5.$$

In the next year, let another 50 per cent of the consumers (making 75 per cent in all) adjust to the new price, so the quantity demanded becomes

$$q_2 = \tfrac{3}{4}(100 - 30) + \tfrac{1}{4}(100 - 40) = 67.5.$$

And in the third year, when all consumers adjust to the new price,

$$q_3 = 100 - 30 = 70.$$

The demand curve for period 1, when only one-fourth of consumers adjust to the current price, is, for all possible prices

$$q_1 = \tfrac{1}{4}(100 - p_1) + \tfrac{3}{4}(100 - 40) = 70 - \frac{p_1}{4},$$

shown as D_1, and that for the second year is,

$$q_2 = \tfrac{3}{4}(100 - p_2) + \tfrac{1}{4}(100 - 40) = 90 - \tfrac{3}{4}p_2,$$

shown as D_2.[7] It is apparent that these demand curves are more elastic, the longer the period of adjustment,[8] and this is surely the general rule.

Expectations of future prices will also influence consumers. A simple example is the annual (usually January) sales of textiles, or the annual sag of new automobile prices as the model year nears its end. Larger price movements are associated with the introduction of new goods: ball point pens, for example, were introduced at a price of $12.50 but within two years were available at less than a dollar.[9] But nonseasonal price movements are probably unimportant in most consumer markets, and for two reasons. Most consumer expenditures—roughly two-thirds in the United States, and more elsewhere—are for nondurable goods and services, which are usually expensive or inconvenient to store, and yet are consumed

---

[7] The general demand curve in year t with annually changing prices is
$$q_t = \tfrac{1}{4}(100 - p_t) + \tfrac{1}{2}(100 - p_{t-1}) + \tfrac{1}{4}(100 - p_{t-2})$$
$$= 100 - \frac{p_t}{4} - \frac{p_{t-1}}{2} - \frac{p_{t-2}}{4};$$
so the current purchases depend upon prices in the two previous periods in this particular example.

[8] At a price of $30, the elasticities of demand are:
1. Long run
$$\frac{dq}{dp} \cdot \frac{p}{q} = -1 \cdot \frac{30}{70} = -0.43.$$
2. First year after the price change
$$\frac{dq_1}{dp_1} \cdot \frac{p_1}{q_1} = -\frac{1}{4} \cdot \frac{30}{62.5} = -0.12.$$
3. Second year after the price change
$$\frac{dq_2}{dp_2} \cdot \frac{p_2}{q_2} = -\frac{3}{4} \cdot \frac{30}{67.5} = -0.33.$$

[9] See Thomas Whiteside, "The Amphibious Pen," *New Yorker* (February 17, 1951).

fairly uniformly through time. In the case of durable goods (houses being the most important and most durable), price expectations have a larger role, and the expectation of continued inflation may have been one factor in the rise of home ownership.[10] These price expectations usually represent extrapolations of recent price trends.[11]

Durable Goods

The demand for durable goods is implicitly a demand for their services—for years of transportation or food preservation or shelter. In any given year, there will be an expected flow of services, to which the consumer attaches a monetary value. If we subtract from this gross value of the services the costs of operation and repair, we shall obtain a set of net services in successive years, say y_1, y_2, y_3, . . . , and a final scrap or trade-in value, s. Distant incomes must be discounted back to the present if we wish the present value of this stream of services. If the appropriate interest rate is i, the present value of the durable good is

$$\frac{y_1}{1+i} + \frac{y_2}{(1+i)^2} + \frac{y_3}{(1+i)^3} + \cdots + \frac{y_n}{(1+i)^n} + \frac{s}{(1+i)^n}$$

if the services have an expected life of n years.[12] If the net value of the services is constant through time, and there is no scrap value,

[10] This is not a simple problem. The chief financial gain from ownership (preferential income tax treatment aside) is in borrowing money at fixed interest rates. But if there is a *general* expectation of inflation (and consumers are usually not the first to expect anything) lenders will demand interest rates which compensate for the decline of the purchasing power of money. Hence the expectation of rising prices of homes will stimulate ownership only to the extent that interest rates fail to reflect the same expectation.

[11] The analysis of price expectations in one simple case may be suggestive. Assume prices have risen and are assumed to do so again in the next period. Then the quantity demanded in the present period is a function of (1) present price and (2) future price. But the future price, say p_{t+1}, is perhaps estimated to equal the present price, p_t, plus some proportion of the previous increase, say $\lambda(p_t - p_{t-1})$. Current demand, in a linear demand function, can then be written as

$$q_t = a + bp_t + cp_{t+1} = a + bp_t + c(p_t + \lambda[p_t - p_{t-1}])$$
$$= a + (b + c[1 + \lambda])p_t - c\lambda p_{t-1}.$$

since c is positive—people buy more now, the higher future prices are expected to be—it is possible for $(b + c[1 + \lambda])$ to be positive even though b is negative.

[12] The formula assumes that the services of the first year will be discounted one year; a slightly more precise discount period would be six months since the first year's services are on average six months away.

this becomes

$$y \frac{(1 + i)^n - 1}{i(1 + i)^n}.$$

The present value of the services is larger, the longer they are received (n) and the lower the interest rate (i).[13]

This is mere arithmetic, but it is not irrelevant arithmetic. It has been said that obsolescence is induced by manufacturers through annual model changes whose only purpose is to make people replace serviceable used items with no more serviceable but somewhat more fashionable new ones. Translated into our arithmetic this means the y_2, y_3, and the like, are now much smaller than y_1. If the life of the good is still n years, the present value of the services is substantially reduced, and the quantity demanded of the durable good will be reduced.[14] Whether such a policy would increase or decrease manufacturers' profits, a question too complex to discuss here, its main effect would be to make transportation more expensive for buyers who wish new cars, and cheaper for those who do not.

One must distinguish the stock of a durable good from the flow of its services. A stock is something that exists at an instant: the family owns n automobiles on January 1, at 10 A.M. A year later it owns m automobiles. We can say, on the one hand, that it has a demand for the *services* of $(n + m)/2$ automobiles on average during the year, and, on the other hand, that it demands $(m - n)$ automobiles *plus* the number worn out during the year.[15]

---

[13] The formula is that of the present value of an annuity of y per year for n years. If the service flow is perpetual (as with land in some uses), the value of the stream is y/i, and $1/i$ ($= 20$ if $i = 0.05$) is called the "years' purchase" price of an income stream.

[14] Alternatively, the price of the use of the services of (say) a new car for one year is increased. This price of the services is the price of a car this year, p_t, minus the discounted price a year hence,

$$\frac{p_{t+1}}{1 + i},$$

which has been reduced by hypothesis.

[15] If we take a commodity that does not depreciate with use, like bonds, the desired stock at time t will be h_t, and at time $(t + 1)$, h_{t+1}. Then the demand for bond purchases during the interval will be

$$q = h_{t+1} - h_t,$$

which will depend upon both the price at time t and the expected price at time $(t + 1)$.

The existence of durable goods raises in unavoidable form a question we have glossed over: to what time period does a demand curve pertain? The answer is one to which the young economist will eventually get accustomed: the time period is governed by the question one asks. One can construct a demand curve for an article of regular consumption for a day, although commonly the time unit is a year to avoid seasonal and minor random variations. But for a durable good, there will be a zero demand for purchase by any one consumer most of the time even though the service of the good is consumed regularly: a family may drive a car every day but buy one once every five years. By a familiar argument the market demand curve for a durable good will be much more stable than the individual's demand curve through time.

PRICES OF OTHER GOODS: COMPLEMENTS AND SUBSTITUTES

The prices of related goods are the second determinant of the demand for any good. The purchases of automobiles will depend upon the price of gasoline (complements) and the price of common carrier services (substitutes). We could, in fact, draw the "cross demand" curve for the quantity of X purchased as a given other price (say p_y) varied. This is seldom done explicitly, but the elasticity of this curve, called the cross-elasticity of demand, is the economist's measure of economic (not technological) substitution.[16] It is formally defined as the relative change in the quantity of X divided by the relative change in the price of Y.

If the consumer considers two goods (say, a company's stock certificates with even and odd serial numbers) identical, the cross-elasticity of demand will be immense (strictly, infinite) and positive. If he considers them very poor substitutes, the cross-elasticity will be small. But there is a certain asymmetry in that perfect complements (right and left shoes) will not have infinite negative cross-elasticities.[17]

---

[16] In terms of our notation for the demand function, the cross-demand curve with respect to p_y would be

$$x = f(\bar{p}_x, p_y, \bar{p}_z, \ldots, \bar{R}),$$

where the bar again denotes that the variable is being held constant.

[17] A fall in the price of right shoes (the left shoe remaining unchanged in price) will lead to a rise in demand for both right and left shoes. But

Whether a commodity has good or poor substitutes (or complements) depends in good part upon how finely the commodity is specified. A particular brand of coffee has a high cross-elasticity with respect to other brands—actually, on the order of $+5$ or $+10$ even within a month or two.[18] Coffee has a much smaller cross-elasticity with respect to other beverages, and beverages presumably have a still smaller cross-elasticity with respect to other categories of expenditure.

A demand curve for a product is specified only if the prices of close substitutes or complements are held constant, and this demand curve merely asserts that various quantities of X will be bought at various prices of X, if the prices of other commodities are unchanged. In fact, the prices of close substitutes or complements of X will inevitably change (at least in the short run) if the price of X changes appreciably: any large change in the price of fuel oil, for example, will cause consumers to buy more or less oil burners (complements) and less or more natural gas (substitutes) and hence affect their prices. But it is necessary to separate these indirect effects of changes in the prices of substitutes and complements simply because they do not always change in the same way when the price of fuel oil changes. At one time a 10-per cent rise in fuel oil prices may lead to a 5-per cent fall in the price of oil burners, at another time to a 9-per cent fall.

This necessity for holding constant the price of a closely related product is important enough to deserve illustration. Let us assume that the demand function for woolen socks is

$$q_w = 30 - 10p_w + 4p_n,$$

where the subscript w denotes wool, and n denotes nylon. If the price of woolen socks (p_w) rises 0.10 dollars, one less pair ($= 10 \times 0.10$) will be purchased, if p_n is constant. If p_n also rises 0.10 dollars, the purchases of woolen socks will fall by only 0.6 pair ($4 \times 0.10 = 0.4$ less); if instead p_n falls by 0.20 dollars, q_w will fall

---

if the elasticity of demand for shoes is K, the cross-elasticity of demand for left shoes with respect to a fall in the price of right shoes will be $K/2$, since the percentage fall in the price of a pair is only half as large as the percentage fall in the price of right shoes. This cross-elasticity may be quite small.

[18] Lester G. Telser, "The Demand for Branded Goods as Estimated from Consumer Panel Data," *Review of Economics and Statistics* (August 1962).

by 1.8. Unless p_n always moves in some strict relationship to p_w, we shall make an error in our estimate of the effect of a change in p_w unless we take explicit account of p_n.

Most empirical studies take into account at most a very few complements or substitutes, but this may be as much a reflection on the studies as a reflection of the world. Aluminum, for example, competes with iron in furniture and kitchenware, with wood in house sidings, with fiberglass in boats, with red lead in paint, with chrome on automobile grills, not to forget the major competition with copper for electrical conduction. Or, to take a consumer good, television competes with movies, radio, phonographs, attending sporting events, books, and for many, homework and sleep.

The reader will observe that we have announced no empirical rule for the effects of prices of related goods similar to the rule that a rise in the price of a commodity reduces the quantity demanded. The closest we can come to such a rule is to say that close technological substitutes—that is, commodities serving much the same purposes—will have positive cross-elasticities, and close technological complements—commodities which must be used jointly in tolerably inflexible proportions—will have negative cross-elasticities. Most pairs of commodities do not fall in either class, and then direct investigation is necessary even to determine the sign of the cross-elasticity.[19]

INCOME

The third determinant of consumer purchases is income. The quantity of a commodity that is purchased at various incomes (prices being constant) may be drawn against income; it has no generally accepted name but we shall call it an income curve. Two income curves are given in Figure 3-3, one illustrating the situation in which purchases rise with income (called a "normal" good), the second illustrating the situation in which purchases fall as income rises (called an "inferior" good). The income elasticity is the relative change in quantity divided by the relative change in income; this elasticity is, of course, positive for normal goods and negative for inferior goods.

[19] For a collection of demand and cross-elasticities, see Richard Stone, *The Measurement of Consumers' Expenditures and Behavior in the United Kingdom, 1920–1938* (Cambridge, England: The University Press, 1954), Chs. 20–23.

As a rule, the dollar expenditure on a commodity, rather than the quantity of the commodity, is drawn against income. Total expenditures and physical quantities are proportional if prices are uniform, but in general prices paid rise with income. Prices rise because better qualities of the commodity are purchased at higher incomes and because more retailing services are purchased (better stores, delivery service, and so forth). Therefore the income elas-

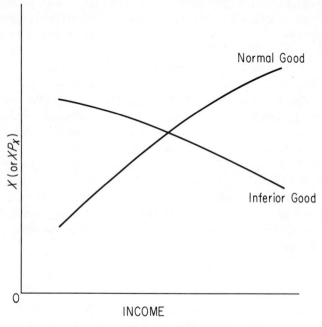

Figure 3-3

ticity of the quantity of a commodity will usually be smaller than the income elasticity of total expenditures on the commodity.

The income of the consumer may be variously defined. In most statistical surveys it is taken as the sum of wages, dividends, and interest, plus an estimated value of the major nonpecuniary services (food grown and consumed on farms, rental value of owned homes) during the year. Capital gains are usually omitted: unrealized gains (such as stocks worth more than they cost when purchased) are hard for the statistician to estimate, and realized gains and losses are often viewed as cancelling (what the seller gains the buyer loses) in the population as a whole. Even if this were true,[20] the households with gains and losses could have different spending patterns. There are also a host of problems, amusing to every one except tax collectors, on what disbursements are deductible as occupational expenses.

A more subtle difficulty is encountered when we consider the time period over which income should be reckoned. Suppose a family has the following sequence of annual incomes: $10,000, $2,000 $10,000, $2,000, and so forth. Should it treat its income as fluctuating between $10,000 and $2,000, or as averaging $6,000? It is obvious that it *can* view its income as averaging $6,000—saving $4,000 in prosperous years and dissaving $4,000 in unprosperous years. And the family should normally do this: it would be foolish, and even expensive, to alternate between a tenement and a nice home, to send its children to college one year and to a coal mine the next. Family incomes do not fluctuate this widely or consistently (except perhaps between seasons of a year) but they do undergo fluctuations of substantial magnitude. Even in a period as short as a year, the incomes of a set of families shift about substantially: the correlation coefficient of successive annual incomes runs from 0.65 (for families with unstable incomes, such as farm operators) to 0.9 (for families whose chief earner is a sales or clerical employee).

Let us label the average income of a family over (say) five years its permanent income and the deviation of its current income from this level as its transitory component of income.[21] We shall illustrate the effect of transitory components with a numerical example. Suppose each family buys a commodity X according to the equation,

$$X = \frac{1}{50} \text{ (Permanent Income)} + 10.^{22}$$

[20] It is not true. For example, a stockholder may take the corporation's income as dividends, or (if the corporation reinvests it) as capital gain, and to this gain there is no offsetting loss.

[21] This terminology, I find, was independently discovered by Milton Friedman in *A Theory of the Consumption Function* (New York: National Bureau of Economic Research, 1957).

[22] There will also be transitory components of consumption of a commodity but if they are not correlated strongly with the transitory component of income, they do not affect the principle and are ignored here.

The distribution of 25 families by their permanent income is shown in Table 3–1. We calculate random components of income for these families by flipping a freshly minted coin, adding $200 for each heads or subtracting $200 for each tails, and terminating the tossing when the coin changes face.[23] The purchases of X are plotted

Table 3–1

FAMILY NO.	PERMANENT INCOME	TRANSISTORY. INCOME	OBSERVED INCOME	PURCHASES OF X
1	$2220	+$200	$2420	54.4
2	2340	+ 200	2540	56.8
3	2450	− 400	2050	59.0
4	2550	+ 600	3150	61.0
5	2640	+ 200	2840	62.8
6	2720	− 800	1920	64.4
7	2790	+ 800	3590	65.8
8	2850	+ 600	3450	67.0
9	2900	− 200	2700	68.0
10	2940	+ 200	3140	68.8
11	2970	+ 400	3370	69.4
12	2990	− 800	2190	69.8
13	3000	+ 800	3800	70.0
14	3010	+ 600	3610	70.2
15	3030	+ 800	3830	70.6
16	3060	− 400	2660	71.2
17	3100	− 200	2900	72.0
18	3150	− 800	2350	73.0
19	3210	− 600	2610	74.2
20	3280	− 200	3080	75.6
21	3360	+ 200	3560	77.2
22	3450	− 200	3250	79.0
23	3550	+ 200	3950	81.0
24	3660	+ 800	4440	83.2
25	3780	− 200	3580	85.6

against current income in Figure 3-4, and the line on which all points would fall if each family had its permanent income is also

[23] Or, more economically, we use runs of odd and even numbers from a table of random numbers. The expected number of heads (or tails) for a family which has a heads (or tails) on the first toss is

$$1 + \tfrac{1}{2} + \tfrac{1}{4} + \tfrac{1}{8} + \cdots = 2,$$

so the average transitory component is plus (or minus) $400.

displayed. It is obvious that the slope of the line which is fitted to the observations has less slope than the true relationship.[24]

The average permanent income of this group is $3,000, and its average current income is $3,079—the difference is due to the small size of the sample and would vanish with a larger group. Yet only 3 families are below the true regression line to the left of the true

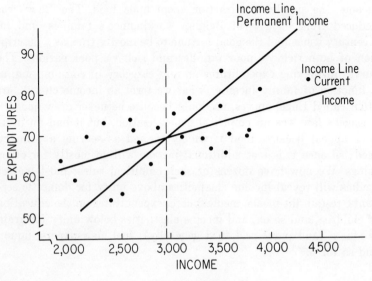

Figure 3-4

mean ($3,000), and only 3 families are above it to the right of this mean. The average transitory components by current income are:

CURRENT INCOME	AVERAGE TRANSITORY COMPONENT
Under $2500	−$520
2500–3000	− 167
3000–3500	+ 233
Over 3500	+ 600

And this sort of pattern is inevitable, because the very fact that a family has a large negative transitory component tends to put

[24] The least squares line is

$$X = \frac{1}{144} \text{(Current Income)} + 48.7.$$

it in a low current income class, and the very fact that the family has a large positive transitory component puts it in a high current income class. For this reason budgetary studies of a group of families at any one time understate the responsiveness of expenditures to changes in permanent income.

A century ago the first important student of family budgets, Ernst Engel, proposed the law: the larger a family's (or a nation's) income, the smaller the fraction spent upon food. The "law" was deduced from budgets of Belgian workingmen's families, and for a century it has had the good fortune to be mostly true, as a description of both rich vs. poor families and rich vs. poor nations. The curves displaying expenditures on any category of consumption, as a function of family income (what we term an income curve), are often called Engel curves, no doubt because he never drew one.

Engel's law was an empirical generalization, but it had an intuitive appeal because food is widely viewed as serving a primary need; so once it is met additional income will go mostly for other things. We now have dozens of such empirical rules: most budget studies will reveal income elasticities above unity for domestic servants, restaurant meals, medical care, expenditures on the education of children, and so on, and income elasticities below unity for grain products (and purchased food generally), fuel, newspapers, liquor, and so forth.[25]

TASTES

The quantity of a commodity demanded at given prices and income depends upon the likes and dislikes of the consumer. These tastes, as they are called, are in turn governed by a great host of circumstances: age, sex, and family composition; cultural tradi-

[25] A collection of such results can be found in S. J. Prais and H. S. Houthakker, *The Analysis of Family Budgets* (Cambridge, England: The University Press, 1955). For the early work in this area see my "Early History of Empirical Studies of Consumer Behavior," *Journal of Political Economy,* **62** (1954). It should be noted that Engel asserted that F/Y falls as Y increases, if F is expenditure on food and Y is income. This is equivalent to asserting that the income elasticity of food is less than unity: if $F = \phi(Y)$,

$$\frac{d(F/Y)}{dY} = \frac{F}{Y^2}\{\eta_{FY} - 1\},$$

so if the expression is negative, $\eta_{FY} < 1$.

tions (Frenchmen drink wine; Americans duel martinis); religion (whose influence goes far beyond dietary rules); and even education. A method of describing tastes quantitatively will be presented in the next chapter.

For a vast array of problems, including most of those we shall encounter, it is customary to treat tastes as fixed. The stability of tastes could be argued *a priori:* tastes depend upon such slowly changing things as demographic characteristics and cultural tradition. Moreover, tastes should not be influenced appreciably by most of the actions the economist studies. It is hard to see how an embargo on oil, for example, should have any important effect upon the demand for gasoline other than through the effects on prices and incomes.

These defenses of the assumption of constant tastes are not wholly implausible, and they are buttressed by a wholly different line of argument. If a prediction is made on the basis of an economic analysis that assumes tastes to be fixed, and if the prediction is confirmed by experience, then the neglect of tastes has been justified. Hence every successful economic analysis of consumer behavior that neglects changes in tastes is support for the neglect.[26]

Let us be more specific: the economist says that if one collects a thousand instances of a price rising 10 per cent, and adjusts for income changes, that in well over 950 cases the quantity purchased will decline. If any student should find this statement to be wrong, will he please notify the profession?

And now to retract. There is no strict boundary over which the economist dare not step, and many studies of tastes have been made. In a study of the long term demand for housing, one naturally investigates changes in family size. In a study of the trend of employment in the medical professions, one considers the age and sex structure of the population and its urbanization. Pertinent components of tastes are introduced whenever and wherever they

---

[26] And every failure of an economic prediction, a showing that tastes have changed? Not quite. Changing tastes can invalidate a prediction, but so too can a mistaken analysis—the neglect of some other important variable, the improper formulation of the theory, clumsy statistical technique. The economist looks for these sources of failure much more often than he looks for changing tastes—simply because they have been found to be more probable than changing tastes.

are helpful, and it is only their enormous variety that keeps them out of the general theory.

Two propositions on tastes are deeply imbedded in economic thought.

The first proposition is that human wants are insatiable—that there is no real income so large that a family would not like more. (The assertion does not tell us whether the liking for more income diminishes as the family becomes richer.) Although this proposition emerged long before the day of statistical analysis, it has always been essentially an empirical proposition—the richest sovereign seemed ever-willing to augment his wealth. The exceptions which are alleged (it is not evident that any exist) have usually been attributed to "primitive" people.

The insatiability of wants is more than a philosophical observation on human nature—it is an integral part of economic analysis. There is no place in economics where it is asserted that if an individual buys some of a commodity at a given price, he will not on average buy more if the price is reduced. Nor are there many economists who would explain the failure of a society's income per head to grow on the ground that all wants were satisfied.

The second proposition is that tastes are extremely varied—that one man's meat is another man's poison. And this proposition lends itself to quantitative measurement. When the purchases of families with equal incomes are compared at a given time (so prices are also held fairly constant because all families buy at about the same prices), most of the original differences in purchases among families still remain. Thus, even with so broad a category as all food, the coefficient of variation of family expenditures is more than 30 per cent, and after eliminating income differences, it is still 25 per cent. In other words, among families which spend an average of $1,600 on food in a year, roughly one-sixth spend less than $1,200 and one-sixth more than $2,000.[27] In the case of more specific commodities, such as white bread and peanut butter and tennis balls, the diversity of family tastes becomes almost astronomical.

The diversity of taste raises some interesting problems in economic organization. Whenever it is uneconomic (expensive!) to supply a good or services on a small scale (opera, unusual automobile

[27] This diversity is exaggerated by the use of current instead of permanent income.

styles, books in Sanskrit on bowling) the individual will be unable to satisfy his wants unless they are shared by a sufficient number of other people. People's tastes in housing differ more than they do in automobiles, and mass production techniques have had much less scope in the construction industry. But as a society becomes wealthier, its citizens can afford to pay the higher costs of specialized goods and a proliferation of varieties takes place.

MARKET DEMAND FUNCTIONS

The demand and income curves so far discussed pertain to an individual household. We shall briefly indicate how to pass from individual to market demand functions, but postpone to Chapter 6 the definition of the market.

Market Demand Curves

Since all individuals in a market buy at the same price or at fixed differentials (see p. 34), we can construct a market demand curve simply by adding horizontally the demand curves of all individuals. A simple example is given in Figure 3-5. Each of the individual demand curves (D_1, D_2, D_3, D_4, D_5) has been drawn to

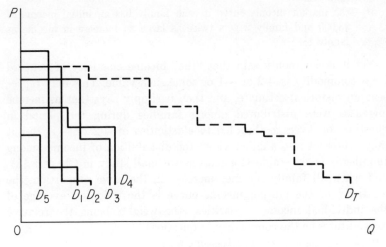

Figure 3-5

display highly discontinuous responsiveness to price simply to show that the market function takes on a smoother form.

It can be shown that the elasticity of the market demand curve is equal to the weighted average of the elasticities of the individual curves, the weights being the relative quantities purchased by each buyer.[28]

Market Income Curves

The aggregate income curve of the market for a commodity, unfortunately, bears a very complicated relationship to that of the individuals who constitute the market. The lack of symmetry to the demand relationship arises from the fact that prices are usually equal (with allowance for transportation costs) for all individuals, whereas incomes are unequal. The effects of an increase in income, therefore, depend upon how income is initially distributed and how the increments of income are distributed.

We may illustrate this complexity by combining the income curves of two families, denoted I_1 and I_2 in Figure 3-6. Only three of the innumerable possible market income curves are drawn:

M_1—the market income curve if the families have equal incomes. It is the sum of I_1 and I_2.

M_2—the market income curve if family 1 always has half the income of family 2.

M_3—the market income curve if each family has an initial income of $3,000 and family 2 gets twice as large an increase in income as family 1.

Yet it is commonly said that "the" income elasticity of demand for a commodity is $+2$ or -1 or some such value. This may represent an historical estimate, and then it simply says that as income increases were distributed among families during the period in question, on average they led to elasticities of $+2$ or -1. But it may represent also another view: the distribution of income among families is fairly stable (for reasons we shall study in Chapter 18), and when all family incomes increase in the same proportion, the elasticity of the market income curve is the weighted average of the individual income elasticities (the weights being the relative expenditures on the commodity in question).[29]

[28] See mathematical note 4 in Appendix B.
[29] See mathematical note 5 in Appendix B.

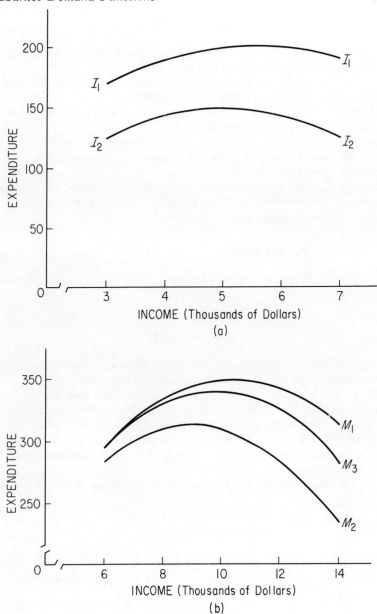

Figure 3-6

RECOMMENDED READINGS

Friedman, M., *A Theory of the Consumption Function*, New York: National Bureau of Economic Research, 1957.

Prais, S. J., and H. S. Houthakker, *The Analysis of Family Budgets*, Cambridge: Cambridge University Press, 1955.

Schultz, H., *The Theory and Measurement of Demand*, Chicago: University of Chicago Press, 1938, Chs. 2–6.

Stone, R., *The Measurement of Consumers Expenditures and Behavior in the United Kingdom, 1920–1938*, Cambridge, England: The University Press, 1954, Chs. 20–23.

Working, E., "What Do Statistical 'Demand Curves' Show?" *Quarterly Journal of Economics*, **41** (1927), 212–35. Reprinted in *Readings in Price Theory*, Chicago: Richard D. Irwin, 1952.

PROBLEMS

1. Make numerical schedules of the demands of two consumers, whose functions are

$$q_1 = 100 - p$$
$$q_2 = \ 50 - p/2.$$

Then add the demand curves horizontally and compare the elasticity of each schedule with that of the combined schedule, at $p = 50$.

2. Budget studies of families made at any one time show that richer families employ more servants than poorer families, and the income elasticity calculated from these cross-sectional data is about $+2$. But over the last half century the income of the average American family has risen while the number of servants has actually fallen. How can these results be reconciled?

3. The equations of the income curves underlying Figure 3-6 are

$$I_1 = -5Y_1{}^2 + 55Y_1 + 50,$$
$$I_2 = -6Y_2{}^2 + 60Y_2,$$

where Y is income in thousands of dollars, and the equations hold over the range from \$2 to \$9.5 (thousand). Verify the shapes of M_1, M_2, and M_3 in Figure 3-6.

4. What is the income elasticity of each of the income curves in Problem 3 at an income of \$5 thousand?

5. Given the demand function which portrays a lagged response of

buyers to price changes (it is given in footnote 7, page 28), draw the demand curve for this year when prices in the two preceeding years were:

(a) $p_{t-2} = 40$; $p_{t-1} = 40$

(b) $p_{t-2} = 40$; $p_{t-1} = 50$

(c) $p_{t-2} = 40$; $p_{t-1} = 30$.

6. Calculate the observed expenditure pattern for the 25 families in Table 3–1 if the transitory component of income is twice as large. That is, add \$400 to each family's permanent income for each consecutive head in a coin tossing, or subtract \$400 for each consecutive tail. Is the observed income elasticity larger or smaller than that of the income line in Figure 3-4?

7. Suppose all consumers have identical demands for a given commodity, but live various distances from the central city. What would happen to the market demand curve reckoned at the central city if transportation costs per unit of the product rise? What will happen to the elasticity of demand if the demand function is linear?

chapter four

The Theory of Utility

Utility theory made its way into economics almost a century ago, when it was still semifashionable psychological doctrine to assert that man's behavior could be explained by his desire to achieve pleasure and avoid pain. It was a natural extension to say that the pleasure (or utility) derived from a commodity varies with the quantity of the commodity, but increases less rapidly than the quantity of the commodity (law of diminishing marginal utility). The maximizing of utility provided a basis for a theory of motivated consumer behavior, thus complementing the pursuit of profits which was the basis for a theory of motivated behavior of entrepreneurs.

For a short time the utility theory was taken very literally: some economists believed that there were definite numbers of units of utility to be attached to the consumption of given quantities of goods, numbers which were in principle measurable. The greatest flowering of this theory was achieved in the famous monograph of Francis Y. Edgeworth entitled *Mathematical Psychics* (1881). Edgeworth, who was one of England's greatest economists, even discussed such problems as whether a woman obtained as much utility from a given income as a man, on which he reached the correct answer.[1]

The increasing criticism of this psychological theory (known as hedonism), and the closer examination of the role of utility in economic analysis (particularly by Vilfredo Pareto), led economists to abandon everything but its substance. The simple measurement of utility, the comparisons of utilities derived by different people,

[1] See *Mathematical Psychics,* p. 78.

the use of utility arguments to support public policy proposals—all were gradually abandoned in part or in whole. What was retained was the concept of what we may term a rational consumer.

THE RATIONAL CONSUMER

The Characterization of Tastes

Before we examine the nature of the rationality attributed to individuals, it is desirable to develop a graphical method of describing the individual's tastes (or preferences or utility function). Let us assume that the individual is offered his choice of the 20 combinations of two commodities, X and Y, which are listed in Table 4–1. The choices could be determined by an actual offer of sale

Table 4–1

Combinations of Two Commodities, X and Y

		QUANTITY OF X		
	9	10	11	12
QUANTITY OF Y		COMBINATION NUMBER		
10	1	6	11	16
11	2	7	12	17
12	3	8	13	18
13	4	9	14	19
14	5	10	15	20

of the various combinations for various sums of money, a method ("revealed preference") which will be discussed later. For the present we simply ask the individual to rank the combinations in the order in which he prefers them for his consumption.

There are several difficulties in actually conducting such an experiment with specific commodities. The first is that the individual will normally have some knowledge of the prices the commodities currently command in the market. If X costs \$1 and Y costs \$5, he will be tempted to calculate the values of the various combinations, and rank combinations in the order of their value—on the ground that even if he personally does not care much for Y (say recordings of zither concertos) he can always exchange them for X, which he does like, in the market. On this approach he would

choose combination 5 in preference to combination 16, even though
he much preferred to consume the latter combination. We must rule
out the values (or resale possibilities) by some artifice which com-
pels him to consume the commodities.

The second difficulty, which is of an entirely different nature,
is that he may be undecided as between some combinations. He
may prefer combination 12 ($11X$ and $11Y$) to combination 11 ($11X$
and $10Y$), but be unable to express a clear preference between combinations 12 and 8 (the latter has $10X$ and $12Y$). In fact, if the
commodities are divisible we can always construct combinations
that seem equivalent to the individual. If, for example, he prefers

$$9X \text{ and } 14Y \qquad \text{to} \qquad 10X \text{ and } 10Y,$$

and

$$10X \text{ and } 10Y \qquad \text{to} \qquad 9X \text{ and } 11Y,$$

we can find a value of Y somewhere between 11 and 14 such that
with $9X$ it is equivalent to $10X$ and $10Y$. We then say that he
is *indifferent* between the combinations.

And this leads us to a third difficulty: what if his rankings
change from one day to the next? This difficulty will be postponed:
we shall assume that his preferences are stable.

The combinations of Table 4–1 are displayed as little circles in
Figure 4-1, Panel A. In Panels B and C we have drawn different
lines through the circles, to display two possible rankings that two
different individuals might make. The lines (called indifference
curves) obey one rule: All combinations on a line are equivalent
to the consumer. And our fundamental argument is that the consumer's preferences can always be characterized by such indifference curves.

In Panel B, the individual (B) requires several units of Y to
compensate for the loss of a unit of X, as between combinations
which are equivalent. In Panel C, the individual (C) requires only
a fraction of a unit of Y to compensate for the loss of a unit of
X, as between combinations which are equivalent. Hence we may
say that B sets a higher preference (utility) on X relative to Y,
than C does.

Only extensive experiments will convince the reader that *any* set

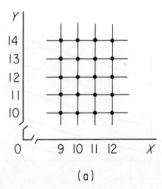

(a)

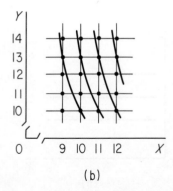

(b)

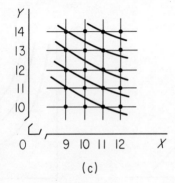

(c)

Figure 4-1

of tastes can be characterized by such indifference curves. In the four panels of Figure 4-2 we show

A. A person who considers X utterly useless: say Y is food and X is tickets to marathon dances.

B. A person who considers X a positive nuisance: say Y is food and X is garbage.

C. A person who considers X and Y absolutely equivalent: say X and Y are objects differing only in color, and this is deemed irrelevant.

D. A person who considers less than 4 units of X desirable, would never be caught dead with 4 to 6 units (a difficult feat), and would find more than 6 a nuisance.

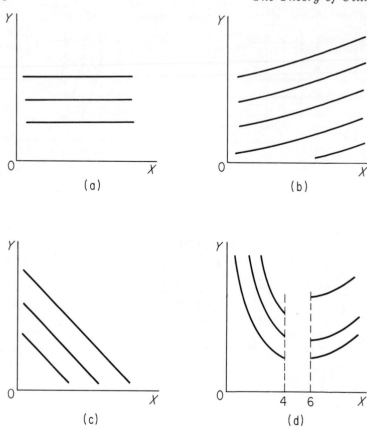

Figure 4-2

In order to simplify the discussion of indifference curves, economists make two assumptions:

1. The consumer finds both commodities desirable.[2]
2. The commodities are continuously divisible—milk and sugar are prototypes.

These assumptions place two limitations on the indifference curves. The latter ensures, obviously, that they will be continuous curves,[3]

---

[2] Any nuisance commodity can be redefined to become desirable: instead of garbage, call it garbage removal; instead of work, call it leisure.

[3] Strictly speaking, continuity requires also that the consumer can discriminate between combinations differing by infinitesimal amounts.

and not simply collections of discrete points. The former ensures that they have a negative slope: if both commodities are desirable, and one combination has more of X, it must have less of Y or the combinations would not be equivalent to the consumer. Moreover, the former assumption insures that as between two indifference curves, the consumer prefers the higher one, because it contains as much X and more Y, or as much Y and more X.

Convexity. The indifference curves, on the conditions stated, are continuous and negatively sloping; in addition it is almost universally assumed that they are convex to the origin. This, let it be noted, is an empirical proposition, not a definition—in fact it is the first empirical proposition encountered in this chapter. How can we prove it?

The line of proof first used by economists was introspective, and in fact was based upon the principle of diminishing marginal utility. The early utility theorists assumed that the utility derived from a commodity depended upon the quantity of that commodity. If we define the marginal utility of a commodity as the increase in total utility divided by the increase in the quantity of the commodity with which it is associated, their proposition was that the marginal utility diminishes as the quantity increases. If $U(n)$ is the utility derived from n units of a commodity, they asserted that the marginal utility of $(n + 1)$ units, $U(n + 1) - U(n)$, was greater than that of $(n + 2)$ units, or, $U(n + 2) - U(n + 1)$. For surely one satisfied increasingly less important desires as the quantity of a commodity increased: the first gallon of water (per week) was necessary to survival, the fourth to cleanliness, the fifth for one's wife, the one-thousandth to a green lawn, and so forth.

If so, indifference curves would be convex. The various combinations on an indifference curve yield equal utility. If we decrease X by ΔX, and require ΔY of Y to compensate for the loss of ΔX, then

$$(\Delta X) \text{ (Marginal utility of } X) = \Delta X \cdot MU_x$$

is the loss of utility from the decline in X, and

$$(\Delta Y) \text{ (Marginal utility of } Y) = \Delta Y \cdot MU_y$$

is the gain in utility from ΔY, and these two must be equal if the utility of the new combination $(X + \Delta X, Y + \Delta Y)$ is to equal that of (X,Y). (Notice that ΔX is negative.) But if

$$\Delta X \cdot MU_x + \Delta Y \cdot MU_y = 0,$$

$$S_{yx} = -\frac{\Delta Y}{\Delta X} = \frac{MU_x}{MU_y}.$$

This last expression is the slope of an indifference curve, and is called the marginal rate of substitution of Y for X; it is illustrated in Figure 4-3. As we continue to decrease X by equal increments, MU_x of the remaining quantity gets larger, and the MU_y of the

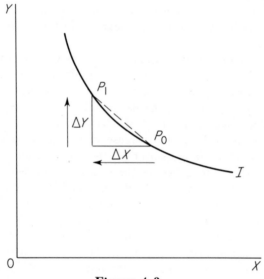

Figure 4-3

increasing quantity of Y gets smaller: the slope becomes numerically greater as we move to the left along the indifference curve. And this is what convexity means.

This proof ruled for a short time in this form, but it had one unsatisfactory aspect. Diminishing marginal utility does not imply convexity if the utility of a commodity depends also upon the quantities possessed of other commodities. In this event the decrease in X may, for example, increase the marginal utility of a given amount of Y, and spoil our argument.[4]

The second line of proof is based upon observable behavior. If the consumer buys some of each commodity, the indifference curves

[4] The precise relationship is given in mathematical note 6 in Appendix B.

must be convex to the origin. (It will be shown that with linear or concave indifference curves, only one of the commodities would generally be purchased.) We shall return to this proof later.

The Budget Line

Indifference curves display subjective attitudes toward objective goods and services. We need to be able to display also the terms on which these goods and services can be acquired, and this is done by means of a so-called budget line. Suppose we add

the amount of x_1 purchased, times its price (p_1);
the amount of x_2 purchased, times its price (p_2);
the amount of x_3 purchased, times its price (p_3);
   (and so forth to the end of the list)
the amount of x_n purchased, times its price (p_n).

The sum must be the total amount of income the consumer possesses, for if our list of commodities is complete the income must be held in some form. Thus we may write the budget equation as

$$x_1 p_1 + x_2 p_2 + \cdots + x_n p_n = \text{Income} = R.$$

Of course many of the x's may be zero for any individual.

Two additional remarks on budget constraints are sufficient at this point. The first is that the budget equation says that transactions are voluntary—that there is no theft or coercion. The second is that the equality of purchases and income is really a matter of definition: we can always find appropriate "commodities" to keep the equation in balance. If our time period were a week (it is usually convenient to make it longer), and the family bought a house, the purchase of the house would be offset by the increase in debt of the family.[5]

The budget line in a two-commodity world would become

$$X P_x + Y P_y = R.$$

If the prices of commodities and the income of the individual are fixed, say at \$2, \$1, and \$30 respectively, this becomes

$$\$2X + \$1Y = \$30$$

or

$$2X + \quad Y = \quad 30,$$

[5] Or, if we wished to avoid introducing stocks into an analysis concerned chiefly with flows, only the cost of the week's shelter would be in the budget equation.

since we may cancel out the common dimension of dollars. This budget line can obviously be drawn on the same scales that we have employed for indifference curves, and this budget (or price) line and a second, in which $P_x = \$3$, are shown in Figure 4-4. The

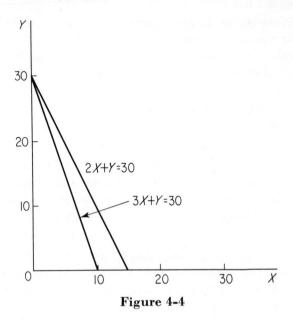

Figure 4-4

slope of the budget line with respect to the X axis is $-P_x/P_y$, as can be seen when it is written as,

$$Y = \frac{R}{P_y} - \frac{P_x}{P_y} X.$$

The collection of possible combinations of X and Y the consumer can possess is the set of points in the triangle bounded by the X and Y axes and the price line. If he spends all his income, an assumption we shall make, he must be on the budget line, for below it,

$$XP_x + YP_y < R.$$

The consumer usually buys at a constant price; he is too unimportant in the markets in which he deals to influence prices. But occasionally price does vary with quantity: a simple example is a schedule of rates for electricity such as 5¢ per kwh for the first

100 kwh and 4¢ per kwh thereafter. In this case (which is left to the reader to draw) the budget line will have a kink at $X = 100$, being steeper to the left of 100 than it is to the right. And there are more complicated price systems, such as that involved in a flat sum for installation of a utility service and another price per unit.[6] We shall put such complications aside, and analyse the constant price case.

Rational Consumer Behavior

Let us now consider more closely the behavior of a rational consumer. There are three characteristics of a rational consumer:

1. His tastes are consistent,
2. His cost calculations are correct,
3. He makes those decisions which maximize utility.

After these characteristics have been explored, some widely held objections to the realism of this theory will be confronted.

Consistent Tastes. One must distinguish sharply between a set of tastes that is consistent and a set of tastes that is admirable. A consistent set of tastes is one in which the order of preference among combinations of goods is well-defined. If combination A (say $7X + 11Y$) is preferred to B (say $6X + 12Y$), and B is preferred to C (say $5X + 13Y$), then A is preferred to C.

Consistency excludes intersecting indifference curves. For consider the two intersecting indifference curves in Figure 4-5. On I_1, Q_1 is equivalent to Q_2; on I_2, Q_1 is equivalent to Q_3. Hence the intersection implies that Q_2 is equivalent to Q_3. But Q_2 contains more of each commodity than Q_3, and on our assumption that all commodities are desirable, Q_2 is preferred to Q_3. Hence the indifference relationship between Q_1 and Q_2 and Q_1 and Q_3 is not *transitive*, the technical name for this consistency condition.

Consistency, to repeat, has only this narrow meaning of well-ordered preferences. Consistency does not mean logically harmonious preferences: it might be consistent, in our narrow sense, for an individual to prefer to pay $10 more to fly in a plane whose chance of crashing was one in 10,000 less than the chance of crash-

[6] In this case the price line can be defined only if the time period over which the utility service will be used is known. If, for example, the period of use is indefinitely long, only interest on the cost plus depreciation should be charged as an annual cost.

ing on a cheaper flight (thus setting a marginal value of $100,000 on his life) while simultaneously playing Russian roulette once for $1,000, thus setting a $6,000 value on his life.[7] For in the latter case, the admiration of a dozen equally shallow-minded observers might be esteemed highly.

Even more, of course, consistency does not imply enlightenment of tastes. The consumer could with consistency prefer to read the telephone book rather than Shakespeare, or to listen to a boiler

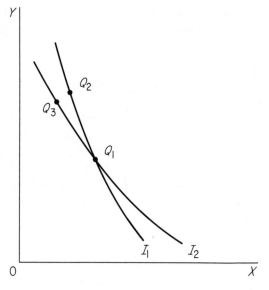

Figure 4-5

factory rather than to Mozart. This is only to say that the analysis of man's behavior is not an ethical study.

Correct Cost Calculations. The costs of various combinations of goods are incorporated in the budget equation, and our second condition of rational behavior is simply the requirement that the cost be reckoned correctly. This condition of proper arithmetic is so obvious as to be vulgar, but let us spell it out in a few cases to show that not all arithmetic is simple.

---

[7] With a six-chambered revolver, the probability of winning is $\frac{5}{6}$ and a $\frac{1}{6}$ probability of death is valued at $1,000.

As a primitive example, a commodity X is sold for $2 at shop A, for $2.10 at shop B. Then the budget equation should read, $2X_a + 2.1X_b$, so far as this item is concerned. If X_a is identical with X_b, in all respects (including the services of the two shops), X_b will drop out of the consumer's purchases, as we shall show later.

At a next level of sophistication, or rather naiveté, the consumer can "buy" a fund of money for Christmas presents by (1) putting money in the bank each month, and receiving interest, or (2) joining one of the Christmas fund plans whereby he is compelled to contribute, and not allowed to make early withdrawals, and receives no interest. The cost of the fund is (say) $100 by the second plan, and $98 (if the interest averages 4 per cent on an average balance of $50) by the first plan. He will obviously choose the former. Yet some people choose the latter.

One can of course explain the participation in a Christmas fund by introducing another item of preference: a desire of people to protect themselves against a future lack of will power (or a desire to be charitable toward bankers). If we stopped the analysis with this explanation, we would turn utility into a tautology: a reason, we would be saying, can always be found for whatever we observe a man to do.

In order to preserve the predictive power of the utility theory, we must continue our Christmas fund analysis as follows. The foregone cost of putting money in a Christmas fund is the interest one could earn by putting the same money in a savings account. If interest rates on savings accounts rise, the cost of buying protection against a loss of will power rises and less of it ought to be bought: relatively more savings will go into savings accounts, relatively less savings into Christmas funds.

As another example of cost analysis, let us assume that a monopolist sells both razors and blades, and that (what is unreasonable), possessing a razor the consumer uses each week either one blade or no blades (if he gives up shaving by razor). Will the consumer care how the two items are priced, given their total cost? The answer is no. If the razor lasts indefinitely, its cost per week is the interest on the investment, or

$$\frac{ip_r}{52};$$

if i is the interest rate, and p_r the price of the razor, and the cost of shaving per week is this interest cost plus the price of a blade, or

$$\frac{ip_r}{52} + p_b,$$

the consumer will be indifferent (at $i = 0.05$) whether blades are 1¢ and razors $10.40, or blades 2¢ and razors free. (If the number of blades is variable, the situation is more complicated.)

Let us finally take a more difficult example. A household rents a home for $200 a month, and contemplates purchasing it for $20,000. Here the monthly cost of home ownership would be the sum of

1. interest per month on the $20,000, whether paid for in cash or mortgaged 100 per cent;

2. taxes per month on the house;

3. *minus* the saving in income taxes because interest payments and taxes are deductible;

4. repair costs per month;

5. depreciation of the house;

6. the costs (agents, fees, worry) of selling the house, if the family moves in the future;

7. *minus* the pleasure of independence, or *plus* the pleasures of insolence.

These costs will vary with the family's situation—for example item 3 varies with the family's taxable income.

Maximizing Utility. We come now to the part of rational behavior that provides purpose to consumer behavior: the maximizing of utility. Let us translate this assumption into terms of indifference curves and budget lines before examining it critically.

On our assumption that the goods are desirable, indifference curves have negative slopes, and the combinations on a higher indifference curve are always preferred to those on a lower indifference curve. Hence to maximize utility is to select from the attainable combinations of goods that combination which is on the highest indifference curve. In Figure 4-6, the combination chosen is Q —combinations R and T, for example, are also available but represent lower levels of utility; combination S is superior to Q but costs more than the available income.

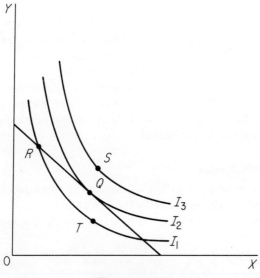

Figure 4-6

The slope of an indifference curve has been defined as the marginal rate of substitution of Y for X. Since a price line is tangent to the highest indifference curve it touches, the price line and the indifference curve have the same slope, so the condition of maximum utility may be rewritten,

$$S_{yx} = \frac{P_x}{P_y}.[8]$$

What can the economist respond to a person (say a psychiatrist) who insists that *he* does not maximize utility? It would be easy to persuade him that he does not minimize utility: after all he is alive, and not drinking crankcase oil. It would also be possible, as we shall see later, to point to empirical implications of the assumption, but since these implications began to be developed only about 40 years after the theory was proposed (1871), what led economists to accept it?

[8] This equation holds only if the price line and indifference curve are tangent. If a price line touches the highest indifference curve on an axis, so only one commodity is purchased (say Y), the condition for maximum satisfaction becomes,
$$S_{yx} < P_x/P_y \quad \text{if} \quad X = 0.$$
Such "corner" solutions abound in "linear programming."

The main reason was introspection. Everyone has irrational foibles: a common one is to refuse to put extra postage on a letter if one does not have the exact denomination, thus saving one or two cents, at the cost of a more expensive special trip to the post office. Yet by and large our actions are geared to the goals we seek to achieve. Introspective evidence will never convince a sceptic, and perhaps the only remarkable thing about introspection on utility maximizing is that virtually every economist found it convincing over so long a period.

Consumer Behavior

We can now proceed to the derivation of consumer reactions to price and income changes. Let us begin with income.

Variations in Income. The budget line, which displays the com-

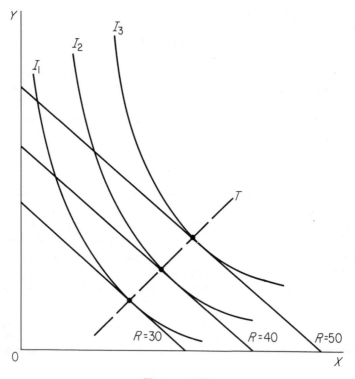

Figure 4-7

bination of goods which (at given prices) the consumer can afford is

$$XP_x + YP_y = R = \text{Income}.$$

As income rises, the budget line shifts to the right, but without a change of slope because prices are being held constant. A whole array of budget lines is shown in Figure 4-7, with incomes labeled.[9]

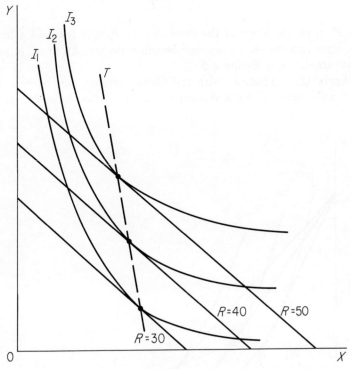

Figure 4-8

Each budget line is tangent to an indifference curve, and this is the point of maximum satisfaction for the consumer. These points are joined by the dashed curve, T. If T is positively sloping, more of each commodity is purchased as income rises. If T has a negative slope, as in Figure 4-8, less of one commodity will be bought as income rises (and such commodities are often called *inferior*).

[9] Income will be proportional to the intercepts on either axis.

Clearly both (or, in the case of more commodities, all) commodities cannot be inferior or the entire income would not be spent.

Variation in Prices. The corresponding derivation of the demand curve requires only that we vary one of the prices, holding income and the other price constant. Let the variable price be P_x, and re-write the budget line as

$$Y = \frac{R}{P_y} - X\frac{P_x}{P_y}.$$

As P_x rises, the slope of the price line $(-P_x/P_y)$ becomes a larger negative number—the price line becomes steeper. An array of price lines are drawn in Figure 4-9.

Again the tangencies with indifference curves can be read off, and are connected by a dashed curve M. As we have drawn the

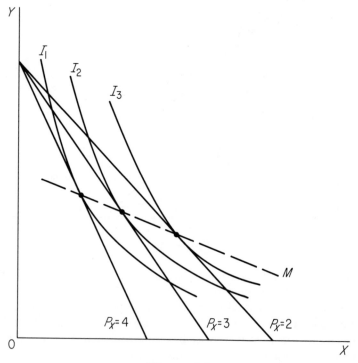

Figure 4-9

indifference curves, the quantity of X purchased diminishes as its price rises, and this is of course the usual state of affairs. But it is possible to draw the indifference curves so more of X is bought as the price rises; we do so in Figure 4-10. This result is paradoxical and what is even more paradoxical is that Marshall believed such

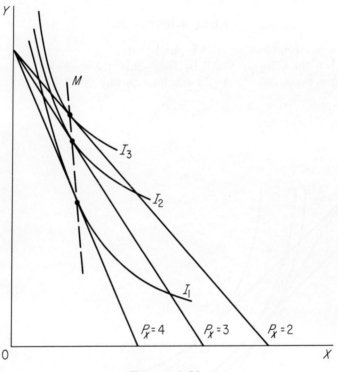

Figure 4-10

a situation once arose. There is some evidence that this "Giffen case" (as it is called) never existed, and none at all that it did.[10] But it *could* exist, and we shall shortly explain why.

Income and Substitution Effects. The logic of the Giffen case, and of these exercises in geometry, will be clarified if we go back to a simple question: what happens when the price of a commodity

[10] See reference, footnote 4, p. **24**.

falls? Suppose the consumer has been on the budget line,

$$0.1X + 0.5Y = 50,$$

(where $P_x = 10¢$ and $P_y = 50¢$), buying $200X$ and $60Y$. This combination is labelled Q_0 in Figure 4-11. If the price of X falls to $6¢$, the budget line becomes,

$$0.06X + 0.5Y = 50,$$

and a new combination (Q_2) is purchased.

When the price of X fell by four cents, the consumer obviously became better off: he could continue to buy $200X$ and $60Y$, and

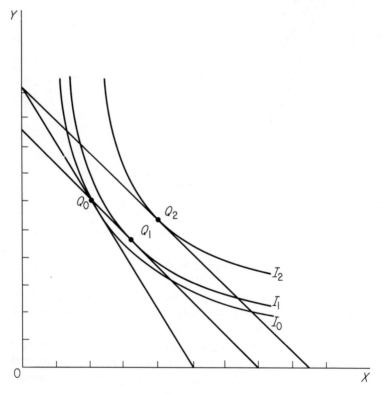

Figure 4-11

still have \$8 (= 200 $\times$ 0.04) left. Suppose, in fact, that simultaneously with the fall in P_x, an \$8 income tax were levied upon him. Then the new price line (with $P_x = 0.06$) would shift to the left and go through Q_0, because $X = 200$ and $Y = 60$ is a point on the price line, $0.06X + 0.5Y = 42$. With such a tax, the consumer would have moved to combination Q_1, because this would be the point where utility was maximized. And clearly Q_1 lies to the right of Q_0: the convexity of indifference curves guarantees that a flatter price line will be tangent at a larger quantity of X. Or, in commonsense terms, since X is relatively cheaper, with a fixed "real" income the consumer will buy relatively more of it than before the price fall.[11] Now let the vacillating tax collector refund the \$8. The price line moves to the right, and the individual returns to Q_2. The move from Q_1 to Q_2 is therefore called the *income effect,* and the move from Q_0 to Q_1 the *substitution effect.*

The substitution effect is always negative: a fall in price always leads to an increase in quantity. But the income effect can go either way. In the normal case it reinforces the substitution effect: the restoration of the increment of real income due to the price fall leads to an additional increase in the consumption of X. But with inferior goods (such as coarse bread, tenements, and old polo ponies) the income effect is negative. It can even dominate the substitution effect, and then we have the Giffen paradox—which is illustrated in Figure 4-12 (an elaboration of Figure 4-10).[12]

A Utility-based Supply Curve. Whenever an individual possesses a stock or flow of anything (potatoes, labor services) he may become a seller as well as a buyer of it. It is easy to enlarge the utility analysis to deal with this situation.

[11] Strictly speaking, Q_1 lies on a slightly higher indifference curve than Q_0 so real income is (by definition) slightly larger at Q_1 than at Q_0. But if the price change is small, the difference between measuring the substitution effect along indifference curve I_0 and between I_0 and I_1 is mathematically negligible (meaning a higher order infinitesimal).

[12] In the preceding chapter complements and substitutes were defined in terms of the cross-elasticity of demand. In the theory of utility, different definitions have been developed that are more logical and less usable. When one thinks of bread and butter as complements, one is thinking of tastes, and it is therefore more appropriate to define the relationship between goods in terms of the indifference curves, quite independently of prices and income. And this is what is done; see, for example, R. G. D. Allen, *Mathematical Analysis for Economists* (London: Macmillan, 1938), p. 512.

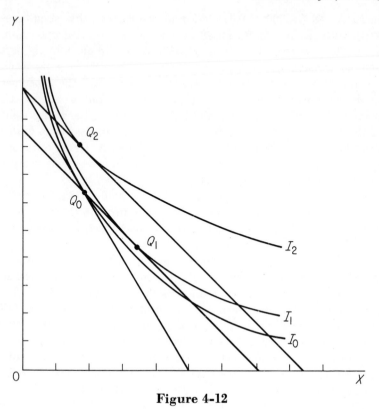

Figure 4-12

Let us assume that the individual possesses an initial stock X_0 of a commodity, and that the quantity he possesses after making any exchanges he wishes is X. Then $X - X_0$ is the quantity demanded if $X > X_0$. The budget equation becomes

$$(X - X_0)P_x + YP_y = R,$$

or

$$XP_x + YP_y = R + X_0 P_x.$$

Hence when the price of X rises, the budget line becomes steeper as before, for its slope is $-P_x/P_y$, but now it also is raised by the amount of the increase in the value of the initial stock.

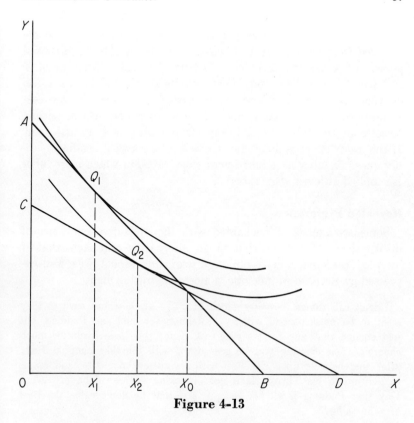

Figure 4-13

The geometrical derivation of the supply or demand curve for X is illustrated in Figure 4-13. At an initial price P_x, with price line AB, the individual is at Q_1—as drawn here he wishes to hold less of X than his original stock, and supplies $X_0 - X_1$. If the price of X falls by half, the budget line becomes CD,[13] and the quantity supplied falls to $X_0 - X_2$.

There is a double income effect with an initial stock of X. A

[13] The intercept of the budget line and the X-axis is now given by
$$X = \frac{R + X_0 P_x}{P_x} = \frac{R}{P_x} + X_0.$$
The corresponding Y-axis intercept is
$$Y = \frac{R}{P_y} + \frac{X_0 P_x}{P_y}.$$

fall in price increases the real income of a given number of dollars. But a fall in price will reduce the number of dollars of income received from the sale of X. If possession of X yields a substantial portion of a person's income, as is true of a wage earner when X is labor (time), the latter effect will be dominant. Hence a fall in wage rates will (1) lead to an increase in leisure (whose cost is foregone wage income), and (2) lead to a decrease in leisure, because of the fall in real income, and leisure is a normal good. If the latter effect is dominant, there is a "backward bending" supply curve of labor as a function of wage rates, in which more labor is supplied at lower wage rates.

Revealed Preference

Some economists, disenchanted with the subjective overtones of utility theory, have resorted to an alternative approach, that of revealed preference. The philosophy of this school was well-expressed by Bernard Mandeville, a most penetrating man:

> I don't call things Pleasures which Men say are best, but such as they seem to be most pleased with; . . . John never cuts any Pudding, but just enough that you can't say he took none; this little Bit, after much chomping and chewing you see goes down with him like chopp'd Hay; after that he falls upon the Beef with a voracious Appetite, and crams himself up to his Throat. Is it not provoking to hear John cry every Day that Pudding is all his Delight, and that he don't value the Beef of a Farthing?[14]

The essence of the approach is to look at observed behavior, and from it deduce certain properties of tastes. The theory is formally independent of utility, but it is inconceivable that the right things would have been observed without guidance of the utility theory.

Suppose we can observe a consumer at many equilibria—each with a different set of prices and quantities. At one time he is at Q_{10} on price line B_{10} (Figure 4-14). The individual prefers this position to any other on or below this budget line, or he would not have chosen it. In principle (a phrase used to denote the combination of incredible circumstances and unbelievable ingenuity) we could observe him at a hundred other different relative prices. Let

[14] *The Fable of the Bees* (1714), (Oxford, England: The Clarendon Press, Kaye edition, 1924), Vol. I, pp. 151–52.

us find the budget line (B_9) which leads the consumer to choose combination Q_9, a combination necessarily inferior to Q_{10}. The choice of Q_9 reveals it to be preferable to every other point on or below B_9, so all these points are inferior to Q_{10}. By similar argument Q_{10} is preferable to every point on or below line B_8. If the

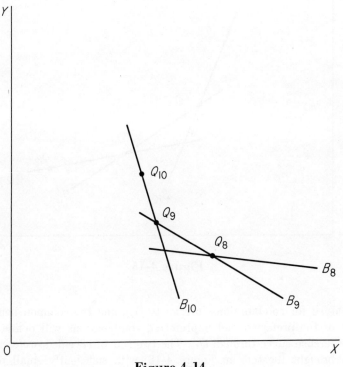

Figure 4-14

relative price changes are made small enough, this procedure will trace out all combinations inferior to Q_{10}.

A parallel procedure will trace out all the combinations superior to Q_{10} (Figure 4-15). On budget line B_{11}, if Q_{11} is chosen it is preferable to Q_{10} and hence to all points on or below B_{11}; similarly Q_{12} is preferred to Q_{11} and hence to Q_{10}. The combinations traced out by this procedure will define a curve which converges to that

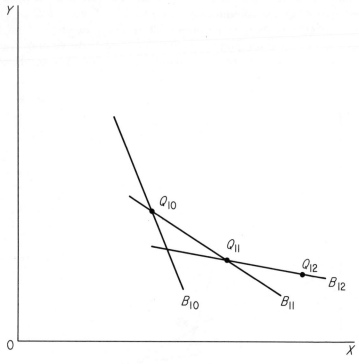

Figure 4-15

obtained for combinations inferior to Q_{10}, and the common boundary of the preferred and unpreferred combinations will define the
indifference curve through Q_{10}. The two sets of revealed preferences
are brought together in Figure 4-16; with sufficiently small price
changes the two sets of lines converge to the indifference curve.

This approach dispenses with almost every requirement except
consistency of preferences of individuals. But since it is obviously
heart-breaking in its data requirements, all the properties
illustrated by revealed preference have of course been inferred from
utility theory. Its chief function is, therefore, to reassure critics
of utility theory that the same results can be reached by another
route, in principle.

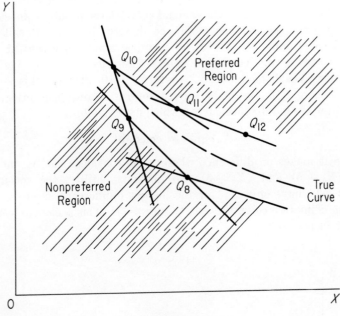

Figure 4-16

APPLICATIONS OF UTILITY THEORY

The elements of the theory of utility are before us: for what can it be used? The uses are of two different sorts. On the one hand, it is possible to make predictions concerning the behavior of individuals, and in this role utility theory provides a set of hypotheses. On the other hand, utility is a bridge between observable phenomena and subjective states of satisfaction, and in this role allows inferences to be drawn concerning welfare effects of policies. Both uses deserve illustration.

Utility Theory as a Hypothesis

The theory of the rational consumer has numerous empirical implications. The most famous one is the assertion, discussed above, that the demand curve for a commodity must have a negative slope if the income effect is small or positive. But it is not a very useful hypothesis, since all known demand curves have negative slopes.

Many simpler hypotheses can be derived, however. Recall our previous example (p. 57) of an identical commodity sold at two prices, where the consumer knows the prices and the fact of identity. The budget line, $2X_a + 2.1X_b = 10$, displays this situation, where B is the higher-priced source. Against this price line we draw the indifference curves, which have the form

$$X_a + X_b = \text{constant},$$

since it makes no difference whether the consumer has X_a and X_b or $(X_a - 5)$ and $(X_b + 5)$. To maximize utility, the consumer obviously buys only X_a, for the highest indifference curve he can reach is intersected on the axis (Figure 4-17). This is easy to test, at least in principle.

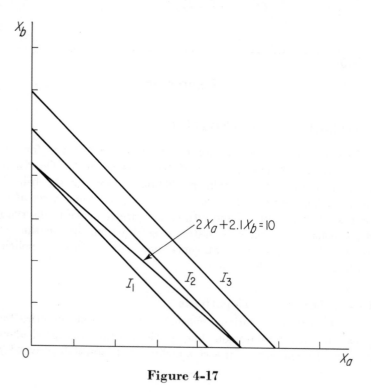

Figure 4-17

Or consider a wholly different area. In addition to a desire for profits, the entrepreneur wishes certain consumption amenities in his business (a noble edifice, a handsome office, a delectable secretary, certain social types of associates). All have costs, of course, and the corresponding budget line and indifference curves are shown in Figure 4-18. He buys $0C$ of the amenities at a cost of BA (of foregone profits). In certain areas (public utilities) the state regulates prices to put a maximum on profits, which are reckoned after

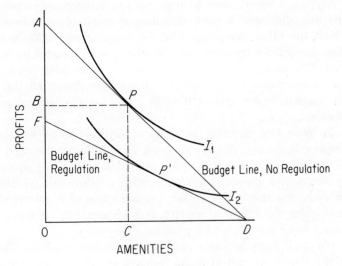

Figure 4-18

business expenses which of course include the costs of these amenities. Hence to the limited degree that the regulation is effective the budget line becomes flatter—there are smaller costs to the amenities in terms of foregone profits. The new equilibrium, P', necessarily has larger amenities.[15]

[15] The new budget line is flatter because the regulatory body objects much less to amenities than to money profits. For an elaboration of the argument and empirical evidence on effects on the racial composition of the labor force, see A. Alchian and R. Kessel, "Competition, Monopoly and the Pursuit of Pecuniary Gain," in *Aspects of Labor Economics* by A Conference of the Universities-National Bureau Committee for Economic Research (Princeton, N. J.: Princeton University Press, 1962).

Only inventiveness is necessary to multiply such predictions of the utility theory.[16] The theory of the rational individual, who seeks to fulfill his goals as efficiently as possible, pertains to a vast area of human conduct, even if it does not provide a complete theory of any part of that conduct. We economists have been remiss, I believe, in developing and testing the implications of the theory; only by such tests, indeed, are we likely to discover a better theory of economic conduct.

Welfare Analyses

Suppose a wholly alien creature were to observe two events. First, one man displayed a card requesting a charitable contribution, to which the other man responded by handing over $20. Next, one man displayed a revolver, and the other man responded by handing over $20. Surely he would be unable to distinguish between the two transactions, and if told that the former donor felt the better for his gift, would feel entitled to infer that the latter donor felt likewise.

To read any meaning in terms of satisfaction or welfare into observable events, clearly we must have a bridge between states of welfare and observable events, and this is the chief role played by the utility theory. Unlike the alien creature, we do not need an elaborate theory (or rather, possess parts of it intuitively) to distinguish the effects of charity and robbery, but for many problems a much more formal apparatus is necessary.

We shall examine three examples of welfare analysis. The first is the theory of cost-of-living indexes, on which economists have long labored. The second example is a famous piece of the apparatus of welfare economics. The final example, price discrimination, is intended chiefly to display a technique with many applications.

Cost-of-Living Indexes. The phrase, cost of living, connotes the amount the family spends on consumption, but this important cost is termed consumer expenditures. The phrase actually means the cost, over time or between places, of living at a constant level—which means, of course, staying on the same indifference curve.[17]

---

[16] Special mention should be made of the important modern literature on utility in relation to risk, to which references are made at the end of the chapter.

[17] To avoid this ambiguity, the official American index is called the Con-

Price indexes developed out of the inflation following the California gold discoveries, and they have not lost their intimate connection with inflation. If an average family earned \$5,000 in 1960 and \$5,500 in 1962, in which year was it "better off"? The answer is that if a (perfect) index of the cost of living rose less than 10 per cent between these years, the family was "better off" in 1962.[18]

One basic assumption must be made before we can make any progress toward an index number: tastes must not change. For no meaning can be attached to the same level of satisfaction when satisfactions change. Suppose Smith is a vegetarian in year 1, and meat-eater in year 2. No matter how the prices of grains and meat move, one cannot measure the cost of living, for there is no quantity of meat which yields the same satisfaction as the previous quantity of grain: the man is different at the two dates, and the question has become the insoluble one of finding the money incomes which will yield equal satisfactions to two men.[19]

Let us assume that in a given year the average family buys two commodities—the argument of course applies to any number—in quantities $_aq_0$ and $_bq_0$ (where a and b are the names of commodities, and 0 the year) at prices $_ap_0$ and $_bp_0$. Then

$$_aq_0 \, _ap_0 + _bq_0 \, _bp_0 = {_0R_0},$$

was the amount spent. The budget line and the observed combination (Q_1) are shown in Figure 4-19. In the next year prices change, and the foregoing combination would have cost

$$_aq_0 \, _ap_1 + _bq_0 \, _bp_1 = {_0R_1}.$$

If we treat this latter expression as a budget line, it will necessarily go through the combination bought in year 0; but its slope will be different if the prices of A and B have not changed in the same proportion.

---

sumer Price Index. On the practice and problems of price indexes, see *Government Price Statistics* (Washington, D. C.: Joint Economic Committee, 1961).

[18] A perfect index would take account of income taxes and public services, which both the official index and the present discussion ignore.

[19] Of course one can postulate that money incomes that will yield the same real income to a vegetarian and a meat-eater, or to a ditch-digger and a prime minister, are equal. This is in fact done in some income-equalizing philosophies, but it is an ethical judgment, not a description of states of real income.

If the family had a money income $_0R_0$ in year 0 and $_0R_1$ in year 1, it must be at least as well off in terms of utility in the latter year. It could buy the original quantities, so it was as well off, and it could probably reach a higher indifference curve with $_0R_1$ by substituting the commodity whose price has fallen relatively (A

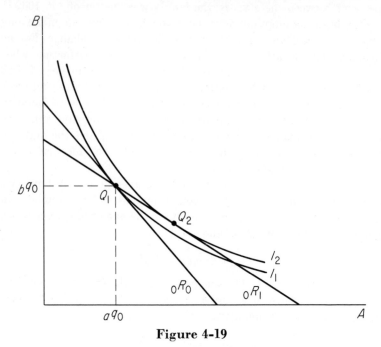

Figure 4-19

in our diagram), say at point Q_2. So we can assert that the cost of living rose from year 0 to year 1 *at most* in the proportion,

$$\frac{_0R_1}{_0R_0} = \frac{_aq_0\,_ap_1 + _bq_0\,_bp_1}{_aq_0\,_ap_0 + _bq_0\,_bp_0},$$

which is generally written

$$\mathcal{L} = \frac{\Sigma q_0 p_1}{\Sigma q_0 p_0},$$

where the summation signs indicate addition over all commodities, and $\mathcal{L}$ is the name (of Etienne Laspeyres) given to this index. This is the form of the index used to measure changes in the cost of living in the United States, with a sample of prices of 400 goods and services and a new set of quantities (weights) every decade.

The Laspeyres index measures the change in the cost of living as the family lived in year 0; obviously another index could be made to measure the cost in year 0 of the way the family lived in year 1. Here in year 1 the family bought quantities $_aq_1$ and $_bq_1$ and prices $_ap_1$ and $_bp_1$, on the budget line

$$_aq_1 \,_ap_1 + \,_bq_1 \,_bp_1 = \,_1R_1.$$

By exactly the same argument used to reach the Laspeyres index, we can say that in year 0 the family would be at least this well off if it had spent

$$_aq_1 \,_ap_0 + \,_bq_1 \,_bp_0 = \,_1R_0,$$

because it could have purchased the year 1 quantity in any case, and usually it could reach a higher indifference curve by buying relatively more of the commodity whose price had fallen relative to the other price. In fact the previous diagram needs no change other than to relabel $_0R_0$ as $_1R_1$, and $_0R_1$ as $_1R_0$. So we conclude that the cost of living in year 0 relative to year 1 rose at most in the proportion,

$$\frac{_1R_0}{_1R_1} = \frac{_aq_1 \,_ap_0 + \,_bq_1 \,_bp_0}{_aq_1 \,_ap_1 + \,_bq_1 \,_bp_1}$$

$$= \frac{\Sigma q_1 p_0}{\Sigma q_1 p_1}.$$

But normally index numbers are reckoned forward in time, so if $_1R_0/_1R_1$ is the maximum relative change in the cost of living (as in year 1) from year 1 to year 0, then its reciprocal,

$$\mathcal{P} = \frac{\Sigma p_1 q_1}{\Sigma p_0 q_1},$$

is the minimum relative rise in year 1 relative to year 0 of the cost of living as in year 1. Here the $\mathcal{P}$ represents Hermann Paasche, who, like Laspeyres, was not the first to propose the index named after him. If we should ever encounter a case where a theory is named for the correct man, it will be noted.

The Laspeyres index, as we have said, is a maximum estimate of the change in the cost of living from year 0 to year 1, and the Paasche index is a minimum estimate. Unfortunately, they do not pertain to the same level of living: the Laspeyres index prices the year 0 budget; the Paasche index prices the year 1 budget. Of course if the same quantities were consumed both years, the indexes would be identical, but in this case the only probable cause is that prices have not changed!

One basic problem in calculating index numbers is the treatment of changes in the qualities of goods. We cannot properly attribute all of the change in price to the cost of living if an improved commodity (a better automobile or improved surgical techniques) is involved. On the other hand, if one prices only those commodities whose qualities do not change, he will find that a large and ever rising share of the consumer's budget must be omitted. A device that can often be employed is a fairly straightforward extension of the basic logic.

Changes in quality are gradual, and they can be at least partially measured by measurable characteristics of the commodity. Automobile quality can be measured by weight, horsepower, length, automatic vs. nonautomatic transmission, and so on. If these measures are properly chosen the differences in prices of various models in any one year will be well explained by these differences in characteristics. We can then say, for example, that 10 horsepower are worth $40, and automatic transmission is worth $180. If next year a given model of car sells for $200 more, but has 10 more horsepower and an automatic transmission, its quality-corrected price actually fell $20.[20] Economists generally believe—certainly this one does—that the official index has considerably overstated the rise of prices because of the failure to cope with quality changes.

Consumer's Surplus. When a reflective man buys a crowbar to pry open a treasure chest, he may well remark to himself that if necessary he would have been willing to pay tenfold the price. When a parched man drinks a free beer on a hot day, he is apt to consider it a bargain. Marshall gave the odd name of "consumer's surplus" to these fugitive sentiments.

Let us define this surplus as the amount over and above the price actually paid that a man would be willing to pay for a given amount of a commodity rather than go without it. Then we may illustrate this surplus by two indifference curves between money income (= all other goods) and the commodity in question (Figure

[20] This method is used in Zvi Griliches, "Hedonic Price Indexes for Automobiles," in *Government Price Statistics* (Washington, D. C.: Joint Economic Committee, 1961).

4-20A). The individual would be as well off with an income of $0A$, and the privilege of buying $0C$ of the commodity at the indicated prices (given by the slope of AB), as with an income of $0E$. Hence AE is a measure of his consumer's surplus. Alternatively, he pays a total of DA for the $0C$ units, and would be willing to pay an

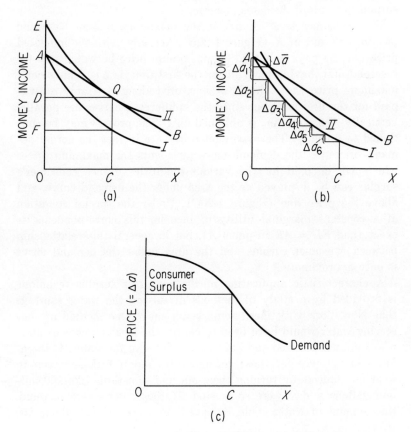

Figure 4-20

additional FD. Therefore FD is the additional amount he would pay if he already has $0C$ of the commodity, whereas AE is the additional amount he would pay if he has none of the commodity and the option is offered to him. The two estimates may differ.

Let us follow Marshall a step further in assuming that the marginal utility of money income does not change appreciably if only a small amount is spent on commodity X. Then every indifference curve will have the same shape but be vertically higher or lower than other indifference curves.[21] Armed with this simplifying property, we can now construct a simple representation of consumer surplus in terms of the demand curve.

If a consumer is at A, Δa_1 is the maximum amount he would pay for one unit of X (Figure 4-20B). Actually, with the indicated price line, he pays only $\Delta \bar{a}$. The maximum price he would pay for a second unit, having paid $\Delta \bar{a}$ for the first unit, is Δa_2. This second maximum price (Δa_2) should be measured along II if only $\Delta \bar{a}$ was paid for the first unit, but since the indifference curves are parallel vertically, the same Δa_2 is obtained on I. The process may be continued to reach Q. The maximum prices are in fact the actual demand prices, so the demand curve represents the maximum prices which will be paid for the various quantities. Hence consumer's surplus can be displayed as the area under the demand curve, and above the price line (Figure 4-20C). Under the special condition of a constant marginal utility of income, this correspondence is exact (and $FD = AE$ in panel A), but in general this relationship between consumer surplus and the area under the demand curve is only approximate.[22]

A characteristic application of the consumer surplus technique is provided by a study of methods of solving the water shortage that New York City faced some years ago.[23] One method of conserving water would have been to charge the large number of users who were not metered and paid only a flat sum for water. It therefore did not pay for those consumers to repair leaks or even to wear out faucets by turning them off, and something like 200 million gallons a day were so wasted. If these users were metered, this amount of water could be saved, at a cost of (1) about $50

[21] Since the slope of an indifference curve is

$$- \frac{\text{marginal utility of } X}{\text{marginal utility of income}},$$

if the marginal utility of income is constant, the slope of the indifference curves will vary only with X.

[22] See J. R. Hicks, "Consumer's Surplus and Index Numbers," *Review of Economic Studies*, 9 (1942), 126–37.

[23] This discussion is based upon Chapter 10 of J. Hirshleifer, J. C. DeHaven, and J. W. Milliman, *Water Supply* (Chicago: University of Chicago Press, 1960).

per million gallons per day for the cost of metering, *plus* (2) the cost of repairing leaks, which we shall ignore, and *plus* (3) the consumer's surplus lost by restricting consumption if the marginal cost of water was raised from zero to say 15¢ per cubic feet (the going rate). If the demand curve is taken as linear in this range, the average value of the water saved was 7.5¢ per 100 cubic feet or $100 per million gallons. Hence the total cost of saving water, including consumer surplus lost, was about $150 per million gallons.[24]

Price Discrimination. As our final example of welfare analysis, we shall examine price discrimination. Price discrimination arises when a commodity is sold at different prices to different people.[25] Suppose, for example, that salt is sold to one person for 10 cents per pound, and to another person for 20 cents per pound; all other prices are equal for the two persons. The buyer at the lower price consumes salt until the marginal rate of substitution of a composite "other goods" (with a price of $1.00 per unit) for salt is 1 for 10, whenever the buyer at the higher price has a rate of substitution of 1 for 5. If they were to exchange salt and other goods at some intermediate ratio, say 1 to 7, both would gain. At the margin the buyer at the higher price would gain 40 per cent ($\frac{2}{5}$) more salt per unit of other goods given up; the buyer at the lower price would gain 43 per cent more units of other goods per pound of salt given up.[26] Price discrimination plays the same role here as a tariff plays in the theory of comparative costs: it is an obstacle to maximizing utility.

This kind of problem is commonly analyzed geometrically by an artifice that is worth describing. Suppose the two parties have a total of $0Y_0$ of other goods and $0X_0$ of salt (Figure 4-21): perpendiculars are then projected to $0'$. The indifference curves of individual A (who gets salt for 20¢) are drawn with respect to $Y_0 0 X_0$, and those of B (salt for 10¢) are rotated 180° and drawn with respect to $Y_0 0' X_0$. Then any point in the rectangle represents a distribution of the given quantities of salt and other goods between

[24] The city fathers, or step-fathers, chose instead to build a new dam, at a cost of $1,000 per million gallons.

[25] A more precise definition will be given later, p. 209.

[26] He now obtains $\frac{1}{7}$ of a unit of other goods per pound of salt, where formerly he received only $\frac{1}{10}$ of a unit, and

$$\frac{\frac{1}{7} - \frac{1}{10}}{\frac{1}{10}} = \frac{3}{7} = 0.43.$$

the two individuals: for example, at S, A gets OM of salt and B gets MX_0.

With price discrimination, the price line of A (drawn with respect to $0X_0$) will have a slope of $-\frac{1}{5}$, the ratio of the price of the salt to that of other goods; it is labeled P_a. The price line of B will have

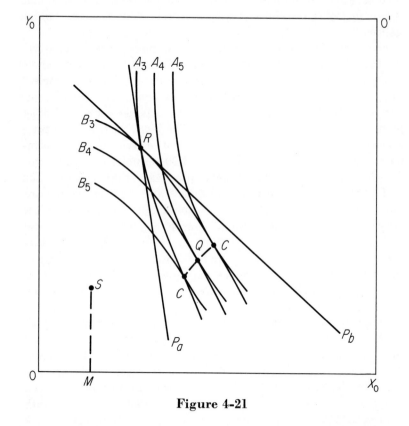

Figure 4-21

a slope of $-\frac{1}{10}$, with respect to $0'Y_0$, it is labeled P_b. If the position with discrimination is one of equilibrium, the two price lines intersect at a point (R) such that each is tangent to an appropriate indifference curve.[27]

[27] At point R, not only is each consumer maximizing utility but the quantities demanded of the two goods equal available amounts.

Now consider a point Q where the two individuals' indifference curves are tangent. Each individual would be better off at Q than at R, for each would be on a higher indifference curve (remembering that the B curves are measured from $0'$). There are many points such as Q, and we have joined them by a curve CC (called the contract curve). Only points on this curve maximize utility for each man, given the level of utility attained by the other, and only with a nondiscriminatory price will the individuals arrive on this curve. Any movement along the contract curve injures one party and benefits the other, but movements *to* the curve can benefit both.[28]

RECOMMENDED READINGS

Alchian, A., "The Meaning of Utility Measurement," *American Economic Review*, **42** (1953), 26–50.

Ellsberg, D., "Classic and Current Notions of 'Measurable Utility'," *Economic Journal*, **64** (1954), 528–556.

Hicks, J. R., *Value and Capital*, Oxford: Oxford University Press, 1939, Part I.

Friedman, M., and L. J. Savage, "The Utility Analysis of Choices Involving Risk," *Journal of Political Economy*, **56** (1948), 279–304; reprinted in *Readings in Price Theory*.

Stigler, G. J., "The Development of Utility Theory," *Journal of Political Economy*, **33** (1950), 369–387; reprinted in *Essays in the History of Economics*, Chicago: University of Chicago Press, 1964.

PROBLEMS

1. Draw the indifference curves which display the following preference system:

(a) Two commodities are useful only in fixed proportions (left and right shoes).

(b) One commodity is fully divisible but the other comes in (or is useful only in) integral units (gasoline and tires).

(c) "I like my martinis drier than you do."

(d) Consumption of one commodity reduces the enjoyment of the other (WCTU tracts and bourbon).

---

[28] The length of the contract curve is given by the "initial" conditions of a problem. Here individual A would prefer discrimination to falling below indifference curve A_3, and B would prefer discrimination to falling (toward $0'$) below B_3.

2. Calculate the Laspeyres and Paasche indexes:

	YEAR 0	YEAR 1
Quantity of bread	200	170
Quantity of beef	100	120
Price of bread	15¢	12¢
Price of beef	20¢	25¢

Illustrate graphically and explain.

3. Suppose the total utilities of X and Y vary as follows:

$$TU_x = \sqrt{X}$$
$$TU_y = 10Y - Y^2 \qquad (Y < 5)$$

(a) Construct indifference curves between X and Y for a level of satisfaction of 24.

(b) Suppose the utility of each commodity doubles (to $2\sqrt{X}$ and $2[10Y - Y^2]$). Construct the indifference curves for a level of satisfaction of 48.

4. Demonstrate that people are better off with rationing by prices than with rationing by fixed allotments, given the distribution of income.

5. A consumer challenges you to disprove empirically his assertion that his indifference curves intersect. If you have an unlimited number of observations on his actual consumption (at all relative prices and incomes), how would you meet the challenge?

6. If the marginal utility of Y is constant, all indifference curves have the same slope at a given X. Prove.

chapter five

Pricing with Fixed Supplies

Once the demand curve of a commodity is established, we know the price at which each quantity can be sold. But we have begged two questions in constructing this demand curve: what is the market, and is it competitive? After we answer these questions we can analyse the pricing of commodities in fixed supply.

THE MARKET

A market, according to the masters, is the area within which the price of a commodity tends to uniformity, allowance being made for transportation costs.

The price of a commodity "tends to uniformity" for one reason: the buyers at point B refuse to pay more than the price at point A plus transportation, and the buyers at A act similarly. Or the sellers act in this manner. The market area may well differ between buyers and sellers.

As the buyer of an automobile, I will perhaps search only over a circle with a 10-mile radius about my home, so I may readily return to the dealer for services. But this cannot mean that the market area is 314.16 sq. miles, for other buyers are located elsewhere and their circles of search overlap mine. The market area, so far as buyers are involved, is the sum of the areas within which the mobility of consumers is sufficient to ensure the tendency to uniformity in price, allowance being made for transportation costs. For automobiles, this area will probably contain a city and its adjacent suburbs; for the services of gardeners it may be a small portion of a city; for goods purchased by mail order it may be nation-wide.

The market area from the sellers' viewpoint will usually be larger than from the buyers' viewpoint. There is no important tendency for people in Minneapolis to buy potatoes in Maine. Yet one of the earliest statistical studies of demand revealed that the price of potatoes in Minneapolis depended upon the nation's output of potatoes, but given this output, was not influenced by whether the local output (in Minnesota and Wisconsin) was large or small.

An investigation was made to determine the effect of variations in the production of Minnesota and Wisconsin taken together on the price of potatoes in Minneapolis and St. Paul. This investigation resulted in the discovery that variations in the production in Minnesota and Wisconsin had no measurable effect on the price of potatoes except to the extent that the production for the entire United States was affected.

Although the fact is surprising, it is very readily explained when once recognized. The explanation will be somewhat clearer if the price situation as shown in [an accompanying figure] is borne in mind. Consider the extreme case of an excess production in Minnesota exactly equaled by a deficiency of production in Maine. In order to take care of the deficiency in the supply for New York City, for example, an unusual quantity is shipped in from New York and Pennsylvania. Large quantities of potatoes having been shipped east instead of west from New York and Pennsylvania, their place is taken by Michigan potatoes. But since Michigan potatoes are being shipped somewhat farther east than usual, Minnesota potatoes can be sold without competition in what is ordinarily Michigan territory. The result is that the Minnesota potatoes sell at practically the same price that would have been obtained if production in both Minnesota and Maine had been normal.[1]

On the other hand, sometimes the market area as defined by sellers is smaller than that of buyers: a cotton farmer will have a relatively small area in which he will sell his crop; the buyers may deal in every cotton-picking state.

Since the market is defined by the uniformity of price, its area will be at least as large as the larger of the areas of sellers' competition and buyers' competition, or the sum of the areas when they partially overlap.

---

[1] H. Working, "Factors Determining the Price of Potatoes in St. Paul and Minneapolis," Technical Bulletin 10, University of Minnesota Agricultural Experiment Station (1922), p. 25.

The size of the market also varies with the time we allow for price adjustments. A perishable good, once it reaches a given city, will be sold there even though it turns out that a higher price could have been fetched elsewhere—but future shipments will iron out the disparity. Once an apartment is built, its rental depends upon the housing demand of the community. But in the long run (meaning a period long enough for the supply of houses to be varied sufficiently), apartments will not be built where rentals are unremunerative, and more will be built where they are remunerative. There is accordingly a tendency for apartments of given quality to have the same rental throughout the country. But this tendency is slow in its workings because the stock of apartments changes very slowly, and it is modified by geographical immobilities of resources (in particular, land) which we shall discuss later. Because of the mobility of entrepreneurs and also of consumers, in the long run most markets are of very large geographical extent.

A perfect market is one characterized by perfect knowledge on the part of the traders. Or stated differently, in a perfect market no buyer ever pays more than any seller will accept, and no seller accepts less than any buyer will pay. These conditions can be met only in a completely centralized market, which is approximated by a few exchanges such as the New York Stock Exchange.

COMPETITION

A competitive market is easily defined only for a perfect market: it is then a market in which the individual buyer or seller does not influence the price by his purchases or sales. Alternately stated, the elasticity of supply facing any buyer is infinite, and the elasticity of demand facing any seller is infinite.

A market may obviously be competitive on only one side: a million buyers can deal with only one seller (monopoly) or a million sellers can deal with one buyer (monopsony). But for the time we shall defer such situations and deal only with competitive situations.

We have defined a perfectly competitive market: what are the conditions under which it will normally arise? The conditions are four:

1. *Perfect knowledge.* If there is not perfect knowledge, there will be an array of prices at which transactions will take place, and almost all real markets display such an array. There will then often be scope for higgling, and to this extent a situation termed bilateral monopoly arises. But if the scope for higgling is small, the departure from competition is small.

2. *Large numbers.* There must be many buyers or sellers if each is to have no appreciable influence upon the price,[2] and they act independently.

3. *Product homogeneity.* If the product is not homogeneous, it is meaningless to speak of large numbers. Hence, if every unit is essentially unique (as in the market for domestic servants), there cannot be large numbers. Yet, if the various units are highly substitutable for one another, the market can approach competition.

4. *Divisibility of the product.*

Perfect competition is a typical example of a concept of everyday life that has been taken over by economists and developed into something almost unrelated to its original form. Originally competition meant a multiplicity of traders, and only that. But when it was discovered that 5 traders might collude, a vast number seemed necessary to guarantee that collusion would not be feasible. When it was realized that even a thousand sellers and buyers were not enough if each pair dealt in ignorance of the others, perfect knowledge was added. The explicit recognition of homogeneity of product came from the fact that even minor differences (a sunny disposition or a fancy container) might lead some people to pay a slightly higher price.

Divisibility has a similar origin. Edgeworth, whom we have met before and shall meet again, was a diabolically clever man. He contrived the following problem: a thousand (or a million) masters hire one servant each—exactly the number available—and no servant can work for two masters. Each master will pay $100; each servant will accept $50—what will the wage rate be? That it will be between $50 and $100, and hence *indeterminate*, is no cause for anxiety. But let it be $50—then a single servant can leave the market and force the wage up to $100—so even perfect knowledge, large numbers, and (let us assume) homogeneity are not enough to de-

---

[2] More precisely, the largest buyer or seller must provide only a small fraction of the quantity demanded or supplied, which involves, in addition to large numbers, no extreme inequality of size.

prive an individual of a large influence over the market price. Hence we assume divisibility, so the departure of one worker leads (say) to about a 30-second lengthening of the working day for other workers, and his power to influence price is destroyed.[3]

If the reader bristles at the acceptance of assumptions such as perfect knowledge and complete product homogeneity, he is both wrong and right. He is wrong in denying the helpfulness of the use of pure, clean concepts in theoretical analysis: they confer clarity and efficiency on the analysis, *without depriving the analysis of empirical relevance.* He is right if he believes these extreme assumptions are not *necessary* to the existence of competition: it is sufficient, for example, if each trader in a market knows a fair number of buyers and sellers, if all traders together have a comprehensive knowledge so only one price rules. The reason for not stating the weakest assumptions (necessary conditions) for competition is that they are difficult to formulate, and in fact are not known precisely. Again, more work for the next generation.

The Demand Curve of the Competitive Firm

Since the competitive firm contributes only a trifling fraction of the total market supply, it has a trifling influence on market price.[4] We may illustrate this influence by considering a market with a unitary demand elasticity ($pq = \$1,000$), in which there are already 100 firms. Each supplies 2 units and the price is therefore $\$1,000/200 = \$5.00$. An additional supplier now appears. If the 100 firms continue to supply 200 units, the new supplier faces the demand schedule:

QUANTITY	PRICE
0	$\$1000/200 = \$5.000$
1	$1000/201 = 4.975$
2	$1000/202 = 4.950$
3	$1000/203 = 4.925$

[3] An eight hour day contains 480 minutes—B.C. (before coffee breaks), so if each of the remaining 999 workers works slightly less than half a minute for the employer of the vanished servant, his employer's need will be satisfied. Or, alternatively, each of the thousand masters hires a worker for 30 seconds less.

[4] The use of "trifling" rather than "absolutely no" is a trifling concession to realism. It would be more precise to use the latter phrase, but then some students would believe that the theory is inapplicable where there is even a trifling influence, and this is not true.

If we compute the arc elasticity of the new supplier's demand at an output of 2, it is roughly

$$\frac{3-1}{3+1} \cdot \frac{4.925+4.975}{4.925-4.975} = -\frac{2}{4} \cdot \frac{9.9}{0.05} = -99.$$

It is, in fact, a general rule that under these conditions the elasticity of the demand curve of a firm is equal to the elasticity of the market demand curve *times* the number of sellers.[5]

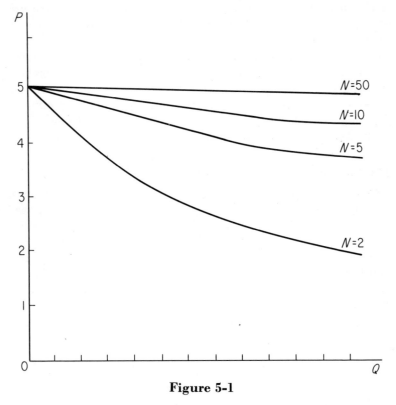

Figure 5-1

We illustrate such individual demand curves for 2, 5, 10, and 50 sellers in Figure 5-1, all on the assumptions that the market demand has unitary elasticity and the output of all firms except one sum to 200. Of course competition connotes fairly numerous sellers, and the demand curves for 2 and 5 sellers are put in only to display how rapidly the individual demand curves become elas-

[5] See mathematical note 7 in Appendix B.

tic. It would require a very large diagram to make the difference between the demand curves for each of 50 and each of 100 sellers perceptible.

These demand curves were derived on the condition that all firms sell at the same price. But suppose 100 firms had agreed to fix the price at $5, and one now contemplated his demand curve if he secretly cut the price to $4.99 to trustworthy buyers. Assuming that the 99 other firms continued to adhere to $5; the demand function of this price cutter would be

PRICE	QUANTITY DEMANDED
$5.01	0
$5.00	2
$4.99	$\dfrac{1000}{4.99} = 200.4$

Now his elasticity of demand is approximately

$$\frac{200.4 - 0}{200.4 + 0} \div \frac{4.99 - 5.01}{4.99 + 5.01} = -\frac{10.00}{0.02} = -500.$$

Of course if he cuts prices secretly and expands sales immensely, the other 99 firms will soon discover their sales are vanishing. But if he is moderate in his sales (perhaps only doubling sales to 4 units) he will reason that the price cutting will not be detected.[6] This reasoning will also be followed by at least 5 or 10 of his rivals, and if 10 double their sales to 4, only 160 (200 − 40) units will be demanded of the other sellers, each of whom will suffer, with rising animosity, a decline of 11 per cent in sales.[7]

This arithmetic portrays the history of a thousand price agreements. We shall discuss monopoly, which is what this is, at a later point, but it seems appropriate to emphasize here that large numbers of sellers not only make the formation of collusive agreements difficult, but also encourage each individual seller to violate the agreement.

PRICE DETERMINATION

Commodities in fixed supply, at least for limited time periods, are very numerous: they include the paintings of Rembrandt, the first editions of Shakespeare, and the number of Fords or Chevrolets

---

[6] After all, each rival will lose only 2/198 units or 1 per cent of his sales.
[7] Sales of each will be 160/90 = 1.78, a decrease of 0.22 from 2.

five years old. They include also the number of shares of common stock in a large industrial company, and the number of dwelling units in a city—at least for a time. Historically the most important example of all has been the stock of an agricultural product between harvests.

The same apparatus of supply and demand can be used for all these markets. But the details of the apparatus vary in an impor-

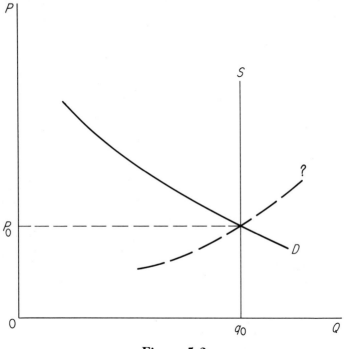

Figure 5-2

tant respect with one characteristic of commodities and services: can they be stored? Let us call commodities which cannot be stored *perishing*. It is customary to describe all goods which will not survive either time or repeated use as perishable, but those which may be used only once (like a bullet) are often capable of storage for a long period.

Perishing Commodities

The traditional case of a perishing commodity was fresh fish or strawberries brought to market before preservation by freezing was possible. The stock was naturally thrown on the market (under competition) for what it would fetch, and we may translate this behavior into a vertical supply curve (S in Figure 5-2). The demand curve is determined by tastes, income, and prices of other goods, as described in previous chapters, and the intersection of the two curves (at p_0, q_0) is the equilibrium price. The quantities would be per day or other period for which the perishing commodity remained salable.

The equilibrium price is the price from which there is no tendency to move, so long as the underlying supply and demand conditions do not alter. It is a stable equilibrium, in the sense that if the market is jarred off equilibrium, the dominant forces push it back toward this equilibrium position. For example, if a rumor of a shortage of the commodity drives the price above p_0, the fact that the quantity supplied exceeds the quantity demanded will drive the price down toward equilibrium.

These terms were obviously borrowed from physics—has the economist made sure that they really make any sense in economics? The answer is, let us hope, yes. The stability of equilibrium is indeed the normal state of affairs in a tolerably stable world, and from it we deduce important properties. For example, there is a mysterious dotted line through (p_0, q_0) in Figure 5-2 which I have not had the audacity to label a demand curve. If it were, the intersection with the supply curve would still be an equilibrium point, but it would be highly unstable: the slightest accidental fall in price, for example, would drive price ever lower, because at each lower price the quantity supplied exceeds the quantity demanded. A stable equilibrium, then, implies that an increase in the quantity supplied must lower the price, so it implies (in this case) a negatively sloping demand curve. Stability conditions are a source of information at many points in the subsequent chapters.

Is stability something we can take for granted? Economists have generally argued its acceptance on the intuitive ground that wildly unstable market prices (and quantities traded) are not often observed. This is a relevant consensus, although not a conclusive one. There are in fact some cumulative processes in economic life (one has the name of galloping inflation), but we shall follow the general practice of assuming that the equilibria are stable.

Now that fish and strawberries can be frozen, are there any perishing commodities left? A few commodities like Christmas trees and cut flowers are perishing, but the important examples are in services. The motel rooms for rent on a given day in a given area are essentially fixed in number and under perfect competition would be thrown on the market each day at an estimated full-occupancy price, so long as the price exceeded any costs of occupancy. There are two reasons why this flexibility of price is not fully attained, although there are seasonal variation in rates, higgling, and so on. The first reason is that some monopoly power may be possessed by the owners, and the second is that the costs of searching are high for the tourist and not negligible for the owner. The symphony concert, the train or plane on a scheduled run, the services of professional men at a given time, the supply of longshoremen on a given day—are all instances of essentially perishing services. Some have prices which do not clear the market because of public or private controls.

But tolerable stability of price is not inconsistent with a price that clears the market. If the demand is steady, the day-to-day fluctuations in price will not be large (unless supply fluctuates). And if demand is postponable (storeable), the same effect can be achieved. Suppose that the supply of cut flowers fluctuates erratically, and that consumers consider flowers tomorrow to be a very good substitute for flowers today. They will then have, on any day, a highly elastic demand for flowers, and the price will be relatively stable.

The usefulness of even the simple graphical analysis of Figure 5-2 is likely to be underestimated by students who have not experienced the ability of men to make mistakes. Consider one of the attacks launched on the "law of supply and demand" by William Thornton just before graphical techniques were introduced in England.[8]

When a herring or mackeral boat has discharged on the beach, at Hastings or Dover, last night's take of fish, the boatmen, in order to dispose of their cargo, commonly resort to a process called "Dutch Auction." The fish are divided into lots, each of which is set up at a higher price than the salesman expects to get for it, and he then gradually lowers his terms,

---

[8] The full attack (not this instance) happens to be famous because it led, or permitted, John Stuart Mill to abandon the wages-fund doctrine. Mill's position in English economics in 1869 was roughly that of Napoleon in the French Army in 1810, so the abandonment was the source of some comment, especially since the criticisms were flimsy. The quotation is from *On Labour*, pp. 47–48.

until he comes to a price which some bystander is willing to pay rather than not have the lot, and to which he accordingly agrees. Suppose on one occasion the lot to have been a hundredweight, and the price agreed to 20 *s*. If, on the same occasion, instead of the Dutch form of auction, the ordinary English mode had been adopted, the result might have been different. The operation would then have commenced by some bystander making a bid, which others might have successively exceeded, until a sum

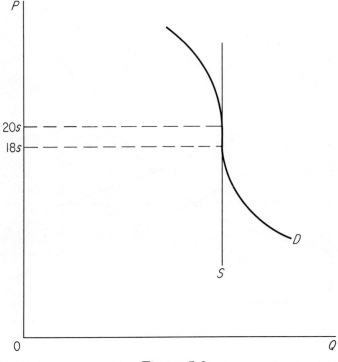

Figure 5-3

was arrived at beyond which no one but the actual bidder could afford or was disposed to go. That sum would not necessarily be 20 *s*: very possibly it might be only 18 *s*. . . . In the same market, with the same quantity of fish for sale, and with customers in number and in every other respect the same, the same lot of fish might fetch two very different prices.

If we translate Thornton's criticism into a diagram (Figure 5-3), we observe immediately that the result is due to the fact that his demand curve has a vertical branch. This is absurd in a competitive *market* demand curve.

Storeable Goods

Let us turn to the more important case of storeable goods, shares of stock or sheaves of wheat or those first editions. Now the supply curve is no longer a vertical line, denoting the total absence of alternatives for the seller—for he has always the alternative of selling tomorrow, or never.

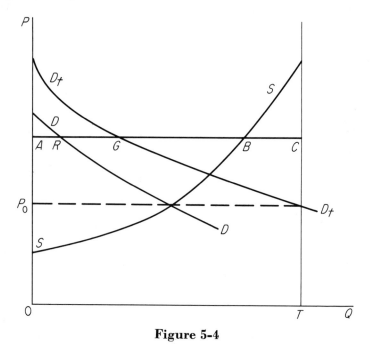

Figure 5-4

In fact the very identity of a seller may be uncertain. Jones may sell his four-year-old car at one price, and buy a second at another. Where this uncertainty arises it can be dealt with by the device of "reversing" the supply curve. Let us arbitrarily divide up traders in a market into "buyers," who have none of the commodity, and "sellers," who posses initial stocks of it (which they may wish either to augment or to sell). The "buyers'" demand curves will be those already discussed in Chapters 3 and 4. The "seller's" supply curve, as we have shown (p. 65), will be constructed in exactly the same way. These curves are shown in Figure 5-4. The total stock is shown as the vertical line TC. At any price $0A$, a definite quantity is demanded by "buyers," AR. At this price a quantity AB is supplied by sellers, but we can alternately say that sellers wish to hold BC at this price, for this is the portion of the stock which they do not offer for sale. Thus if the total stock $(0T)$ is 150, and sellers offer 110 (AB) at price $0A$, they are implicitly demanding 40 units (BC). If we add AR and BC, to get AG, we have the total quantity demanded at this price by "buyers" and "sellers." Applying this procedure at all prices, we obtain the aggregate demand curve D_t, and its intersection with the total stock line sets the equilibrium price P_0.

This construction does more than evade the minor problem of classifying buyers and sellers. It illuminates a common fallacy. Many people have said that if a stock sells for \$40 a share on a given day that this is not the "true" price because only a modest number of shares were traded—if a huge block had been thrown on the market, the price would have fallen drastically. Indeed it might have, but if a huge block had been thrown on the market this would have meant that many holders now believed the stock was a poor investment at the price. In effect a large decrease in demand has been implicitly assumed. Since the large block of stock was not thrown on the market, the holders thought it was worth at least this much. The fact that one could not buy a large block of the company's outstanding stock at the market price, similarly, merely means that one cannot double the demand without influencing the price.

The holder of a durable commodity has to take account of two elements of return:

1. The marginal utility (measured in money terms) he derives from holding the commodity. Examples are the pleasure of driving a car or of admiring a painting or of cashing dividend checks paid on a stock.[9]

[9] The condition for maximum satisfaction is

$$\frac{\text{Marginal Utility of } A}{\text{Price of } A} = \frac{\text{Marginal Utility of } B}{\text{Price of } B}.$$

This ratio is called the marginal utility of income because it is the amount of utility received per dollar of expenditure at the margin. If we divide the marginal utility of (say) a painting by the marginal utility of income, we obtain the marginal utility of the painting expressed in dollars.

2. The change in the price of the product from now to (say) next year, which may be positive or negative.

The total return from holding the commodity then consists of the sum of the utility (u) and the expected increase in price (Δp). The owner of a first edition of Ricardo's *Principles of Political Economy and Taxation* (1817), of which there are probably 400 copies in the world, expects its price to rise because the number and wealth of potential owners are increasing. But the price cannot on average rise so fast as the interest received on sums of money invested in securities comparable in riskiness to holding Ricardo's *Principles*. If it did, economists would buy the book and have the pleasure of owning it without cost, while receiving the increment of value. In equilibrium, in fact, $u + \Delta p$, the (marginal) return to the holder, must equal the cost of holding the durable good. This cost is composed of the amount that could be earned on the sum elsewhere, ip (where i is the appropriate interest), plus any cost of possession of the good (insurance of a painting, and so forth).

It follows that the greater the utility to be derived from holding a commodity, the lower must be its rate of increase of price. People will not hoard a keg of nails unless its price is expected to rise by i per cent; they will hold the Ricardo if it rises by only $\Delta p = ip - u$, or $\Delta p/p = i - u/p$ per cent, where u/p is the annual utility of possession per dollar invested in the commodity.

Speculation

A more interesting and important pricing problem is posed by the existence of stocks of goods which are periodically produced—agricultural products are of course the leading example. The tasks in rationing a fixed supply until the new crop is harvested are two: to provide supplies throughout the period of fixed supply, so that the entire stock will not be consumed early in the year; and to provide a carry-over as insurance against future crop failures, increases in demand, and the like.

The former task is relatively the easier one: the demand for foodstuffs and textiles is tolerably stable over the period of a year, although there are some fluctuations in demand due to fluctuations in consumer income, seasonal changes in tastes, changes in foreign demands, and so on. If demand (as a schedule or curve) were absolutely identical in every month, and no carry-over was needed, the price would rise each month by the costs of holding the stock. For, if the price were uniform, any holder this month would have the choice of selling his stock now at a given price, *p*, or of holding it a month and receiving only $(p - c)$, where *c* is the cost of carrying the good a month. Therefore he would sell now, until the current price was depressed, and the price next month elevated, enough to cover the costs of carrying a stock for a month. This gradual rise in price is in effect the method of charging consumers for the service of holding the stock.

The second task, providing a stock for emergencies, is less simple. As of any time there are an immense array of possible events, each of which will influence the price at any future date. Let our commodity be wheat, with a current price of \$2 a bushel; then the possible events may include:

1. A future crop failure, which can be large or small, leading to prices ranging up from \$2 to \$4, with smaller probabilities of the bigger failures and higher prices.

2. A future bumper crop, also of variable size, with corresponding future prices from \$2 down to \$1.

3. A business depression, leading to a modest decline in price and quantity demanded.

4. A war, leading (perhaps through conscription of farm workers) to a reduction in output and a higher price.

5. A fair prospect of increased or decreased demand for exports.

6. A possible shift in consumer tastes away from wheat toward meat.

The only thing a holder of wheat can be quite certain of is that something unusual will happen.

The carry-over will be held in warehouses, but who will own it and take the risks of profits or losses? The natural answer is: a group of people who specialize in predicting future demands and supplies. This group, called speculators, develops skill in collecting and assessing current evidence on future conditions, and therefore on average can perform this task more efficiently than, say, the processors of wheat (grain mills).

Each speculator may be described as making a set of estimates of the probabilities of various conditions of supply and demand

at a given future date. These estimates may be assembled into a
frequency distribution such as:

PROBABILITY	EXPECTED PRICE
0.05	$3.00
0.10	2.50
0.20	2.25
0.35	2.00
0.20	1.80
0.10	1.60

The average expected price is then simply the sum of the products
of the expected prices and their probabilities, which is **$2.07** in this
case. The confidence with which this estimate is held may be measured by the dispersion about this expected average; obviously the
speculator will have more confidence in this price (**$2.07**) being
approached with the above distribution than with

PROBABILITY	EXPECTED PRICE
0.38	$3.00
0.62	1.50

which also has a mean of **$2.07**. Presumably he will make larger
commitments on his prediction the greater his confidence in it.

If the commodity is one that has no futures market—no market
in which contracts for future delivery are bought and sold—the
trader will buy wheat if the present price *plus* carrying costs is
less than **$2.07**; he will get out of the market if this is not the
case.[10] With a futures market, however, he will sell contracts for
future delivery if the price he expects is below the futures price
currently quoted (and buy futures contracts in the converse case),
with the hope of covering the contract (with a "spot" purchase)
when it matures at the expected lower price.

Each speculator has a different set of expectations, and a different
demand-supply function for futures contracts. We may add them
together to get the aggregate demand for (say) May futures in
the previous December, as a function of the price of futures contracts; it is denoted D in Figure 5-5. If the futures price is above

[10] Thus, if real estate prices are expected to fall, it is impossible to sell
land "short" because it is not homogeneous and therefore one cannot promise
to deliver a particular piece at some future date.

the price that speculators anticipate, they will supply futures contracts, and at lower futures prices they will demand contracts.

The supply of futures contracts is provided by hedgers—of whom it is sufficient to notice those who buy the wheat from farmers and supply storage. If they do not wish to speculate, they can eliminate their risks by selling futures contracts at prices equal to at least the current price plus carrying costs. Their supply together with the speculators' demand (D) fix the present price of futures contracts.[11]

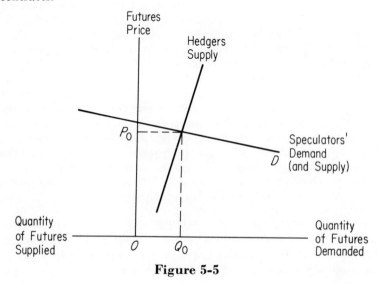

Figure 5-5

The skill with which this delicate task of reading the future is performed is a much-debated point. It is undeniable that if anyone can predict future prices more accurately than the professional speculators, he can make a vast amount of money rather quickly. It is also undeniable that most nonprofessionals (who, by Barnum's law, are constantly being replenished) manage to keep alive by borrowing money from relatives.

The public, and especially farmers, have nevertheless always been hostile toward the speculators, and wave aside the economist's arguments on the need for someone predicting the future and taking

[11] This is a much simplified picture; see L. G. Telser, "Futures Trading and the Storage of Cotton and Wheat," *Journal of Political Economy,* **66** (1958), 233–55.

risks that the predictions are wrong. Ancient laws against forestall-ing, engrossing, and regrating—buying foodstuffs on the way to market or in a market with a view to resale—are an adequate proof of this popular suspicion. This policy led Adam Smith to say,

> It supposes that there is a certain price at which corn is likely to be forestalled, that is, bought up in order to be sold again soon after in the same market, so as to hurt the people. But if a merchant ever buys up corn, either going to a particular market or in a particular market, in order to sell it again soon after in the same market, it must be because he judges that the market cannot be so liberally supplied through the whole season as upon that particular occasion, and that the price, there-fore, must soon rise. If he judges wrong in this, and if the price does not rise, he not only loses the whole profit of the stock which he employs in this manner, but a part of the stock itself, by the expence and loss which necessarily attend the storing and keeping of corn. He hurts himself, therefore, much more essentially than he can hurt even the particular people whom he may hinder from supplying themselves upon that particu-lar market day, because they may afterwards supply themselves just as cheap upon any other market day. If he judges right, instead of hurting the great body of the people, he renders them a most important service.
>
> The popular fear of engrossing and forestalling may be compared to the popular terrors and suspicions of witchcraft.[12]

Smith's comment needs only a minor qualification. The proposi-tion that speculators cannot as a group make money by inducing price fluctuations or withholding supplies is correct if they possess no monopoly power. In actual fact, any large or persistent degree of power to control prices has not been attainable in the large com-modity markets, simply because the trade of buying and selling is one which it is easy for anyone to enter. Smith is too kind to those who suspect speculators, however, when he compares their at-titudes with those once held toward witches, for there was no proof that the witches had not entered into compacts with the devil.

RECOMMENDED READINGS

Hardy, C. O., *Risk and Risk-Bearing*, Chicago: University of Chicago Press, 1933, Chs. 11, 12.

Working, H., "The Theory of Price of Storage," *American Economic Review*, **39** (1949), 1254–63.

[12] *The Wealth of Nations* (New York: Modern Library ed.), p. 500.

PROBLEMS

1. You are given the information: the total stock of a commodity is 100, the demand function is $q = 80 - p$, and the supply function is $q = 5 + p$. Derive the combined demand curve of buyers and sellers.

2. Mountifort Longfield (1834) argued that the practice by the rich of buying wheat in years of small crops and reselling it to the poor at half price did not reduce the cost of wheat to poor consumers, as compared with having the poor buy directly at market prices. Compare your analysis with his (*Lectures on Political Economy*, London School Reprints, 1931, p. 56).

3. The market demand curve is $p^2q = 1000$ (a constant demand elasticity of -2). Derive the demand curve for one of 2, 10, and 40 firms, all of equal size, with the aggregate industry output of 200 when the firm in question is operating at the same output as other firms. (Thus with 10 firms, each of the other 9 firms has an output of $20 = 200/10$.)

4. On a certain morning you find the following foreign exchange rates quoted:

	PRICES		
	U. S. *Dollars*	£ *Sterling*	*Francs*
Pound Sterling	2.80	1.	14.0
French francs	0.2025	0.0714	1.0
American dollars	1.	0.36	5.0

(a) What do you do to make money?

(b) Suppose no one bothered with arbitrage, and the rates persisted. What, if any, economic objections are there to these nonequilibrium quotations?

5. The larger the number of traders in a market, and the larger the dollar volume of transactions, the smaller will be the spread between bid and ask prices for a commodity. Explain why.

6. It has been observed that the best grades of products (oranges, apples, and the like) are sent to large cities and are not readily available to consumers in the areas in which they are produced. Explain why.

7. In a market in which carrying costs are negligible (such as common stocks), you are told the price of the commodity at time t—say, $P_t = \$100$. If the market consists of intelligent traders, will it be of any value to a speculator to know what the price was a time unit earlier? (That is, would it be useful to know whether P_{t-1} had been $50 or $200?) More generally, can repetitive patterns of prices over time exist?

chapter six

Costs and Production

It is necessary now to look more closely at the nature of costs.

THE NATURE OF COSTS

Occasionally one walks into the shop of a lazy man and observes identical goods with two prices, and is told that the lower priced items were in an earlier shipment that cost less. This is foolish merchandising unless the cost of remarking the price is more than the rise in price. It is also symptomatic of the layman's tendency to identify "cost" with outlays actually incurred or historical costs.

Historical costs have powerful sway over untutored minds. The Internal Revenue Service insists that corporation assets be so valued. The public utility commissions consider historical costs a relevant or even decisive item in setting rates. Men incur additional losses trying to "get their money" out of a venture. They all fly in the face of a basic principle of rational behavior, "By-gones are forever by-gones."

It is easy to manufacture cases in which historical costs are seen to be irrelevant to price. Smith produces a commodity for $3, Jones for $4—will they receive different prices? Johnson builds a house for $20,000 which termites mostly devour—will it sell for $20,000? I buy a rock for $10, and it proves to be a diamond of remarkable purity—will I sell it for $10? Some Indians of questionable character sold Manhattan Island (which they did not own), for $24, a typical exploitation of tourists. The examples are sufficient to show that actual historical outlays need not govern values.

In every case, of course, there was a miscalculation of some sort: Jones should have been more efficient; Johnson should have beaten off the termites; the seller should have known it was a diamond (and possibly nature should have hidden it deeper in the ground); the Dutch should have bought the Great Lakes. But even with perfect foresight historical costs can be irrelevant: they exclude interest (as accountants reckon costs) whereas a wine should sell for C per cent more after a year, if C is the carrying cost (as a per cent of last year's value).

The basic concept of cost is therefore something different: the cost of any productive service to use A is the maximum amount it could produce elsewhere. The foregone alternative is the cost. Note that the alternative cost sets the *value* of the resource to use A; it does not by itself set the cost of producing A's product. To determine the cost of production of A's product, we must know also the amounts of resources used to produce a given amount of A, and this additional relationship (summarized as "the production function") is examined later.

The alternative uses of a resource depend upon the use for which the cost is being reckoned:

1. The cost of an acre of land to agricultural uses is the amount the land could yield in nonagricultural uses (residences, parks, and so on).

2. The cost of an acre of land to the wheat-growing industry is the amount it would yield in other agricultural crops (oats, corn, and so on), as well as in nonagricultural uses.

3. The cost of an acre of land to wheat farmer X is the amount the land could yield to other wheat farmers, as well as all nonwheat uses.

If all land were homogeneous in all relevant respects (including location, fertility, and the like), obviously all three of these alternative costs would be the same. For if land yielded more in nonagricultural uses than in agricultural uses, some of it would be transferred to the nonagricultural uses, and the transfer would go on until the yields in all uses were equal (under competition). Equality of yields of a resource in every feasible use is necessary to maximum return for the individual owners of the resource; any discrepancy in yields is (with competition) an opportunity to someone to increase his income.

But if the land is not homogeneous, it is not necessary that these alternative costs be equal. Suppose that due to locational and other factors, an acre of one type of land will yield $50 in wheat, $30 in other farm crops, and $5 in nonagricultural uses. Then the cost of the land to the wheat industry is $30 an acre—the best foregone alternative.[1] This cost is decisive to the land's use: even if a declining demand forces the yield in wheat down to $31, the land will not be transferred to other uses. But from the viewpoint of any tenant wheat farmer, a rent of $50 is the cost because at $49.99 it will be rented to another farmer.[2]

This definition of cost clearly avoids the paradoxes encountered by historical costs. All productive services which are identical necessarily have the same alternative cost, no matter what the differences in their historical costs. It is also a powerful weapon in analyzing fallacies, of which a few samples may be appropriate.

With conscription an army pays its soldiers whatever it wishes, and it is sometimes said that the relatively high wage rates of American soldiers make national defense more expensive for the United States than for other countries. The cost of a soldier to an economy, however, is his foregone product as a civilian, and this is not directly affected by his rate of pay.[3] The dollars which are given to the soldier involve a real cost to the community only to the extent that higher wage rates lead to the employment of more tax collectors.

A variant of this same argument is encountered in the request of various groups (Rural Electrification is one) to borrow from the

[1] The surplus of earnings over what can be earned in the best alternative is called a *rent*. As the name suggests, economists first attached this concept of returns beyond those needed to hold a resource only to land. The concept has since been generalized to include such returns even when received by laborers or owners of specific capital goods.

[2] A superior farmer, it might be believed, can get more than the average yield from the land. So he can, but as will be shown later, it is the (value of the) *marginal* product of land that constitutes its yield, and this marginal product will not differ in equilibrium between superior and inferior farmers.

[3] Since no conscription system ignores certain factors (such as occupation) which are partially controllable by the individual, the higher the rate of pay the fewer eligible conscripts will seek to alter these factors to postpone military service. This sort of burden-avoiding behavior leads to some misallocation of resources.

federal government rather than directly in the capital market because federally guaranteed bonds can be sold at lower interest rates. Here again the true cost of the capital to the society is what it would produce elsewhere.[4]

The alternative uses of a resource will often be different, and in fact fewer, in the short run from what they are in the long run. This is obviously true of specialized machinery: during its life it can be used only for the purpose for which it was designed, or as scrap. But over time it earns depreciation reserves which can be reinvested in other forms of capital. The same situation holds with respect to labor: a carpenter has as alternative occupations only those fields which require his skills or are less skilled (he can become an unskilled laborer, for example). But given sufficient time to be retrained, he can work in a sash and door plant or become an electrician. Given still more time, every young man who otherwise would have entered this occupation will enter one of a hundred others with demands for a comparable quality of labor.

We have already referred to the "short run" and the "long run," for example in connection with demand curves; let us look more closely at these concepts. They do not refer to clock time, but to the time necessary for people to adapt fully to new conditions. When automatic machinery took over the making of glass containers, there was a great reduction in the demand for glass blowers, who until then had been among the elite of the artisans. Those in the occupation experienced great reductions in earnings, and the younger (and more easily and profitably retrained) members went into other occupations. The older workers held on until earnings fell even below what they could earn as unskilled laborers. Eventually all disappeared, except for a handful who continue to produce custom products. The true long run—the period when all reactions to the decrease in demand for glass blowers had been completed—varies with the question we ask. If we ask about the long run with respect to the number of glassblowers, it is a period sufficiently long to allow enough withdrawals so those remaining in the occupation earn enough to attract young apprentices. This

[4] An egregious example of this fallacy is contained in the following passage: "By taking upon themselves a large share of economic functions the State and municipal authorities to that extent released a vast amount of private effort and capital." [W. H. Dawson, *The Evolution of Modern Germany* (London: T. F. Unwin, 1914), p. 208.]

might be 30 years. If we ask about the long run with respect to the retraining and relocation of young glass blowers, the period may have been seven years. The short run is easier to define: not all adjustments to the force we are studying have been made; or more simply, it is a period shorter than the long run.

There is a widespread tendency to look at only the short run alternatives in judging the cost of a commodity (when alternatives are considered at all). When France froze rents during a substantial inflation, there seemed to be no serious costs in the alternative sense. Dwellings are durable and specialized, so the supply can be assumed to remain the same with low rents as with high. For a week this is true. Over time, however, a landlord can and will (and did!) reduce maintenance, as a device for withdrawing capital from this unprofitable field of investment. Over a still longer period the supply of houses will shrink—none will be built (privately) and the elements will erode those in existence. In the long run houses can be built and maintained only with resources that have many other uses, and no scheme of financing can avoid the alternative costs of these resources. The alternative cost theory is sometimes rephrased as the theorem that there is no such thing as a free lunch even in France.

Nonmonetary Alternatives. The alternatives to a given use of a resource often include also nonmonetary elements. In the employment of labor, they include riskiness, the conditions of work (cleanliness, 3 vs. 9 coffee breaks, and so forth), prestige, and similar factors, but *not* the prospective increase in earnings with time, which is a monetary element. In the employment of capital, riskiness is the main factor, although in some areas the ability to withdraw funds rapidly (liquidity) is also important. These nonmonetary elements obviously must be reckoned with monetary returns in analysing the allocation of resources among uses.

It would be an immense boon if one could always translate nonmonetary elements into "monetary equivalents." We would obviously prefer to say that the alternative cost of a man to the legal professions is $14,000 or its equivalent, rather than $12,000 plus the amenities of being a professor.

Within limits it is possible to make direct estimates of the monetary value of these elements. For example, the longer vacation of an occupation can be appraised at the time rate of the basic salary,[5] and income in kind (as food grown and consumed on farms) can be appraised at appropriate market prices.

This method is not available for elements such as prestige[6] or risk of death. Here we may *deduce* the monetary equivalent by comparing returns to the factors in equilibrium if there is free competition. If in equilibrium a professor earns $3,000 less than a dentist, after adjustment for differences in training, income in kind, and so on, we may assert that this is the money value of the nonmonetary returns of the one occupation relative to the other. There are difficult, but not insoluble, problems in determining whether an equilibrium has existed during a given period. A more important limitation in principle is that the occupations may not be equally open to men of equal and appropriate ability: this is obviously the difficulty with comparing Supreme Court Justices and lawyers or comparing airline pilots (who have a strong union) and other pilots.

The equilibrium difference in money returns will measure the difference in nonmonetary elements only at the margin. If the equilibrium money labor income of a farmer is 20 per cent less than that of a comparable urban worker, there will be many farmers for whom nonmonetary returns are larger, and some who would not leave farming if incomes fell to 50 per cent of the urban level. In our terminology, the earnings of these ardent farmers contain rents.

The nonmonetary returns are seldom an invariable part of the use of a resource. If men love a rural setting, industrial plants will move to the country to supply this desire (or, what is simply another way of viewing it, to pay lower wages). If workers wish the opportunity to acquire additional training, the employers will institute programs or allow time off to take courses. If lenders are fearful of losing their capital, they are supplied with senior obligations by the borrower.

[5] This is presumably the proper basis because the alternative cost of leisure (at the margin of working another week) is the salary that could be earned. The question of whether working time is actually subject to the worker's control is discussed later.

[6] This is possibly an overstatement. Wealthy donors have often been incited and rewarded with knighthoods, ambassadorships, LL.D.s, and the like. These markets are believed to be somewhat imperfect, but have not yet been studied in adequate detail.

For a gratifyingly large number of economic problems, the non-monetary elements need not be estimated. Often they are essentially irrelevant, as in the choice whether to grow rye or wheat on a farm, or to invest funds in chemicals or paper and pulp. Often they are stable over substantial periods of time, so that the more volatile monetary elements will dominate the movements of resources. For example, one would have expected the preference for investing at home rather than abroad to be stable as between Canada and the United States, so total returns would move from year-to-year by the same amount as monetary returns—until the recent era of discriminatory rules imposed by the two nations under the benevolent influence of economic nationalism.

Private Costs and Social Costs

A chemical plant, let us assume, collects waste products and discharges them into a stream which flows by the plant. The cost to this plant of disposing of waste is then the cost of pumping the waste to the stream (or, in more precise language, the cost is the foregone alternatives of the resources necessary to do the pumping). If pollution of the stream reduces the income of other people (destroying recreational uses, making the water unpotable, and so on), there are additional costs borne by others. The costs to the individual firm are termed *private* costs, while the sum of costs to everyone is called the *social cost* of waste disposal.[7]

There can be no doubt of the existence of these external effects of an individual's behavior. In fact, in strictest logic there are very few actions whose entire consequences accrue to the actor. If I educate my children well, the community (it is hoped) will benefit by reduced crime, more enlightened citizenship, and so forth. If I grow an attractive lawn, my neighbors are pleased; if Smith dresses shabbily, the other members of the United States Senate become annoyed.

One of the most tendencious questions in economics has been: when social and private costs diverge appreciably, will competition lead to correct amounts (and prices) of goods? Will not the chemical plant, under competition, sell at a price which does not cover

---

[7] The terms are due to A. C. Pigou, *The Economics of Welfare,* 4th ed. (London: Macmillan, 1932), Part II, Ch. 9.

the costs of pollution, so its costs will be too low and its output too large (with given demands for chemicals)?

To answer the question, let us shift to another example, which happens to have a long legal history, that of wandering cattle.[8] In a region hitherto devoted to unfenced farms growing grain, a cattle raiser comes. His cattle will, unless fenced in, occasionally wander into the neighboring grain fields and damage the crops.

Taking account of this damage, from the social viewpoint the use of the farm for cattle is desirable only if the additional net income of the land is larger than that in growing grain by the lesser of the two amounts: (1) the annual cost of fencing the cattle farm, or (2) the damage to the neighboring crops. Let us assume that cattle raising just meets this test.

If the cattle raiser has no responsibility, or only partial responsibility, for the costs imposed upon others by his wandering cattle, it appears that he will earn a larger rent in cattle than in grain. As a result, more farms will be converted to cattle, and there will be too much meat and not enough grain in the community.

We mean a specific thing by too much meat and not enough grain. Suppose the social costs of 100 bushels of wheat and 400 pounds of meat are the same—the same resources can produce either. Then if their prices (for these quantities) are not equal, consumers will buy relatively more of the cheaper product. Perhaps the equilibrium is reached when 500 pounds of meat sells for the same price as 100 bushels of wheat. The consumer is then indifferent if one bushel of wheat is added and 5 pounds of meat taken away from him. But given the social costs, it would be possible by reducing meat output 5 pounds to obtain 1.25 bushels of wheat, and the consumer would consider this 0.25 bushels a clear gain.

This is in fact an instance of a general theorem: consumers will be best off (on the highest indifference curves) when the relative prices of goods are equal to their relative (marginal) social costs. Where private costs differ from social costs, obviously this optimum position will not be reached, because producers will gear output to their private costs.

In our case of wandering cattle, it is clear that a legal require-

---

[8] The discussion to follow is based upon the profound article of Ronald Coase, "The Problem of Social Cost," *Journal of Law and Economics,* 3 (1961).

ment that the cattle raiser bear the cost of fencing or damage to crops will make private and social costs equal; a contrary law (it would appear) will not. But suppose, to reverse the whole situation, that the area had originally been devoted to cattle raising and now a wheat farmer enters. The argument is completely analogous, but this time we reach the conclusion that the wheat farmer should pay for the fencing! It is his arrival which creates the problem of wandering cattle, and therefore to get the true (social) cost of his wheat we should take account of the damage he inflicts on cattle raisers if they should for example have to erect fences. We need two laws: one imposing fencing costs on grain growers, the other imposing the costs on cattle raisers.

The fundamental symmetry in the relations of cattle and grain farmers, no matter where the law places the liability for damages, deserves elaboration. Let us consider more closely the intruding cattle raiser. He has, let us assume, the following production schedule (all quantities per year):

CATTLE	TOTAL NET PRIVATE RETURN	DAMAGE TO GRAIN FARMERS
9	$ 94	$ 0
10	100	2
11	105	3
12	109	6
13	111	10
14	112	15
15	111	21

If he considered only his private net returns, he would have a herd of 14 cattle, for then his return is maximized. But since he must compensate for damage to grain, he will stop before this point. If he has (say) 12 cattle and contemplates a 13th, he will have to pay grain growers an additional $4 for the additional damage. Similarly, he will reduce payments for damages to $3 if he reduces the herd to 11. (If fencing costs, say, $6 a year, the alternative will be adopted and a herd of 14 reared.)

When the cattle raiser increases his herd from 10 to 11, his revenue rises by $5, but this is at a cost of $1—the marginal damage to grain growers. Hence his net gain is $4. Similarly he adds $4 to revenue, and $3 to cost (for damages) by the 12th animal, a net gain of $1. The thirteenth animal adds more to cost ($4) than to revenue ($2), and will not be reared.

If the law puts the burden of damage on the grain grower, the herd will still be 12. For now the grain growers will offer him sums equal to the marginal damage if he does not increase the herd. If the herd is 12, for example, they will offer up to $4 if he will not add a thirteenth animal. Since he foregoes this receipt by adding the 13th animal this is the cost (for costs are foregone alternatives). The manner in which the law assigns liability will not affect the relative private marginal costs of production of cattle and grain.

But this procedure obviously leads to the correct social results—the results which would arise if the cattle and grain farms were owned by the same man. The Coase theorem thus asserts that under perfect competition private and social costs will be equal. It is a more remarkable proposition to us older economists who have believed the opposite for a generation, than it will appear to the young reader who was never wrong, here.

The proposition that the composition of output will not be affected by the manner in which the law assigns liability for damage seems astonishing. But it should not be. Laws often prove to be unimportant: the laws which specify that the seller or, alternatively, the buyer should pay a retail sales tax are wholly equivalent in effect. The assignment of responsibility for damages, similarly, can be ignored: assume that the same farmer grows grain and cattle, and it is obvious that his determination of output will be independent of the assignment. Either it will be profitable to raise both cattle and grain, and then one "product" will "pay" the amount necessary to maximize the sum of outputs of the two (no matter what the legal arrangements), or it will be unprofitable, and one of the products will not be raised.[9]

The proposition must, to be sure, be qualified by an important fact. When a factory spews smoke on a thousand homes, the ideal solution is to arrange a compensation system whereby the homeowners pay the factory to install smoke reduction devices up to the point where the marginal cost of smoke reduction equals the sum of the marginal gains to the homeowners. But the costs of

[9] One product, say cattle, may impose (for every possible number of cattle) more costs on grain than the net yield from the cattle. However, the cattle land is either (1) already in grain, and could not be competed for by cattle, or (2) has no use except to grow cattle, and then the payment must be made (with this assignment of liability) for foregone profits from cattle grazing, and in either case the use of land is not affected.

this transaction may be prohibitive—of getting the people together, of assessing damages, and so on—so only a statutory intervention may be feasible. The statutory policy is itself far from simple to devise: the amount of smoke reduction that is socially optimal depends upon the technology of smoke reduction, the number of people involved, and so forth, and none of these factors remains constant over time.

The differences between private and social costs or returns have provided a fertile field for public control of economic activity. In fact one can attribute most limitations on private ownership or control of property to this source.[10] These controls are of every degree of perspicacity, ranging from traffic controls (where private contracts between rapidly converging drivers would be difficult to arrange) to petroleum import restrictions (designed to conserve the supply of domestic petroleum!).

Isolating the Product of One Factor

If the alternative cost of a unit of a productive resource is its maximum product elsewhere, it is necessary to isolate its separate contribution from that of the other resources with which it is almost invariably used. Can this be done? On its face this seems difficult, and a considerable number of people have said that since wheat cannot be harvested unless there is land in which to plant it and men to reap it, any division of the product between land and men is arbitrary. Let us see.

Variable Production Coefficients. Let us define the production coefficient of land in growing wheat as the amount of land necessary to grow one bushel of wheat—it is a number such as 1/60 acre year. Similarly the production coefficient of tractors might be 1/6,000 tractor year, and that of labor 1 man hour (or 1/2,000 man year). These production coefficients are merely accepted names for input-output ratios.

The production coefficients are in general variable: there is no unique quantity of land (or other input) necessary to produce a bushel of wheat. One can use less land if he uses more fertilizer

---

[10] Although most public controls are due to this source, they are not always the most important controls. Some measures have purely ethical bases—the redistribution of income, the censorship of some forms of behavior (gambling, for example).

or labor, and less labor if he uses more machinery. The phenomenon of substitution is well-nigh ubiquitous. One can substitute newspaper advertisements for salesmen, in selling goods. Aluminum can be substituted for stainless steel, more efficient engines can be substituted for fuel, more durable machines can be substituted for repairmen.

With variable production coefficients it is possible to write down a schedule of outputs corresponding to various amounts of any one input, for example:

QUANTITY OF INPUT A	OUTPUT
35	60
36	61.5

where the quantities of the other inputs have been held constant. We define the marginal product of input A as the increase in total product divided by the increase in the quantity of A—here it is 1.5 units of product per unit of A.

The marginal product is then the (marginal) contribution of a unit of any input to the total product, and the total contribution is the quantity of the input times its marginal product (or $36 \times 1.5 = 54$).[11]

At this point an experienced teacher is torn between two desires. One is merely to say rather complacently that thus the separation of the contribution of one input has been achieved, and that is that. Most reasonable men will accept this conclusion, especially since it provides a tool—the marginal product—that turns out to be immensely useful. The other desire is to explain the variety of objections that have been made to this procedure, and answer each one—knowing full well that once seeds of doubt have been sown, they love to grow. I shall compromise by giving two examples of the critiques.

The first critique asserts that the extra product of 1.5 obtained by using the 36th unit of A is also "really" due in part to the other inputs which are being held constant in quantity. If our example is in farming, it is said that the land is being worked a little harder if we add a unit of labor. This is quite true, but the contribution of the other inputs to the increment of product is so

---

[11] The question whether the total contributions of all the inputs will exactly add up to the total product is considered in subsequent chapters.

small as to be negligible. Unfortunately the proof of this assertion must be mathematical.[12]

The second critique asserts that although the 36th unit of A may produce only 1.5 units, the previous units of A produced more, and it is improper to appraise their contribution by the contribution of this least important unit. This argument implicitly assumes either that the production coefficients are not variable or that the entrepreneur who is conducting the enterprise has made a mistake. It would be possible to have 35 men engaged in sowing and reaping, and use the 36th man only to repair scarecrows, which (let us assume) yields a much smaller marginal product. But then labor is being used inefficiently: if the 36th man's work is less efficient than that of his fellow workers, his tasks should be reassigned. Perhaps he should spend half of his time in sowing and reaping, and make only basic repairs in scarecrows. Whatever the assignment, as long as the men are homogeneous, each one should be making the same marginal contribution. It is for this reason that the correct phrase is "the marginal product of 36 men," *not* "the marginal product of the 36th man."

This leads us to a basic problem: there are many ways to grow wheat, even using the same inputs. The farmer can plow shallow or deep, he can fertilize uniformly or unevenly, he can harvest early or late, and so on. Which method will he use of this vast array of feasible techniques? Each technique may have a different marginal product for each input, so our concept of costs ultimately rests upon the choice of productive techniques.

The economists' answer is to assume that the entrepreneur will use the best known technique, which is the technique which yields the largest product with these given inputs. This is of course a substantial simplification of the problem, and in effect says: let us put the problem of advances of technological knowledge into a separate compartment, to be studied later—preferably by someone else, since it is a very difficult problem; and let us only gradually introduce the differences in technical knowledge possessed by different firms in an industry. Provided we eventually redeem these pledges, no one can quarrel seriously with the "best technology" assumption.

Fixed Production Coefficients. The question of whether production coefficients are variable or fixed has had a long history in economics.

---

[12] See mathematical note 8 in Appendix B.

The classical economists, for example, assumed that capital and labor were used in a fixed proportion but (through substitution for land) in variable proportion to output. In this case a marginal product can be found for a combined dose of "capital and labor," but not for each separately. Walras used, as a first approximation, universally fixed coefficients of production. By 1900 most economists used universal variable production coefficients. In recent years there has been a revival of fixed production coefficients, in connection with so-called "input-output" and linear programming analyses.

The question is mostly one of fact, and of a kind of fact not easily enumerated in a census. Moreover, while it is easy (I conjecture) to show that every important production coefficient has varied since 1925, only those variations that occurred in the absence of technological progress are in question, and they do not carry separate labels.

Perhaps a majority of economists—certainly a majority if it would be a tie without my vote—believe that almost all production coefficients are variable. They reach this conclusion on various bases. One is that counter-examples are hard to find. Pareto, for example, said that only so much gold leaf can be hammered out of an ounce of gold, so the coefficient of production of gold in gold leaf was fixed.[13] But actually it is variable: in Germany, where labor was cheaper relative to gold, it was pounded thinner, so there were 350,000 leaves to the inch; in the United States, where labor was more expensive, there was less pounding and only 262,000 leaves to the inch.[14] But this game of specific cases never ends. Moreover it is a game that is rather unfair: a possible case of fixed production coefficients can be invented in a minute, and may require a month to refute.

The more important reason for believing that the production coefficients are variable is that a vast amount of experience suggests this to be so. We observe that farmers use more fertilizer when a crop restriction program reduces the land they may till. We observe that some firms in an industry use better labor than others, or mechanize different processes, or use different raw materials, or employ different advertising media, or display a hundred other forms of substitution of one input for another. We even have some

[13] *Cours d'économie politique* (Paris, 1897), II, §714, 717.
[14] U. S. Tariff Commission, *Gold Leaf* (1926), p. 6.

formal statistical findings to this effect, but on the whole they constitute a very tiny and relatively recent part of the evidence for variability.

Even if all production coefficients are variable—and this of course no one can know—there remains the question: how variable? If a technical coefficient ranges only between 1/11 and 1/12 (roughly the average technological coefficient of professors per student), it may be simpler for many questions to assume it is fixed. How, if it is fixed, can we isolate the contribution of one input to the product? Not by marginal analysis, for then when we increase one input by a unit, the product rises in proportion (if there are unused amounts of other inputs) or not at all.

Even with rigidly fixed proportions, however, it is possible to determine the contribution of each input, essentially by a comparison of different industries. The logic of this approach may be presented by means of the analysis of a very simple economy. Suppose that in this economy there are 1,000 men and 100,000 acres of land, each homogeneous. There are only two possible outputs each produced by a different combination of men and land, with no substitution possibilities:

1 man +   50 acres produces 100 bushels of rice;

1 man + 200 acres produces 100 bushels of wheat.

If the economy concentrated on rice, half the land would not be employed; if it concentrated on wheat, half the men would not be employed.

Suppose, in fact, that rice has been selling for $2 a bushel, wheat for $3 (and these constant prices are given by the export market). Then if only rice were produced, it would have an aggregate value of 1,000 (farms) $\times$ 100 bushels $\times$ $2 = $200,000. If 1 man were shifted to wheat, his product would be 100 bushels $\times$ $3, or $300, and the reduction in the value of rice would be 100 $\times$ $2, or $200, so national income would rise $100. Let this shift continue until 333.3 men are raising wheat on (333.3 $\times$ 200) = 66,667 acres, and 666.7 men are on the remaining 33,333 acres. Now if one more man shifts from rice to wheat, he will still produce a product of $300, but the 200 acres he requires will lead to a reduction of 4 rice farms, whose product is $800. So we are at equilibrium with full employment, with two-thirds of the labor force on rice farms. National income is $233,333.

If 150 acres were to be added to the economy, say by giving up golf courses, one more man could shift to wheat, and national income would rise $100. Hence this is the sum that would be paid for the use of 150 acres, and the implicit rent is $0.67 per acre. If, on the other hand, 3 more men were to withdraw from work, then one more wheat farm would be possible, and its higher yield ($300) would partially offset the decline of rice output (4 *times* $200), and national income would decline by $500—hence a man's services are worth $500/3 = $167.

These implicit prices represent alternative products in the proper sense: they measure the value of output foregone when a unit of a resource is withdrawn from any use. The reason we have been able to find these products is that the various uses of the resources allow us to substitute between products even if not directly in the production of any one product.

This method of isolating products is intimately related to a method known as linear programming, and the "shadow prices" of that method are the implicit alternative costs of inputs.[15]

RECOMMENDED READINGS

Coase, Ronald, "The Problem of Social Cost," *Journal of Law and Economics*, **3** (1961).

"Economic Empty Boxes," symposium in *Economic Journal* by J. H. Clapham (September and December 1922), A. C. Pigou, and D. H. Robertson (March 1924). Reprinted in *Readings in Price Theory*.

Knight, F. H., "Fallacies in the Interpretation of Social Cost," *Quarterly Journal of Economics*, **38** (1924), 582–606. Reprinted in *Readings in Price Theory*.

PROBLEMS

1. Under what conditions would historical costs always equal alternative costs?

2. Does it cost a surgeon more to operate on a rich person than a poor person?

[15] See almost any other book on economics; also P. A. Samuelson, "Professor Knight's Theorem on Linear Programming," *Zeitschrift für Nationalökonomie,* **18** (1958), 310–17.

3. What would happen to the value of men and acres in our example (p. 118) if the labor force increased to 1,200 men?

4. You are told that 100 bushels of wheat can be produced by either 4 man-hours and 2 acre-years or by 3 man-hours and 3 acre-years. Can the marginal products of men and land be determined with this information?

5. Explain or denounce the propositions:

(a) There is no such thing as a free lunch.

(b) There cannot be two expensive lunches.

chapter seven

Production: Diminishing Returns

At a given time there is a set of "technological" possibilities open to any potential producer of any commodity. These possible techniques are commonly labeled "technological" without quote marks, and we shall henceforth dispense with them, but the quote marks should serve to remind us that the methods of converting coffee beans at a port warehouse into coffee ground to specification at a grocery store consist of more than the technical details of the ways of roasting coffee, putting it into bags, and transporting it to buyers. Production involves also the carrying of inventories which are not too large (for they are expensive) or too small (or sales will be lost), the hiring of workers of all descriptions and getting them to work well, borrowing money and collecting debts, advertising and quarrelling with the Federal Trade Commission, detecting changes in consumer tastes, and making out tax returns. The plebian phrase, "know-how," better describes this set of possibilities.

An inventory of all known ways of producing goods—using production in its widest sense to include methods of organizing economic activity—is referred to as the "state of the arts." This inventory contains many methods that no one will use because they are obsolete: they yield goods that are no longer desired; or yield desired goods but require larger amounts of all inputs than other known methods. It contains also many methods that cannot be ranked unambiguously as superior and inferior: process A uses more machinery, process B more labor—so which is more efficient will depend upon the prices of machinery and labor. This inventory of knowledge grows over time as new discoveries are made. We shall nevertheless assume that it is fixed.

Even in the absence of new discoveries, the "state of the arts" is an immense collection of possibilities, and of the most varied sorts. In fact it contains all published knowledge and the vast empirical experience reposing only in men's heads. It is similarly indescribable in its variety: it contains the methods of making doughnuts (on a large and small scale) and airplanes, of collecting delinquent accounts and recruiting employees, and what not.

The student should therefore be suitably impressed to learn that economists discovered a general law relating the quantities of inputs and the quantity of output for any productive process. The discovery of this law, due to T. R. Malthus (of population fame) and Edward West (who deserves to be as famous) in 1815, was one of the heroic advances in the history of economics.

It turns out that much more can be said about the relationship of output to one of several inputs than about the relationship of output to all inputs, so we begin with this case. This relationship—the law of diminishing returns—answers the question: in what *proportion* should the various inputs be combined?

DIMINISHING RETURNS

The law of diminishing returns may be stated quite briefly:

As equal increments of one input are added, the inputs of other productive services being held constant, beyond a certain point the resulting increments of product will decrease—that is, the marginal products will diminish.

The law is not a tautology, but an assertion about the real world. As such, it must be interpreted in a particular way—even the physical law that freely falling bodies have constant acceleration does not work well if the body is in a tub of molasses. In our case the conditions are:

1. That there be other inputs whose quantities are held constant. If all inputs vary, we have the problem of economies of scale, discussed in the next chapter.

2. The state of technological knowledge is given. The various input-output possibilities are all available at the same time. Obviously if an additional unit of labor is applied to a farm next year, and a new invention makes the product rise more than it did when a man was added this year, this is no contradiction of the law.

3. The proportions in which inputs can effectively combine are variable, or in other words, the coefficients of production are variable (p. 114). The law has relevance even if this condition fails but we shall discuss only the important situation of continuously variable proportions.

Production is a process, not an act, so all of the inputs and outputs are rates of flow per unit of time: man-years, bushels per year, and so on. If economists used completely meticulous language, they would therefore emphasize this flow nature by speaking, not of hiring 7 men, but of hiring the services of 7 men for a year; not of producing 2,000 bushels, but 2,000 bushels per year. They are not this meticulous, and it is customary to refer to productive "factors" rather than their services.

This carelessness has on occasion led to error. For example, it has been said that labor (service) is perishable but capital (a building or machine, say) is not. Yet surely if the services of a man or a machine are not used this year, there is a loss in either case. It will be roughly true that the man's future services are no larger because of this year's unemployment, but machines also rust or become obsolete and in any case a year's services which are postponed 10 years are worth much less than they would be this year.[1] We shall not examine the relationships between services and the capital goods which yield them until we reach the theory of quasi-rents.

Elaboration of the Law

Let us begin with a simple numerical illustration of the law of diminishing returns. In this numerical example (Table 7–1), a series of amounts of labor (M = man years) are used in cooperation with an amount of land (L = acre years) which we hold constant. Diminishing returns sets in with the fifth unit of labor.

---

[1] Future services must be discounted to obtain their present value, so a dollar of services 10 years hence is worth only $\$1/(1 + 0.1)^{10} = \$0.39$ if the interest rate is 10 per cent.

Production: Diminishing Returns

It will be noted that the average product of labor begins to diminish only after six units of labor are employed, so average and marginal products begin to diminish at different points and diminish at different rates. Until well into the present century the law of diminishing returns was often stated in terms of both average and marginal products, and they were treated as equivalent. We see that

Table 7–1

MAN YEARS	TOTAL PRODUCT	AVERAGE PRODUCT PER MAN YEAR	MARGINAL PRODUCT OF A MAN YEAR
0	0	0	—
1	5	5	5
2	13	6.5	8
3	23	7.7	10
4	38	9.5	15
5	50	10	12
6	60	10	10
7	68	9.7	8
8	75	9.4	7
9	81	9	6
10	86	8.6	5
11	89	8.1	3
12	91	7.6	2
13	92	7.1	1
14	92	6.6	0
15	91	6.1	−1
16	88	5.5	−3
17	84	4.9	−4

they are not equivalent, and in fact only marginal products are of interest to the economist.

We can demonstrate the importance of marginal products at once by asking the simple question: if the wage rate of labor is 6 units of product, how many laborers should the owner of a plot of ground hire? The arithmetic is performed in Table 7–2, which is based squarely on the data of Table 7–1. The owner will wish to maximize his surplus, which is achieved when he hires 9 men—which is of course where the marginal product of labor equals its cost. Marginal products are always the guide to maximum profits or minimum cost: wherever a productive service has a different marginal product in two uses, we can increase total product. Thus, if labor had a marginal product of 10 on one farm, and 8 on another, transferring one laborer from the latter to the former farm would increase total product by 2, and the gains continue (at a declining rate) until the marginal products are equal.

Table 7-2

NUMBER OF MAN-YEARS HIRED	TOTAL WAGE BILL AT 6 PER MAN-YEAR	TOTAL PRODUCT	SURPLUS OVER WAGE BILL
1	6	5	−1
2	12	13	1
3	18	23	5
4	24	38	14
5	30	50	20
6	36	60	24
7	42	68	26
8	48	75	27
9	54	81	27
10	60	86	26
11	66	89	23
12	72	91	19

When we are speaking of "applying" laborers to a plot of land, we can equally well speak of "applying" a plot of land to the laborers. When the marginal product of men declines in Table 7–1, we can say it is because there are more men per acre, or fewer acres per man—only the proportions are important. The law of diminishing returns is completely symmetrical, and it is a matter of indifference which input we hold fixed and which we vary.

The symmetry can be illustrated by deducing the marginal product of land from Table 7–1, on the assumption that 10 acres of land were in the plot. We may proceed along these lines: As an approximation (to be discussed in Chapter 8), if eight units of labor on 10 acres yield 75 units of product, then 9 units of labor on $\frac{9}{8} \times 10$ (= 11.25) acres will yield $\frac{9}{8} \times 75$ (= 84.375) units of product. (That is, proportional increases of all inputs lead to proportional increases of output.) The table tells us that 9 men on 10 acres yield 81 units of product. We may now calculate the marginal product of land by comparing the outputs with 10 and 11.25 acres, holding labor at 9 units:

$$\frac{84.375 - 81}{11.25 - 10} = \frac{3.375}{1.25} = 2.7 \text{ per acre.}$$

When we move from a ratio of labor to land of $\frac{8}{10}$ to one of $\frac{9}{10}$, we found that the marginal product was 6 per man. Now, as we reverse the movement and go from a ratio of labor to land of $\frac{9}{10}$ to one of $\frac{9}{11.25} = \frac{8}{10}$, we find that the marginal product of land is 2.7 per acre.

We give both marginal product curves (with $L = 10$) and the total product curve in one diagram (Figure 7-1, based on Table 7-1). As we move to the right, the ratio of labor to the land rises; as we move to the left, the ratio of land to labor rises. The diagram is divided into three stages, which correspond to three possible stages of returns:

1. In the first stage the marginal product of the land is negative.

2. In the second stage the marginal products of both factors are positive and diminish as the factor increases.

3. In the third stage the marginal product of the labor is negative.

The first and third stages are thus completely symmetrical.[2]

The entrepreneur will seek to be in the second stage, where neither input is being used in so large a quantity as to reduce the level of output. Even if labor is free, he will go only to the end of the second stage, and even if land is free he will stop at the beginning of the second stage. This latter condition was approached in colonial days, when land was almost free. The colonists were properly lavish in their use of land relative to labor, despite the frequent complaints of European visitors who were accustomed to the more intensive utilization of more expensive land and trans-

---

[2] These precise relationships between average and marginal products hold only if a given proportional change in all inputs leads to an equal proportional change in output; see mathematical note 9 in Appendix B.

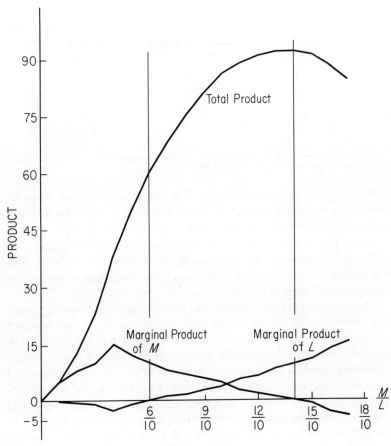

Figure 7-1

ferred their notions of appropriate technique to inappropriate relative prices of labor and land.

In our examples we have assumed that if the ratio of labor to land is sufficiently small, no product will be obtained. This is not impossible: one man-hour applied to an entire 160 acre farm will yield nothing but a brisk stroll. Nor is it necessary. Suppose we apply a variable amount of fertilizer to given quantities of land and labor. If no fertilizer is used, some product will nevertheless be obtained, so the total product curve begins some distance above the origin. An example is given in Table 7–3.

Production: Diminishing Returns

Table 7–3

POUNDS OF FERTILIZER	BUSHELS OF WHEAT PRODUCED	MARGINAL PRODUCT*
0	18.3	—
43	28.6	10.3
86	37.1	8.5
129	39.0	1.9
172	39.5	0.5

* Per 43 pounds of fertilizer.
SOURCE: The example is taken from F. L. Patton, *Diminishing Returns in Agriculture* (New York: Columbia University, 1926), p. 34.

We have so far assumed also that there is an initial stage of increasing marginal returns to labor and this is also possible but unnecessary. Marginal product may begin to diminish with the first units of the variable service; this is also illustrated in Table 7–3, although the size of the increments of fertilizer is so large that we cannot be sure that an initial stage of increasing marginal returns has not been overlooked.

The converse is also possible: the initial stage of increasing marginal product may be so broad that the demand for the required product is obtained before the second stage is reached. But if the productive service being held constant is divisible it would be unnecessary even in this case to employ it with a negative marginal product. Suppose we need only 13 units of product, given the production schedule of Table 7–1. Using again the approximation that proportional changes in all inputs yield proportional changes in output, we may proceed as follows: 6 units of the variable service with 10 units of the constant service yield 60 units of product, so $\frac{13}{60} \times 6$ (= 1.3) units of the variable service with $\frac{13}{60} \times 10$ (= 2.17) units of the constant service will yield $\frac{13}{60} \times 60$ (= 13) units of product. Hence by throwing away $(10 - 2.17) = 7.83$ units of the constant service we can save $(2 - 1.3) = 0.7$ unit of the variable service, still obtaining 13 units of product. If the fixed service is divisible, the entrepreneur will not operate in a region of increasing marginal returns to the variable service (and of negative marginal returns to the constant service).[3]

---

[3] It would be imprecise to say that by this device we have converted increasing returns into constant marginal returns to the variable service, for we are not holding the quantity of land in use constant.

The phrase "diminishing returns" has become part of ordinary language, so people now say that they stopped reading a book because they reached the point of diminishing returns. It is hopeless to fight against popular usage, but one should at least notice that almost always this usage is nonsensical unless reference is being made to diminishing *total*, not marginal, returns. One should indeed stop reading a book (even this one) if he is losing ground, unless it is ground that is a positive nuisance, but commonly the person means that the additional (marginal) pleasure or instruction is not sufficient to justify the time for further reading. I recommend the following language, especially with elderly aunts: I stopped reading the book because its marginal utility per minute had fallen below the marginal utility of alternative uses of my time, including sleep. This language is not only correct but has the interesting effect of always shifting the conversation to sleep.

The Role of Adaptability

The law of diminishing returns requires that we hold constant the quantity of one (or more) productive factors as we vary the quantity of the factor we are studying. In its most literal sense, this constancy implies that the quantity and form of the constant productive factors be unchanged: if we vary the number of men building a house, we nevertheless hold the number and type of tools constant. This is perfectly possible, and will of course usually yield fairly sharply diminishing returns, because if the tools appropriately equip n men, a larger number will have to resort to more primitive methods of work or tool-sharing.

There is another sense in which a factor may be held constant: its economic quantity (or value) can be held constant. We can hold the house-building tools at $2,000, say, but vary their form so that they are most appropriate to whatever quantity of labor we employ. With fewer men, we use fewer and more elaborate tools; with more men, we use more, but less elaborate, tools. Or conversely, if we are examining the marginal productivity for tools, we can hire fewer but abler workmen (with the same aggregate payroll) with fewer tools, and more but less able workmen with many tools.

This broader sense of "constancy" is obviously more appropriate when we are studying the behavior of an entrepreneur who seeks to maximize the output from given resources, if he can in fact change the form of the constant factors. And normally he can make this change if given time: sooner or later the particular factors need to be replaced and they can then be replaced by more appropriate "constant" factors.

If the fixed productive factor need not be changed in form when the quantity of the variable productive factors is changed, the fixed factor is called adaptable. Adaptability is complete when the form of the constant factors is such that, whatever the quantity of the variable factors, the maximum output (with the known technologies) is achieved.

The difference between the products obtainable with partial and complete adaptability is illustrated in Figure 7-2. The extreme case of zero adaptability, it may be noted, would arise with fixed proportions—where the constant factor was literally incapable of being used with more or less than a critical quantity of the variable factor—and in this case the total product "curve" would simply be point P_0.

We shall later argue that the productive service which we arbitrarily hold constant in order to exhibit diminishing marginal returns is often actually fixed for the entrepreneur in the short run. Then he cannot make any magical transformation of the constant productive factor—it requires time to wear out such factors (if they are durable) or to rebuild them. Since the firm will nevertheless usually have a fluctuating output even in the short run, the entrepreneur will seek to have a flexible productive system—one which operates with tolerable efficiency over a considerable range of outputs. This flexibility can usually be achieved (at a cost): for example, it is possible to design an oil refinery so it can vary substantially the proportions in which gasoline, fuel oil, and other products are obtained from given crude oil. In terms of our diagram, the flexible plant will have a lower output at X_0 because, if versatility is expensive, a larger quantity of the constant factor is needed, but the marginal product will not fall so rapidly when the variable productive service is increased.

The Proof of the Law

The law of diminishing returns is, as we have said, an empirical generalization, not a deduction from the laws of matter. An empirical law (as we learned from the law of demand, p. 24) cannot

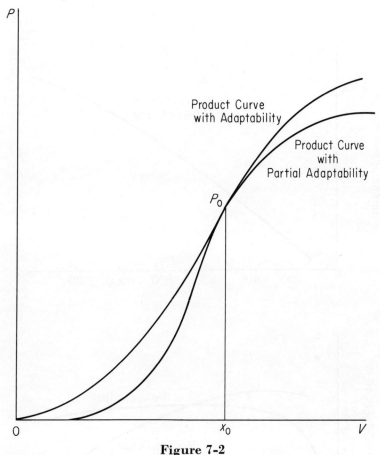

Figure 7-2

be proved by producing instances of its operation. This is not to say that such direct empirical evidence is irrelevant: in particular the law was immediately accepted by economists when it was first proposed simply because it seemed so clearly operative in agriculture. We could now produce a vast number of illustrations and in fact do give two samples in Figure 7-3 and Table 7–3.[4] A method

[4] Figure 7-3 is based upon "Trials of the T.S.M.V. Polyphemus," *The Institution of Mechanical Engineers, Proceedings,* **121** (1931), 183 ff. The equation of the total product curve is

$$Y = -128.5 + 2.740X + 0.0005110X^2 - 0.0000005579X^3,$$

where Y is brake horsepower and X is fuel input (pounds per hour).

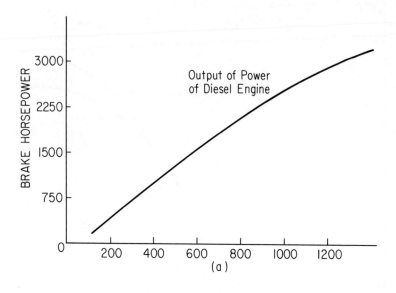

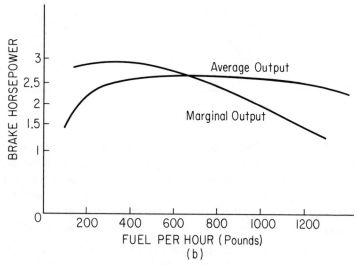

Figure 7-3

of testing the law that is especially relevant to economic analysis
will be provided later in the chapter.

A large number of attempts have been made to prove the law
by deriving it from self-evident facts. Perhaps the most famous
proof assumes the opposite of diminishing marginal returns, and
deduces that all the wheat in the world could be grown in one flower
pot. It proceeds like this: suppose we have increasing marginal
products on a 10 acre farm:

VARIABLE SERVICE	TOTAL PRODUCT
0	0
1	5
2	15
3	30
4	50

(The total product is then $\frac{5}{2}V + \frac{5}{2}V^2$ where V is variable service.)
We proceed:

If 2 units of V on 10 acres yields 15,
1 unit of V on 5 acres yields 7.5.

Again:

If 4 units of V on 10 acres yields 50,
2 units of V on 5 acres yields 25,
1 unit of V on 2.5 acres yields 12.5.

It is evident that by decreasing the quantity of land we are increasing the total product from given quantities of the variable
service. Using our equation for total product,

1000 units of V on 10 acres yields 2,502,500,
1 unit of V on $\frac{1}{1000}$ acres yields 2,502.5.

Since $\frac{1}{1000}$ of an acre is still a very big flower pot, let us do this
once more:

1,000,000 units of V on 10 acres yields 2,502,002,500,000,
1 unit of V on 10^{-5} acres yields 2,500,002.5.

It is clear that we are doing very well by reducing the quantity
of land: 10^{-5} acres is a plot of 5.2 sq. inches. The result should
not surprise us unduly, however: if there are constant returns to
scale (so reducing every input by K per cent reduces the product
by K per cent) and if there are increasing average returns to one

factor, there must be negative marginal returns to the other, so reducing the latter naturally increases the total product (p. **127**). But unfortunately for the proof, there is no basis for saying that there must be constant returns to scale, as we shall see in the next chapter. So the proof is inconclusive, as proofs concerning the real world have a habit of being.

SHORT-RUN COST CURVES

In order to isolate the marginal product of a productive service, we have held the quantities of the other factors constant. This procedure can be applied to any combination of factors: any one input (or group of inputs) could be varied, the remainder being held constant.[5]

In actual life, however, it is usually the case that the entrepreneur can vary the quantities of some inputs much more easily and quickly than the quantities of others. The proprietor of a factory can vary within a few days the number of employees he hires, the rate of supply of raw materials, the number of hours he operates the plant. It may require weeks, however, to hire specialized executives, or to obtain specialized machinery (which may have to be built to order), or to enlarge the factory building. The proprietor of a retail store can increase quickly the number of sales clerks and the supplies of goods, but it will take longer to enlarge the store. The proprietor of an electric generating company can expand quickly his use of fuel, but requires several years to obtain an additional generator.

This is loose language: when a proprietor says that he can quickly buy more steel sheet, but requires **7** months to obtain a new stamping machine, he is not being precise. At a sufficiently high price, one can buy a stamping machine from another company and have it installed in **24** hours; at a very high cost one can have a new machine built in a month by working around the clock. When we say that in the short run some inputs are freely variable, we mean that their quantity can be varied without affecting their price (for given quality). When we say that other inputs are not freely variable we mean that their quantities can be varied within the

---

[5] When more than one productive service is variable, they must be combined in the most efficient proportions, which may vary with the rate of their use. This problem is discussed below, p. **146**.

given time unit—be it a week, a month, or a year—only at a considerable change in their price: if we try to sell the specialized machine, it has little value in other uses; if we try to buy more, price rises sharply for early delivery.

Fixity and variability are matters of degree. The plant's supply of electricity can be increased instantaneously (without a change in price); it may require five years to find a gifted designer. In order to simplify the formal theory, economists define "the" short run as a period within which some inputs are variable, others fixed. Clearly there are many short runs, and the number of freely variable productive services increases as the period of time is lengthened.

The rate at which a firm expands its use of "fixed" factors depends not only on the cost of rapid change but also upon how long output is expected to run at a high or low rate. Suppose a firm has a "plant" (fixed factors) appropriate to a rate of production of 100 units of output per week. (The determination of the right amount of plant is taken up in the next chapter.) If now 130 units is the desired output (due to a rise in price), the firm will immediately begin to increase its plant if this new rate of output is expected to last for years. But if it is a short term fluctuation, which will probably be followed by an output rate of 70, it will be supplied only by varying the use of variable factors (and probably by inventory changes). In general no variation in plant size will be made if the fluctuation in output is expected to be temporary. In addition, even a permanent change in output, if it comes unexpectedly, will for a time be handled primarily through changes in the "variable" productive services.

The cost curve appropriate to these temporary changes in output is the short run marginal cost. We may prove the primacy of marginal cost from first principles. The cost of any action (such as increasing output 10 units) is the alternative use of the resources required to achieve this action. The short run fluctuations of output by definition involve no change in the "plant" (fixed factors), so there is no foregone alternative to the more intensive use of the plant.[6] The only foregone alternative is the amount spent on additional units of variable services.

---

[6] If the plant will wear out faster at higher rates of output, the extra cost is chargeable to the increased output. This cost (called user cost) is usually minor.

The definition of marginal cost is

$$MC = \frac{\text{Increase in Total Cost}}{\text{Increase in Output}}.$$

Since the increase in total cost is equal to the increase in the number of units of variable services times their price (which is constant to the firm under competition), we may rewrite this definition as

$$MC = \frac{\begin{array}{c}\text{Increase in Quantity}\\\text{of Variable Services}\end{array}}{\text{Increase in Output}} \times \text{Price of Variable Services}$$

$$= \frac{\text{Price of Variable Services}}{\text{Marginal Product of Variable Services}}.$$

Hence marginal cost varies inversely to marginal product, and the law of diminishing marginal product is equivalent (under competition) to the law of increasing marginal cost.

For reasons which do not bear close scrutiny, it is conventional to define a considerable variety of short run cost curves for the competitive firm. They may be illustrated with the arithmetic in Table 7–4, which is based upon the production schedule in Table 7–1, plus the assumption that units of the variable service cost $5 and units of the constant service $4. The definitions of the various costs are:

1. Total fixed cost = quantity of the fixed productive service times its price.

2. Total variable cost = quantity of the variable productive service times its price.

3. Total cost = total fixed cost plus total variable cost.

4. Marginal cost = increase in total cost divided by the increase in output.

5. Average fixed cost = total fixed cost divided by output.

6. Average variable cost = total variable cost divided by output.

7. Average cost = average fixed cost plus average variable cost = total cost divided by output.

The last four curves are illustrated in Figure 7-4.

We have said that only the marginal cost curve is relevant to short run changes in output: we can go a step farther and say that only that portion of the marginal cost curve *above* average

Table 7-4

UNITS OF VARIABLE SERVICE	UNITS OF FIXED SERVICE	TOTAL PRODUCT (= OUTPUT)	TOTAL VARIABLE COST	TOTAL FIXED COST	TOTAL COST	AVERAGE VARIABLE COST	AVERAGE FIXED COST	AVERAGE COST	MARGINAL COST
0	10	0	0	$40	$40	—	∞	∞	—
1	10	5	5	40	45	$1.00	$8.00	$9.00	$1.00
2	10	13	10	40	50	0.77	3.08	3.85	0.62
3	10	23	15	40	55	0.65	1.74	2.39	0.50
4	10	38	20	40	60	0.53	1.05	1.58	0.33
5	10	50	25	40	65	0.50	0.80	1.30	0.42
6	10	60	30	40	70	0.50	0.67	1.17	0.50
7	10	68	35	40	75	0.51	0.59	1.10	0.62
8	10	75	40	40	80	0.53	0.53	1.07	0.71
9	10	81	45	40	85	0.56	0.49	1.05	0.83
10	10	86	50	40	90	0.58	0.47	1.05	1.00
11	10	89	55	40	95	0.62	0.45	1.07	1.67
12	10	91	60	40	100	0.66	0.44	1.10	2.50
13	10	92	65	40	105	0.71	0.43	1.14	5.00
14	10	92	70	40	110	0.76	0.43	1.20	∞

Production: Diminishing Returns

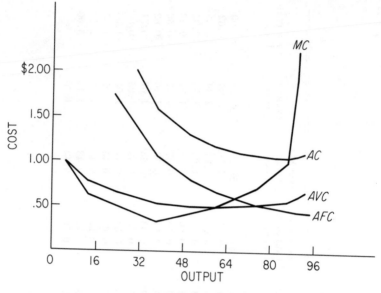

Figure 7-4

variable cost is relevant. To show this, we must first show that a competitive firm will operate where marginal cost equals price. It operates at this output because profits are then maximized. The demand curve of a competitive firm is a horizontal line: its output is too small to affect the market price. Hence, when the firm increases output by one unit, it increases

1. Receipts by the price of the unit.
2. Costs by the marginal cost of the unit.

Hence profits will rise after a unit increase in output if price exceeds marginal cost; and profits will rise after a *decrease* of a unit in output if price is less than marginal cost.[7]

[7] The rule may be derived algebraically. When output rises by Δq, profits rise by

$$p\Delta q - [C(q + \Delta q) - C(q)],$$

where $C(q)$ is the cost of producing q. If profits are at a maximum, they will not either increase or decrease with a small change in output, so this expression must equal zero. Rewriting it,

$$p = \frac{C(q + \Delta q) - C(q)}{\Delta q},$$

and the expression on the right is of course marginal cost.

We illustrate this rule in Figure 7-5. When the price is P_1, if the firm expands its output from X_0 to A, it will add RST more to costs than to receipts; if it contracts output to B, it will reduce receipts by RMN more than it reduces costs. (Recall that the area under a marginal curve between two points is the change in the total between these points.)

But if price falls below P_0, the firm faces a different choice. When price is P_2, if the firm operates at X_1 (where marginal cost equals

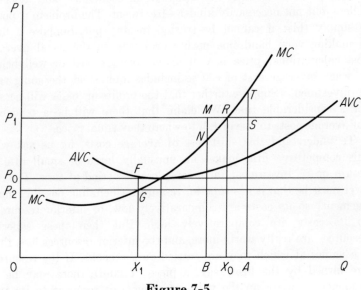

Figure 7-5

price) it will have total variable costs of $0X_1$ times X_1F, which exceed the receipts ($0X_1$ times P_2). By closing down the plant temporarily (recall that short run curves are appropriate only to temporary fluctuations), it will save money. Hence the firm will not operate below a price of P_0.

We define the supply curve of a competitive firm as the amounts it will supply at various prices. This supply curve is (in the short run) the firm's marginal cost curve above minimum average variable cost.

The Suspicious Character of Average Costs

Four cost curves were presented in Figure 7-4: average fixed, average variable, average and marginal costs. Average fixed cost is wholly uninteresting: it is the cost (per unit of time) of the "fixed" factors divided by output. It is always a rectangular hyperbola, and it is always useless. Average variable cost, we found, had one use: to determine the minimum effective point on the marginal cost curve; otherwise it too is dispensable.

Average cost is rather more popular in economics, and deserves fuller—but not necessarily kinder—treatment. The problem it poses is simply this: it cannot be trusted to stay put. Suppose a firm is making very handsome profits or losses on the usual average cost calculations: price is well above average cost or well below it, where average cost of course includes interest at the going rate on investment.[8] Suppose further that the profits or losses will persist for a considerable time. We claim that there will be a tendency for average costs to rise or fall to where they equal price.

To understand this shiftiness of average costs, let us ask why this competitive firm makes an unusually large or small rate of return on its investment for a considerable period of time. The answer must be that it has superior resources (including possibly management) so its costs are comparatively low, or inferior resources, so its costs are comparatively high. But then these superior resources are really worth more, and the inferior resources less, than the values at which they are carried on the books. If the resources are owned by the firm (say, a piece of land), there may be no tendency to write up the value of a superior resource to its true value, because accountants are conservative. On the other hand, the accountants will not object strongly to writing down the value of the inferior resource.

Whether the resources are revalued or not, another factor leads to movements of average costs. If the firm is sold, its price will be determined by its expected earnings. If these earnings are high, the firm will sell for more than book value, and if earnings are low it will sell for less than book value. If the buyer values the

---

[8] The "of course" should not lead the student to believe that it will be included in usual accounting procedures; accountants have been unwilling to include interest on investment (other than interest on debt) in cost.

enterprise at its cost to him, then by definition it will earn the going rate of return—average cost will move to equality with price.

If a firm used no specialized resources, the valuation of inputs would be much simpler, for then by definition the alternative product of a resource would be its cost to the firm (and industry). Once specialized resources enter, however, there is no valid basis for fixing their value other than discounting their future earnings—and average cost begins to follow price.

Revaluations of assets will not affect marginal costs because the revaluations do not depend upon the firm's output. Suppose there is a rise in the industry's output because of an increase in demand, so a given superior resource (say, a piece of land) should be cultivated more intensively for maximum profit. If the plot is cultivated more intensively, it will have a larger marginal product (by the law of diminishing returns; see MP_L in Figure 7-1), and should be revalued upward. But even if the owner of the plot mistakenly failed to use it more intensively, its value would rise—for the value of an asset is determined by what others would pay for it. Hence the asset becomes more valuable whether or not its owner varies output.

The actual amount of asset revaluations is unfortunately almost completely unknown.[9] The effects of restraints imposed by accountants and tax laws are in the direction of preserving historical costs (costs as historically made and recorded). Historical costs, if rigorously adhered to, eliminate certain methods of capitalizing gains and losses, but introduce other departures from the alternative cost concept appropriate to maximum profit behavior.[10]

The Proof of Rising Short-Run Marginal Costs

We have pointed out that marginal cost varies inversely with the marginal product of the variable factor, so the law of diminishing returns implies that the short-run marginal cost curve has a

[9] The most extensive study is Solomon Fabricant's *Capital Consumption and Adjustment* (National Bureau of Economic Research, 1938), esp. Ch. 12. Of 272 corporations reporting during 1925–34, 66 made capital write-ups, 140 capital write-downs—the period was obviously dominated by the Great Depression.

[10] Many of the problems encountered in analyzing historical costs are dealt with in the literature on national income and wealth.

positive slope. It would appear that this ends the matter of proof, but it does not.

A series of statistical studies have found that short-run marginal cost is approximately constant until "capacity" is approached. Capacity in turn is usually defined as the output at which marginal costs become very inelastic.[11] The typical marginal cost curve, according to this literature, is that illustrated in Figure 7-6. Clearly

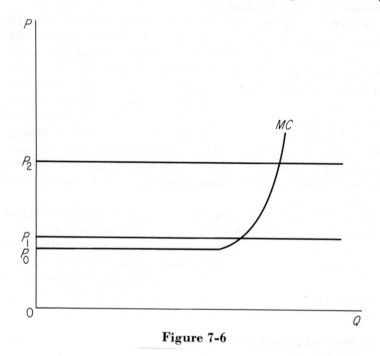

Figure 7-6

this literature denies the short-run validity of the law of diminishing returns.[12]

Rather than delve into the statistical studies which yield horizontal short-run marginal costs,[13] it is possible to test the validity

[11] We shall quarrel with this definition later.

[12] Numerous examples and references are given in J. Johnston, *Statistical Cost Analysis* (New York: McGraw-Hill, 1960).

[13] The studies have been criticized as having linear biases in the statistical procedures, and defended against this charge, with no clear victory for either side.

of this cost curve indirectly. If marginal costs are essentially constant up to the output at which they rise rapidly, under competition a firm's output (set where marginal cost equals price) will be nearly constant at all prices above this constant marginal cost, and zero at lower prices. Thus in Figure 7-6, the output of the firm varies little at prices between P_1 and P_2, but falls to zero at prices under P_0. Where marginal costs display this behavior, then, short-run variations in the output of the industry will come about almost exclusively through variations in the *number* of plants in operation. But if marginal costs rise steadily with output, much of the industry's fluctuation in output will come from fluctuations in the rate of output of each plant, and little from fluctuations in the number of operating plants.[14]

In this form, the hypothesis that short-run marginal costs are constant can be tested against readily observable facts. As an example, consider the American cotton spinning industry. The output of the industry may be measured by spindlehours, the "plant" by active spindles, and the output per plant by "hours per active spindle". Then the percentage change in output (spindle hours) from one quarter year to the next will be approximately equal to the sum of the percentage changes in active spindles and in hours per spindle.[15] This calculation has been made by quarters from August 1945 through June 1959, separately for the southern states (where the industry has grown slightly) and for the New England states

---

[14] The argument, it may be noted, can be extended also to noncompetitive firms which operate more than one plant within a market area. Unless the plants have equal constant marginal costs, a monopolist will minimize costs by operating the lower marginal cost plant at "capacity" and making all adaptations to changing output in the plant with higher marginal costs.

[15] The output of an industry is $Q = Nq$, where N is the number of plants operating, q the output per plant. By definition,

$$\Delta Q = N\Delta q + q\Delta N$$

and

$$\frac{\Delta Q}{Q} = \frac{\Delta q}{q} + \frac{\Delta N}{N}.$$

Hence the relative change in output is equal to the sum of the relative changes in N and q—the magnitudes used in our test. For large changes in output, a term $\Delta q\Delta N/Q$ should be added, and (as is customary with such formal partitions) divided arbitrarily between N and q. Here the cross product term is neglected.

(where the industry has been declining very substantially). We may tabulate the average of the 55 quarterly changes:[16]

	PER CENT OF CHANGE IN SPINDLE HOURS DUE TO	
	Change in Active Spindles	*Change in Hours per Spindle*
Section		
Southern states	9.2	90.5
New England	21.8	76.5

The conclusion is clear: even in the declining branch of the industry the overwhelming part of changes in output is achieved through variations in the rate of operation of plants (here, hours per spindle), not by variations in number of active plants (here, active spindles).[17] In this industry short-run marginal costs are rising: I suspect that in most industries they do so.

RECOMMENDED READINGS

Friedman, M., *Price Theory*, Chicago: Aldine, 1962, Chs. 5, 6.

Stigler, G. J., "Production and Distribution in the Short Run," *Journal of Political Economy*, **47** (1939), 305–27. Reprinted in *Readings in Income Distribution*.

Viner, J., "Cost Curves and Supply Curves," *Zeitschrift für Nationalökonomie*, **3** (1932), 23–46. Reprinted in *Readings in Price Theory*.

PROBLEMS

1. A producer with two plants wishes to produce a given output at the lowest possible cost. Under what conditions will he close down one of the plants?

---

[16] The source of the data is: U. S. Bureau of the Census, "Cotton Production and Distribution," Bulletins **186**, **189**, **193**, and **196** (Washington, D. C.: U. S. Government Printing Office).

[17] In the declining branch of the industry, one would expect a larger role for plant reductions simply because the industry is declining. And when short-run output changes are divided into increases and decreases, we find that the role of plant changes is more important in the case of declines of output:

New England States

Direction of Change in Quarterly Output	PERCENT OF CHANGE IN SPINDLE-HOURS DUE TO	
	Change in Active Spindles	*Change in Hours per Spindle*
Increase	20.3	82.2
Decrease	23.9	68.6

Problems 145

2. You are given the following production function:

INPUT OF A	0	1	2	3	4	5	6	7
OUTPUT	100	101	103	105	106.8	108.4	109.9	111.3

(a) Draw the marginal and average products of A.

(b) Draw the marginal and average products of B (the other productive factor). Ten units of B underly the foregoing schedule. Use the constant returns to scale equation (p. 133).

3. An economy consisting of farms has the unusual production function for each farm:

NUMBER OF MEN	MARGINAL PRODUCT
1	20
2	15
3	19
4	14
5	18
6	13
etc.	etc.

If you had 10 farms and 40 employees how would you allocate them among farms? If wages are $40, construct the marginal cost schedule of output.

4. The law of diminishing returns was originally stated as an historical law, that is, it asserted that the marginal product of labor on land would decline as population grew. If true, what would have happened to (1) aggregate agricultural land values, and (2) prices of farm products relative to manufactures, over long periods?

chapter eight

Production: Returns to Scale

No such sweeping generalization as the law of diminishing returns has been found for the relationship of output to inputs when all inputs are varied. We are accordingly driven to consider alternative possibilities: when all inputs are increased in a given proportion, output may increase in a greater or lesser or equal proportion. The economist must then determine, when he is analyzing the automobile or shoe or radio repair industry, whether it has increasing, decreasing, or constant returns to scale, and we shall discuss later the methods of empirically determining economies of scale.

THE PROPER COMBINATION OF INPUTS

Let us begin by asking a basic question: if we wish to produce at a certain rate, in what proportion shall we use the various inputs? This question is not answered directly by the law of diminishing returns, for it told us only how many men were needed to produce a given product, given that they worked on 10 acres of land, or (since the law is reversible) how many acres were needed, given a labor force of 8 men. There are many different combinations of inputs that will yield the desired product, and obviously the cheapest combination will maximize the producer's profits.

The cheapest combination obviously depends upon the relative prices of the inputs and in fact the least cost combination is given by the rule: a dollar's worth of any input should add as much product as a dollar's worth of any other input. For if a dollar's worth of input A has a marginal product of (say) 5 units, and that of B only 3 units, then we can

(a) Buy \$1 less of B, suffering a decline of product of 3 units,
(b) Buy \$0.60 more of A, obtaining 3/5 of the marginal product of a dollar's worth, or 3 units of product, and
(c) Pocket the \$0.40.

This rule may be stated as an equation of minimum cost:

$$\frac{\text{Marginal Product of } A}{\text{Price of } A} = \frac{\text{Marginal Product of } B}{\text{Price of } B},$$

$$= \frac{\text{Marginal Product of } C}{\text{Price of } C},$$

for all inputs, no matter how many.

When the price of one input increases, this rule of minimum cost tells us that we must use less of this input (thus increasing its marginal product) and more of the other inputs (thus decreasing their marginal products).

This analysis has obvious analogies to the problem of the consumer dividing his income among commodities in order to maximize satisfaction. In fact the same apparatus of indifference curves can be used, with the obvious modification that now we shall call such curves isoquants (equal quantities), and define the isoquant (Figure 8-1) as those combinations of inputs which yield the same product. When we reduce the quantity of one input (A) by a small amount (ΔA), we reduce the product by ΔA times the marginal product of A ($= MP_a$). Thus if the marginal product of men is 6, when we reduce the quantity of labor by 0.25 (one-fourth of a day, say), we reduce the total product by $0.25 \times 6 = 1.5$. In order to offset this reduction, we must increase the other input (B) by such an amount (ΔB) as to produce this much, so

$$\Delta A \cdot MP_a + \Delta B \cdot MP_b = 0 \qquad (\Delta A < 0),$$

along an isoquant. Hence the slope of an isoquant is

$$\frac{\Delta B}{\Delta A} = -\frac{MP_a}{MP_b}.$$

Corresponding to the consumer's budget line, there will be an outlay line for the entrepreneur. With a given expenditure E_0, he

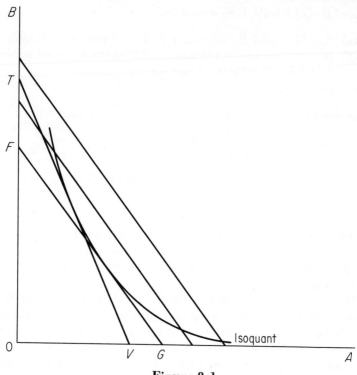

Figure 8-1

can buy all combinations of A and B such that

$$E_0 = AP_a + BP_b,$$

and there will be a different outlay line for every amount of expenditure. We draw three outlay lines in Figure 8-1 (temporarily ignoring TV), each higher one representing a larger total expenditure. The entrepreneur will choose outlay line FG because this is the lowest line which touches the isoquant, and in general the lowest outlay line to yield the desired product is tangent to the isoquant. But the slope of the outlay line is[1]

$$-\frac{P_a}{P_b},$$

---

[1] For a constant outlay,

$$\Delta A \cdot P_a + \Delta B \cdot P_b = 0,$$

so

$$\frac{\Delta B}{\Delta A} = -\frac{P_a}{P_b}.$$

and the tangency implies that

$$\frac{P_a}{P_b} = \frac{MP_a}{MP_b},$$

another form of our condition for minimum cost. The proposition that less will be used of an input if its price rises is illustrated by increasing the price of A, leading to the new outlay curve, TV, which is necessarily tangent to a convex isoquant to the left of the original equilibrium.[2]

The student will find many different uses of this technique, which is generally employed where one wishes to analyze three variables without recourse to solid geometry. (Here the three variables are two inputs and output; with consumer indifference curves they were two commodities and utility.)

CONSTANT RETURNS TO SCALE: THE SIMPLEST CASE

The simplest possibility with respect to economies of scale is that there are none: when output is increased in any proportion, exactly equal proportionate increases of all inputs are required. Then if the prices of productive factors are not affected by the firm's rate of output, as they will not be under competition, total costs vary proportionately with output.

Constant returns to scale are commended upon a very simple ground: if we do a thing once, we can do it twice. If we use A and B to produce P, why should not $2A$ and $2B$ produce $2P$? Perhaps they should, but it must be emphasized that there may be cheaper ways of producing $2P$. Where painting was done by hand, it may now be feasible to use a spray gun; where a man performed tasks X and Y, it may now be feasible to have him specialize in task X with a gain in efficiency. These are questions of fact, and we cannot state that in general they will be, or will not be, possible. If these examples suggest that *at most* we must double inputs to double output, that also is not true. For the tasks of coordinating a larger enterprise may increase so rapidly that large enterprises are inefficient. We shall examine these possibilities of increasing and decreasing returns shortly.

---

[2] See mathematical note 6 in Appendix B on the relationship of diminishing returns to convexity.

If there are constant returns to scale, obviously marginal costs will be constant for all outputs when the inputs are in proper proportion. For K per cent more output requires K per cent more of each input, and since the prices of productive factors are constant to a competitive firm, total costs also rise by K per cent. Hence average and marginal costs are constant.

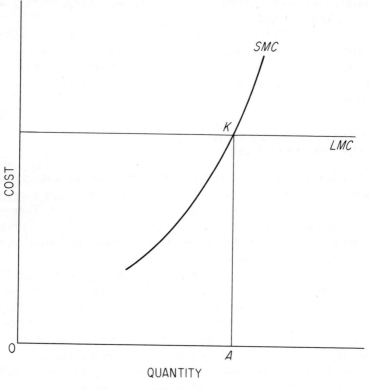

Figure 8-2

We have identified cost curves which reflect complete adjustment of all inputs with the "long run", and those which reflect changes in part of the inputs with the "short run" (p. 134). Hence "short-run" marginal costs will rise (because of diminishing returns) even though "long-run" marginal costs are constant. Consider Figure 8-2. At output A, a certain quantity of each input yields minimum marginal (and average) cost, AK. If we vary part of the inputs, we shall obtain the marginal cost curve, SMC.

It is evident that short-run marginal costs may be greater or smaller than long-run marginal costs, depending upon the rate of output. At the point where the two curves intersect, the marginal product of the plant ("fixed factors") divided by its price is equal to the marginal product of the variable factor divided by its price. At larger outputs the marginal product of the plant rises and the marginal product of the variable factor falls, so the long run minimum cost condition is not fulfilled; the opposite relation holds below the intersection.

Even though the long-run average and marginal cost curves of the firm are horizontal (and in fact identical) under constant returns to scale, no such relation need hold for the industry. As we shall see in Chapter 10, the industry cost curves are affected also by changes in the prices of inputs (which are constant to the individual firm). Nevertheless, even for the industry constant returns to scale is the overwhelmingly popular assumption in scientific work. The so-called Cobb-Douglas function is

$$P = aC^\alpha L^{1-\alpha},$$

where P is product, C is capital, and L is labor. This production function yields constant returns to scale,[3] and it has an almost monopolistic position in economic literature. Its popularity is not due to its demonstrated validity as a description of actual production functions, however. Rather, it is used because (1) it yields diminishing returns to each productive factor separately, (2) it is simple to handle, being linear in logarithmic form, (3) in many investigations the precise nature of returns to scale is not very interesting, and constant returns is a convenient simplification, and (4) of a remarkable property of constant returns to scale which we must now mention.

Euler's Theorem. Euler's theorem on homogeneous functions is the august name attached to this final property of constant returns. The theorem is a simple one: it says that if there is constant returns

---

[3] If we vary each input in a given proportion, say changing C to (λC) and L to (λL), we get

$$a(\lambda C)^\alpha(\lambda L)^{1-\alpha} = a\lambda^{\alpha+1-\alpha}C^\alpha L^{1-\alpha} = a\lambda C^\alpha L^{1-\alpha} = \lambda P,$$

so the product increases in the same proportion.

to scale, then the total product is equal to the sum of the marginal products of the various inputs, each multiplied by the quantity of its input.[4] Thus if the production function is

$$P = f(A, B, C, \ldots)$$

and there is constant returns to scale,

$$P = A \cdot MP_a + B \cdot MP_b + C \cdot MP_c + \cdots.$$

Since the theorem has been in the mathematical books for two hundred years, we can assume its truth, and here present only an example. Consider the simple production function

$$P = C^{1/4}L^{3/4},$$

which Paul Douglas believed to be descriptive of American manufacturing; here P, C, and L are product, capital, and labor, all in index number form. If $L = C = 200$,

$$P = 200^{1/4}200^{3/4} = 200.$$

Increase labor to 201, and the product rises to

$$P = 200^{1/4}201^{3/4} = 200.749.$$

If now C is increased to 201, with L held at 200,

$$P = 201^{1/4}200^{3/4} = 200.249.$$

Hence the marginal product of L is $200.749 - 200 = 0.749$, and that of capital is $200.249 - 200 = 0.249$. The sum of marginal products times quantities of factors is

$$200 \times 0.749 + 200 \times 0.249 = 199.60,$$

which is approximately what Euler's theorem asserts. The small discrepancy in product arises because we use finite increases in the inputs: the theorem holds strictly only for infinitesimal changes.

Euler's theorem entered economics in order to solve the problem whether, if each productive factor is paid at the rate of its marginal

[4] The definition of a homogeneous function of degree k is that if

$$P = f(A, B, C, \ldots),$$
$$\lambda^k P = f(\lambda A, \lambda B, \lambda C, \ldots),$$

where λ is any positive number. When k is unity, the function is homogeneous of the first degree, and this is our definition of constant returns to scale.

productivity, the total product would be sufficient and only sufficient. It was received with considerable hostility: Edgeworth remarked that "Justice is a perfect cube, said the ancient sage; and rational conduct is a homogeneous function, adds the modern savant." The modern savant, Philip Wicksteed by name, abandoned the argument, but the simplicity and manageability of the homogeneous functions have overcome any scruples on realism and they are immensely popular among economists to this day.

Variable Returns to Scale

Phrases such as "economies of mass production" testify to the widely held belief that as an enterprise expands its scale of operations, it will be able to reduce average costs. Popular beliefs are seldom a safe guide in economics, and here they are especially suspect. Laymen observe that more electricity (or transistor radios or electric dishwashers) are made than formerly, and that prices have fallen (or, in a period of inflation, risen less than a comprehensive price index). These observations are correct, but the passage of time also allows technological advances to take place, so the effects of scale of operations and technological advance are not separated. Returns to scale (like diminishing returns) refer to the behavior of output relative to inputs when the "state of the arts" is given.

Increasing returns to scale arise when a doubling of output does not require a doubling of every input. The causes of increasing returns are:

1. There may be some unavoidable "excess capacity" of some inputs. A railroad has a tunnel which is essential for given traffic, but can handle twice as much traffic. The emphasis here is on "unavoidable." If the railroad has unused locomotives, in the long run they can be sold or worn out, and hence do *not* give rise to increasing returns.

2. Many inputs become cheaper when purchased on a larger scale. There are quantity discounts because of economies in larger transactions. Often equipment costs less per unit of capacity when larger sizes are ordered (see Table 8–1).[5]

---

[5] Containers have the property that their contents increase as the cube of dimensions, the surface (and material required) as the square.

Table 8–1

Prices of Ball-Bearing Induction Electric Motors, 1800 rpm
(February 1950)

HORSEPOWER	PRICE	PRICE PER HORSEPOWER
1.0	$59	$59.00
1.5	69	46.00
2.0	80	40.00
3.0	89	29.67
5.0	106	21.20
7.5	139	18.53
10.0	176	17.60
25.0	327	13.08
50.0	559	11.18
100.0	1073	10.73
150.0	1633	10.89
200.0	2085	10.42
500.0	3207	6.41
1000.0	5819	5.82

3. More specialized processes (whether performed by men or machines) are often possible as the scale of operations increases: the man can become more expert on a smaller range of tasks; the machine can be special purpose.

4. The statistical laws of large numbers give rise to certain economies of scale. For example, the inventory of a firm need not increase in proportion to its sales, because there is greater stability in the aggregate behavior of a larger number of customers.[6]

If these forces are dominant, the long-run marginal cost curve of the firm will have a negative slope—there will be economies of scale. An illustrative long-run marginal cost and several short-run marginal cost curves are given in Figure 8-3: each short run curve represents a different amount of "fixed plant." The corresponding aver-

[6] See W. J. Baumol, "The Transactions Demand for Cash: An Inventory Theoretic Approach," *Quarterly Journal of Economics* (November 1952). A similar argument may be made with respect to risks of failure. See also the results on servicing of machines in W. Feller, *An Introduction to Probability Theory and Its Applications,* 2nd ed. (New York: Wiley, 1957), Vol. I, pp. 416–21.

age cost curves are also given in Figure 8-3. These average costs are exclusively alternative costs—the input prices are those necessary to keep the resources in this industry and exclude all "rents."

Decreasing returns to scale arises out of the difficulties of managing a large enterprise. The larger the enterprise, the more extensive and formal its administrative organization must be in order to pro-

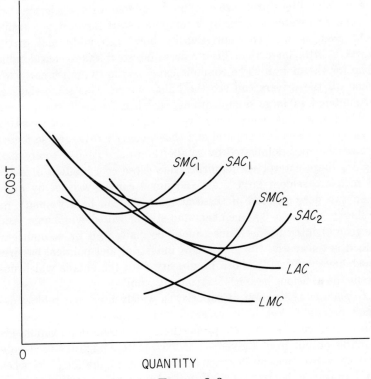

Figure 8-3

vide the information necessary for central decisions and the sanctions necessary to enforce these decisions. A large organization must be less flexible—policies cannot be changed frequently and still be carefully controlled.

The decentralization of a large organization might be considered a way in which to avoid the rigidity of size, and this has indeed become a fashionable practice at times. A fundamental contradiction is encountered here, however: as the parts of a large enterprise are decentralized, the gains of economies of scale are simultaneously sacrificed. It would be possible to give each manager of a store complete autonomy, but then the organization which owned a thousand stores would become a mere investment trust: there could be no gains from quantity purchases or joint advertising.

This source of inefficiency of large size is given little weight in the popular literature: size is almost equated with efficiency. Yet anyone who watches a line of automobiles start forward as a traffic light changes will be impressed by how each additional driver starts a little later than his predecessor, so it takes considerable time for the motion to be communicated to the twentieth car, even when all the drivers can see the light change. This same slack is encountered in large organizations, so when frequent changes are called for, a large company is very inept. The industries making style goods (women's apparel and shoes, novelty toys, and so forth) are consistently dominated by smaller and more flexible companies. Again, those enterprises requiring very close coordination of skills of men are seldom large scale: no novel can be written by more than two persons (and of these at most one can be a woman), no orchestra can have 300 members and still be called symphonic. And in general intricate decisions cannot be made well by committees, which is the reason the greatest of industrial and political empires must have one head, whose familiarity with the details which underlie his decisions becomes vanishingly small.

Capacity. The notion of capacity is widely used, but seldom defined precisely. Yet it is an ambiguous concept even at best. In the normal case of variable proportions, the absolute maximum attainable output from a given set of fixed factors might be used—obviously a firm has no "capacity" limitation in the long run when all inputs can be increased. But the maximum attainable output is never known—it is, for example, the output of a farm or a factory when "no expense [or variable factor] is spared," and no one has been foolish enough to devote unlimited resources to this end.

Sometimes the technology of production seems to invite a fairly clean notion of capacity. For example, a blast furnace runs day and night, so it would appear to have a definite limit on output per month. Actually it does not: the charge can be varied; oxygen can be used, and the shut-down period can be shortened, so plants have operated for considerable periods at more than 100 per cent of capacity. Yet the qualifications are minor, and in the short run "capacity" has a reasonable determinate meaning here. Such cases are uncommon.

It seems clear that capacity should be defined in a way that takes account of costs—no one cares about the output that could

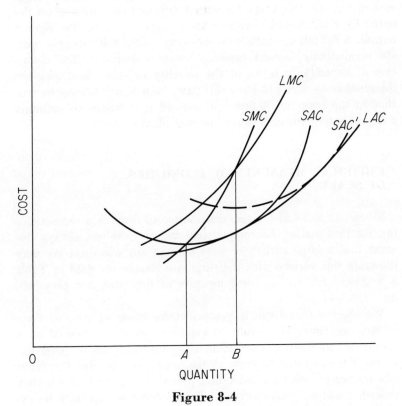

Figure 8-4

be obtained only at literally prohibitive costs. Two definitions have been proposed: capacity is (1) the output at which short-run average costs are at a minimum, and (2) the output at which short- and long-run marginal costs are equal. The definition of words is necessarily arbitrary, but there is a persuasive argument for the latter definition—it is more relevant to entrepreneurial decisions. We may illustrate its relevance by Figure 8-4.

On the minimum cost definition, capacity is OA; on the marginal cost definition it is OB. Suppose an entrepreneur with the plant represented by the short-run average cost curve wished to operate permanently at OB. On the minimum cost definition he is operating beyond capacity, and this suggests that, given time, he will build a larger plant. But he will not: this plant has the minimum average cost of any possible plant for output OB, and the larger plant denoted by SAC' would obviously have higher costs for the desired output. A definition which leads us to say a firm will willingly operate permanently beyond capacity seems undesirable. The definition of capacity in terms of the equality of short- and long-run marginal costs does not have this flaw: then it will always be true that in the long run a firm will expand if it wishes to maintain a rate of output which is beyond present plant capacity.

EMPIRICAL MEASURES OF ECONOMIES OF SCALE

When one looks at the size distribution of firms in a competitive (or, for that matter, noncompetitive) industry, he will always discover that a large variety of sizes exist at any one time. We may illustrate this variety with the corporate income tax data in Table 8–2. Assets are not an ideal measure of firm size, but they will do.

We observe that there is a considerable range of sizes of firms at any one time. This could be explained by the failure of some companies to reach the optimum size, due to errors of judgment or the time required to grow to the optimum size. But the range of sizes persists over a considerable period of time (a longer period, indeed, than our tables reveal). This persistence can only be explained by the fact that there is more than one optimum size.

The optimum size of a firm—we shall define "optimum" shortly—depends upon the resources which a firm uses. All firms in an industry do not have identical resources. Some have managers who are effective in running a small concern; others have managers who capably run a large concern. Some have large holdings of natural resources, others buy their raw materials. Some are located where labor is cheaper, others where electrical power is cheaper.

Table 8–2

**Percentage Distribution of Assets by Company Size in
Selected Manufacturing Industries
(1954 and 1958)**

Asset Size Class	1954	1958
A. Knitting mills		
Under $100,000	2.4%	3.4%
$100,000– 500,000	13.6	14.9
500,000– 1,000,000	12.0	13.1
1,000,000– 2,500,000	19.2	18.1
2,500,000– 5,000,000	14.8	16.3
5,000,000–10,000,000	13.7	12.5
10,000,000–25,000,000	12.8	19.4
Over 25,000,000	11.5	2.4
TOTAL	100.	100.1
B. Engines		
Under $500,000	.1	1.2
$500,000– 1,000,000	.6	.4
1,000,000– 2,500,000	2.4	1.6
2,500,000– 5,000,000	5.5	3.3
5,000,000– 10,000,000	6.1	0.
10,000,000– 25,000,000	32.5	20.2
25,000,000$ 50,000,000	35.1	31.1
50,000,000–100,000,000	16.6	42.3
TOTAL	99.9	100.1

SOURCE: *Statistics of Income*, 1954, 1958.

Such differences are compatible with all firms having equal long run marginal costs.[7]

If we observed the distribution of firms by size in an industry over a period of years and it did not change (random fluctuations aside), one could make several valid inferences. First, the firms of every size would on average be operating in a region of constant or rising long-run marginal costs—for if marginal costs were declin-

---

[7] The optimum size of firm is commonly defined as that which has minimum long-run average costs. As soon as we allow resources to differ, it is not possible to say that long-run average costs *excluding* rents will be equal for the different firms. The varying qualities and types of resources imply that some are specialized to the industry—that is, some resources will earn more in the industry than they could earn elsewhere. Average costs *including* rents can of course be equal.

ing to any size, these firms would expand and acquire a larger share of the industry's output. And second, the firms of various sizes would be equally efficient, because if any size were more efficient, this size would be more profitable and firms would tend either to move to this preferable size or to leave the industry.

In fact the basic definition of a firm of optimum size is that it can maintain itself indefinitely in competition with firms of other sizes. This test of optimality is all inclusive: it takes account of the ability of the firm, not merely to produce goods efficiently, but also to introduce new technology at the proper rate, cope with changes in consumer tastes, adapt to a changing geographical market in the product or resources, and so on. A test of comparative efficiency that is not all inclusive would not allow us to predict the survival of the most efficient size of firm.

Some sizes of firms decline as a share of the industry; for example, corporations with assets under $10,000,000 making engines had 14.7% of industry assets in 1954, only 6.5% in 1958 (Table 8–2). When the decline is large enough or persistent enough to overcome the possibility that it is due only to random fluctuations,[8] as is true in this case, we may conclude that these size classes are comparatively inefficient. On this interpretation, the large firms in the engine industry were more efficient than the smaller firms: there were economies of scale. In the knitting industry, on the contrary, there was a decline in the role of larger firms, so there were diseconomies of scale.

RECOMMENDED READINGS

Douglas, P. H., "Are There Laws of Production?" *American Economic Review* (March 1948).

Marshall, A., *Principles of Economics*, London: Macmillan, 1922, Bk. IV, Chs. 8–13; Bk. V, 3–5.

Robinson, E. A. G., *The Structure of Competitive Industry*, London: Nisbet, 1935.

Stigler, G. J., "The Economics of Scale," *Journal of Law and Economics*, **1** (1958).

---

[8] Random forces would be accidental events unrelated to the size of firm over a long period: floods or other catastrophes, an unusual number of deaths of entrepreneurs in a given period, unusual interruptions of supplies of materials, and so forth.

PROBLEMS

1. Prove that long-run and short-run marginal costs are equal where long- and short-run average cost curves are tangent.

2. Suppose a production process, contains three "machines": A, with a "capacity" of 20 units; B, with a capacity of 75 units; and C with a capacity of 210 units. Each machine has costs of $10 plus 10¢ per unit up to these limits of capacity, after which an additional machine must be employed. Calculate the average costs for outputs of 10, 20, and so on, up to several hundred units. Then determine minimum cost output. The problem of reconciling processes with different efficient sizes is called "balance of processes."

3. Using a Cobb-Douglas function, $P = C^{1/4}L^{3/4}$ calculate isoquants for $P = 100$, 200, 300. (For the first isoquant, since $P = 100$, log 100 $= 2 = \frac{1}{4}$ log $C + \frac{3}{4}$ log L and assign various values to C or L.) Draw some price lines tangent to these isoquants, $P_L = 1$ and $P_c = 2$. (Perhaps P_L is wage rate per hour and P_c rental cost of machinery per hour.) Calculate also the long-run average cost curve.

4. Statistical studies of costs of firms or plants of different size often commit the regression fallacy—which has already been encountered in the discussion of the consumption function. It yields economies of scale simply because of random fluctuation, even though there "really" is constant returns to scale. It may be illustrated as follows:

(a) Consider 10 firms, with average outputs of 100, 200, . . . , 1000, respectively.

(b) Each firm's costs in any one year are $5 per unit (variable costs) plus $5 times its average output. Thus the firm with an average output of 300 has costs of $300 \times \$5 = \$1500$ plus $5 times the output in the given year.

(c) Output in a given year consists of average output plus or minus a random fluctuation.

(d) The random fluctuation is obtained by flipping a coin, adding 10% of average output for each consecutive heads (if heads appear first) or subtracting 10% for each consecutive tails (if tails appear first). Terminate the flipping when the run of heads or tails ends.

Calculate the costs in a given year. Compare graphically with average costs when there are no random fluctuations in output.

chapter nine

Additional Topics in Production and Costs

The cost curves developed in the preceding chapter are those commonly used in economic analysis. Yet they deal with only a particular kind of production process, and there are many problems for which they require modification or extension. In this chapter we discuss three such extensions: multiple products; external economies; and finite production runs. Each is sufficiently important to deserve attention, and in the process more will be learned of the standard cost curves.

MULTIPLE PRODUCTS

Multiple products made their entrance into economic analysis in Great Britain, so the traditional example of multiple products has been the steer, which yielded a hide and beef. It is at least approximately true that these products are yielded in fixed proportions: a steer has only one hide. Hence if we attempt to construct a cost curve for (say) hides, we shall find that we cannot do so: we cannot vary the output of hides, holding the output of beef constant. The only possible cost function is that for a composite unit of (hides and beef), and given competition, it will be a matter of indifference to producers whether hides sell for $20 and carcasses for $1, or hides sell for $1 and carcasses sell for $20. Demand conditions will determine relative prices.

The case of multiple products produced in fixed proportions is, in fact, really not a case of multiple products so far as production is concerned. In a cost diagram, we may relabel the output axis $(A + B)$, and now employ the cost curves of the single product firm. There is no difference between calling (beef and hide) one product and calling H₂O water.

As a general rule, however, the products of a firm can be produced in variable proportions. This is obviously true in many cases: a department store can sell more or less of any one product; a shoe factory can make more or less of one kind of shoe; a farmer (the nation's agricultural policy permitting) can grow more soybeans and less wheat. Variability is also possible in many more subtle cases: a petroleum refinery can vary the proportion of crude oil distilled into gasoline. Conversely, what looks to be independent productive activities—a firm produces steel and cement in different plants—may be related by some common element: for example, the cost of raising capital for the cement plant will probably be lower, the larger the steel plant.

When the proportions among the products are variable, it is possible to derive a separate marginal cost for each product. Consider the hypothetical data for a petroleum refinery in Table 9–1. We

Table 9–1

OUTPUT OF FUEL OIL	OUTPUT OF GASOLINE (GALLONS)			
	100	110	120	130
100	$2.45	$3.55	$4.85	$6.35
110	3.90	4.80	5.90	7.20
120	5.45	6.15	7.05	8.15
130	7.10	7.60	8.30	9.20

define the marginal cost of gasoline as the increase in total cost divided by an increase in the output of gasoline, the quantity of fuel oil being held constant. For example, the marginal cost of 110 gallons of gasoline, when the output of fuel oil is 120 gallons, is

$$\frac{\$6.15 - \$5.45}{10} = \$0.07 \text{ per gallon.}$$

There will be a marginal cost curve for gasoline, or in general for any one product, corresponding to each possible output of the other product or products. This poses no real problem in the theory: we can simply write (in the competitive case)

$$MC_G(G, F) = P_G,$$

that is, that at equilibrium the price of gasoline will equal its marginal cost, which depends upon the quantities of gasoline (G) and fuel oil (F) produced, and similarly for fuel oil:

$$MC_F(G, F) = P_F.$$

The two equations can then be solved simultaneously.

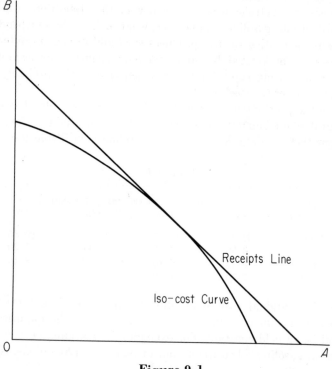

Figure 9-1

An equivalent geometrical procedure is to construct indifference curves (called isocost curves), which represent the quantities of the products which can be produced at a given total outlay. We display one such isocost curve in Figure 9-1. It is concave to the origin because as one continues to substitute one product for the other in the production process, smaller amounts of the other are obtained for given decreases of the one—marginal costs of each product are rising.[1] Under competition the receipts from the sale of the products by a firm can be drawn in the diagram as a straight line: receipts are $Ap_a + Bp_b$, and prices are constant. The firm will operate where the isocost line touches (is tangent to) the highest possible receipts line, and this is equivalent to equating marginal cost and price.[2]

There is no corresponding possibility of calculating the average cost of one of several products. It is worth noticing that even though impossible, it is done every day. The costs which are common to several products—a machine or raw material used in producing both, an executive who manages the production of both—are often divided among the products in proportion to their separable variable costs, or in proportion to their sales. Such an allocation must be arbitrary, for there is no one basis of allocation that is more persuasive than others. Indeed *any* allocation of common costs to one product is irrational if it affects the amount of the product produced, for the firm should produce the product if its price is at least equal to its minimum marginal cost.

EXTERNAL ECONOMIES

An external economy is a source of reduction in cost which is beyond control of the firm. One firm in a competitive industry has no influence upon the prices of inputs, so if their prices fall as the industry expands, this is an external economy. Conversely, if input prices rise as the industry expands, the rise in cost of a firm represents an external diseconomy. The external factors may work upon coefficients of production as well as on input prices: for example the growth of traffic congestion in a community may force a firm to use more trucks to deliver a given quantity of goods.

---

[1] The argument of mathematical note 6 in Appendix B is applicable with changes of language.

[2] The slope of the price line is

$$\frac{\Delta B}{\Delta A} = -\frac{p_a}{p_b}.$$

An isocost curve is given by $\Delta A \cdot MC_a + \Delta B \cdot MC_b = 0$, or

$$\frac{\Delta B}{\Delta A} = -\frac{MC_a}{MC_b}.$$

Cost Curves for Industry-wide
Output Changes

The cost curves of a firm presented in Chapters 7 and 8 were constructed on the assumption that the firm has no influence upon the prices of the factors of production it uses.[3] Under competition this is of course (by definition) the proper assumption. But when all the firms in a competitive industry simultaneously increase or decrease output, their aggregate effect is often to change the prices of inputs. Since we are normally interested much more in the behavior of the industry than of the firm, it is desirable to have cost curves which take account of the impact of the industry's rate of output on input prices.

The direct method of dealing with this dependence of the costs of one firm on the rate of output of the industry is to draw a different cost curve for the firm for each possible price of productive services. For example, when the price of the product is $0A$ and the output of the firm $0T$, the price of raw materials may be \$1 a pound, and the firm's marginal cost curve M_1 (Figure 9-2). When the price of the product is $0B$ and the output of the firm $0R$, the price of the raw material may be \$2 and the marginal cost curve of the firm M_2. Let us join points like T_1 and T_2 (and the innumerable other points we could find for other prices of the raw material) and label the curve M. Then M_1 and M_2 are the type of cost curves derived in preceding chapters, and M is the type of cost curve which we wish to employ in many areas. The distinction between the two types of marginal cost curves is clear:

M_1 (or M_2) is the marginal cost curve when the prices of productive services are constant.

M is the marginal cost curve when all firms in the industry are varying their rate of operation so marginal cost equals price.

Let us call the latter type of curve marginal cost for industry-wide changes. We argued that marginal cost curves of type M_1 have a positive slope under competition in both short and long run. If

[3] Implicitly it was also assumed that variations in the industry's output did not affect the coefficients of production. Exactly the same technique which will be presented to include the effects of changes in input prices on the cost curves will also take account of changes in production coefficients.

this is true, marginal cost curves for industry-wide changes will also have positive slopes unless, when the industry expands, the prices of productive services fall, in which case these curves may (not must) have a negative slope (we discuss this case later).

It should be kept in mind that curves of type M_1, which might be called marginal costs for single-firm changes, are the only type

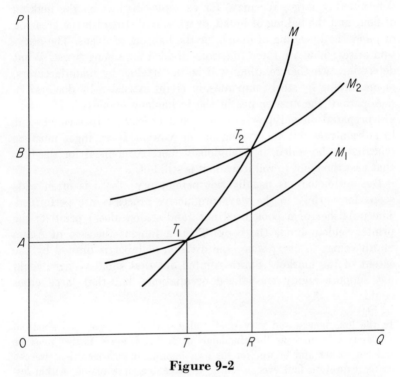

Figure 9-2

that the entrepreneur can individually move along: he cannot control the rate of output of the industry and thus the prices of productive services. The type M curves display the combined effects of the entrepreneur's selection of minimum-cost combinations of inputs (portrayed by M_1) and the repercussions on the firm of profit-maximizing behavior of other firms in the industry, over which the entrepreneur has no control. In this sense the type M curves are shorthand methods of describing the whole array of possible marginal cost curves of the firm (corresponding to all possible prices of productive services), for they pick out the points (like T_1 and T_2) which are relevant to industry-wide changes.

The Functions of the Firm

The number of processes to which a raw material is subjected in its transformation into a finished consumer commodity is indeterminably large. We may, for example, distinguish the making of flour and the baking of bread, or we may distinguish the greasing of pans, the kneading of dough, or the lighting of ovens. The question arises: how are these functions divided up among firms? What determines whether retailing will be undertaken by manufacturers, or ore mining by steel companies, or credit extension by doctors?

A part of the answer lies in the technology employed. If letters are prepared on a typewriter, it would be extremely inconvenient to subcontract out the typing of the vowels. If an ingot must be reheated to be rolled, it is obviously more economical for the firm that cast the ingot to roll it while it is still hot.

But technology is usually not peremptory: there is often wide scope for variety in the ways productive processes are performed. The publisher of a book need not (and seldom does) print it; the printer seldom binds the book. Then a famous theorem of Adam Smith comes to our rescue: the division of labor is limited by the extent of the market.[4] Smith pointed out that small villages could not support highly specialized occupations, but that large cities could:

In the lone houses and very small villages which are scattered about in so desert a country as the Highlands of Scotland, every farmer must be butcher, baker and brewer for his own family. In such situations we can scarce expect to find even a smith, a carpenter, or a mason, within less than twenty miles of another of the same trade. The scattered families that live at eight or ten miles distance from the nearest of them, must learn to perform themselves a great number of little pieces of work, for which, in more populous countries, they would call in the assistance of those workmen. Country workmen are almost every where obliged to apply themselves to all the different branches of industry that have so much affinity to one another as to be employed about the same sort of materials. A country carpenter deals in every sort of work that is made of wood:

[4] *The Wealth of Nations* (New York: Modern Library ed., 1937), pp. 17–21. I earnestly recommend that all of this book except p. 720 be read.

a country smith in every sort of work that is made of iron. The former is not only a carpenter, but a joiner, a cabinet maker, and even a carver in wood, as well as a wheelwright, a ploughwright, a cart and waggon maker. The employments of the latter are still more various. It is impossible there should be such a trade as even that of a nailer in the remote and inland parts of the Highlands of Scotland. Such a workman at the rate of a thousand nails a day, and three hundred working days in the year, will make three hundred thousand nails in the year. But in such a situation it would be impossible to dispose of one thousand, that is, of one day's work in the year.

The gains from specialization operate in the same manner in a modern industrial society. As an industry grows, more and more activities are performed on a sufficient scale to permit firms to specialize in their full time performances: the making, and repairing, of machinery, the designing of plants, the testing of products, the recruiting of labor, the packaging of products, the collection of information on supplies, markets, and prices, the holding of trade fairs, research on technical problems, and so forth.

We may illustrate this development geometrically. Suppose the firm engages in three processes: processing raw materials (Y_1), assembling the product (Y_2), and selling the product (Y_3). For simplicity, assume that the cost of each function is independent of the rate of the other processes, and that the output of each process is proportional to the output of the final product.[5] The average cost of each function is shown separately, and the combined costs are the average cost of output for the firm (Figure 9-3). As we have drawn the figure, process Y_1 is subject to increasing returns, process Y_2 is subject to decreasing returns, and process Y_3 is subject first to increasing and then to decreasing returns. This situation may be perfectly stable in spite of the fact that the firm is performing function Y_1 at less than the most efficient rate and Y_2 at more than the most efficient rate.[6]

As the industry's output grows, the firms will seek to delegate decreasing and increasing cost functions to independent (auxiliary)

[5] This second assumption allows us to measure all processes along one axis; it has no effect on the argument.

[6] If the firm is a monopoly, it cannot specialize in process Y_1 and sell to other firms. It would be cheaper to buy Y_2 from several other firms than undertake it subject to decreasing returns, but if the costs of the other processes would be higher if Y_2 were not performed (contrary to the simplifying assumption in the text), Y_2 cannot be delegated.

industries. For example, when one component is made on a small scale it may be unprofitable to employ specialized machines and labor; when the industry grows, the individual firms will cease making this component on a small scale and a new firm will specialize in its production on a large scale. Thus, when the firm buys

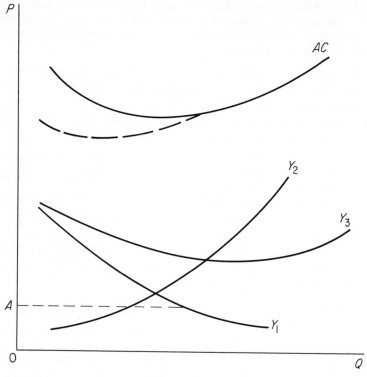

Figure 9-3

Y_1 at price $0A$, its average costs fall to the broken curves shown in Figure 9-3. Conversely, the firms will make only a part of the processes (Y_2) subject to increasing cost, and buy the remainder from independent firms.

A related explanation of the division of functions among firms is that those activities will be undertaken by a firm which are cheaper to administer internally than to purchase in the market. The transactions between firms are not free: there are costs attached to searching for prices, closing contracts, collecting payments, and so on.[7] Of course the coordination of activities within the firm is also not free: men and machines must be assigned tasks in an efficient manner and supervised to ensure that the efficient plan is followed. When a firm supplies only a part of its needs for some process (curve Y_2 in Figure 9-3) the rising costs of internal coordination are in fact the basic explanation for partial recourse to purchase. The cheaper market transactions become (due to improved knowledge of prices and greater security of contracts) the greater will be the comparative role of market coordination—firms will become more specialized.

Some external economies depend less on the growth of the industry than on that of the entire industrial system. As the economy grows, it becomes possible to establish a much more complete transportation system, a complex of types of banks and other financial institutions catering to specialized needs, an educational system that can train highly specialized personnel, and so on. These external economies are perhaps the decisive reason that the law of diminishing returns does not hold for an entire economy; it is highly probable that the American economy would be less productive if it were smaller.

FINITE PRODUCTION RUNS

The traditional laws of production are oriented to the problem of infinitely continued production: the farm will grow wheat this year, next year, and so on indefinitely. Many production decisions, however, involve a given volume or period of production. For example, the firm is to print 10,000 copies of a book, or produce 300 planes of a certain type; or, in the event of a fixed period, it is to supply (at a fixed annual rate) some item for 2 or 5 years.

The traditional theory does not directly cope with production for a finite run. For this theory is based upon continuous, unending flows of productive services, and under this condition it is a matter of minor detail whether the productive resources which yield the flows are durable or perishable: in either case they will be replaced when necessary. If the farm is to produce for only 10 years, how-

[7] See R. Coase, "The Nature of the Firm," *Economica* (1937); reprinted in Stigler and Boulding (eds.), *Readings in Price Theory*.

ever, and then be abandoned, it is clearly more efficient to use up the natural fertility of the soil than to maintain it. If only 5 units of a product are to be made, less specialized or less durable machinery will be used than if 500 units are to be made.

In the case of finite production runs, a theory of costs of great interest has been devised by Armen Alchian.[8] His analysis rests on the variation of total output (volume = V), the rate of production per period (q), and number of periods over which the item will be produced (m); in the simplest case these variables are connected by the equation, $V = mq$. Alchian has proposed a series of propositions concerning the behavior of total cost of the volume to be produced, of which the following are the most important:

1. The average and marginal cost per unit of total volume decreases as the total volume increases, holding the rate of production per unit of time constant.

Let the cost of a given total volume be the sum of discounted future expenditures. Then the proposition may be illustrated by the printing of a given book: once the plates have been made, additional copies (a given number per period) can be struck off at a relatively constant additional cost. The total cost (ignoring interest) will be approximately

Composition Costs + Number of Copies $\times$ Printing Costs per Copy

so the average cost will be

$$\frac{\text{Composition Costs}}{\text{Number of Copies}} + \text{Printing Costs per Copy},$$

which decreases as the number of copies printed increases. There are usually some producers' goods which partake of the nature of stamping dies. In addition there are economies from "learning": as the length of the production run is extended (as it must be if V increases but q is held constant)—a variety of economies are uncovered by experience.

2. The marginal cost of output rises with the rate of output if volume is held constant.

[8] "Costs and Outputs," in *The Allocation of Economic Resources* (Palo Alto, Calif.: Stanford University Press, 1959); see also J. Hirshleifer, "The Firm's Cost Function: A Successful Reconstruction?" *Journal of Business* (July 1962).

If total volume is held constant, an increase in the rate of output per period implies a shortening of the number of production periods, so the proposition asserts that it is cheaper to produce a given number of units in (say) 4 years than in 3 years. This proposition is essentially an assertion of diminishing returns.

These marginal cost curves are illustrated in Figure 9-4. The marginal cost of volume is of special interest—it is the theoretical

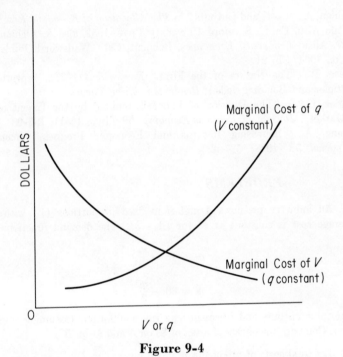

Figure 9-4

explanation for the almost universally observed phenomenon of quantity discounts. Whether we look at aggregate volume—the cost of a book of which 1,000 or 100,000 copies are printed—or at the size of an individual transaction—it costs less per copy to sell five copies than one—we find strong confirmation of the effects of volume on cost.

The relationship of marginal costs to aggregate volume has special relevance to the introduction of new commodities. These new commodities fall in price more rapidly through time than do the prices of established goods, and the more rapid fall is due to the large increase in volume. Once the production of the commodity has achieved a substantial scale, these economies are exhausted and the traditional cost curves of infinite production runs become appropriate.

RECOMMENDED READINGS

Alchian, A., "Costs and Outputs," in *The Allocation of Economic Resources*, Palo Alto, Calif.: Stanford University Press, 1959, also A. Alchian and W. Allen, *University Economics*, Belmont, Cal.: Wadsworth Publishing Co., 1964, Ch. 21.

Coase, R., "The Nature of the Firm," *Economica* (1937); reprinted in Stigler and Boulding (eds.), *Readings in Price Theory*.

Stigler, G. J., "The Division of Labor is Limited by the Extent of the Market," *Journal of Political Economy*. **59** (June 1951), 185–93.

Young, A., "Increasing Returns and Economic Progress," *Economic Journal*, **38** (1928), 527–42.

PROBLEMS

1. An industry produces A and B in fixed proportions ($1A$ with $3B$). Average cost is constant at $5 for $1A + 3B$. The demand functions are:

$$p_a = 48 - \frac{q_a}{10},$$

$$p_b = 60 - \frac{q_b}{3}.$$

Determine outputs and prices in long run equilibrium (assuming competition). Compare the effects of a tax of $3 on A and $1 on B.

2. Let total costs of producing A and B be

$$C = 10 + \frac{A}{2} + \frac{A^2}{10} + \frac{B}{5} + \frac{B^2}{25} + \frac{AB}{10}.$$

What is the marginal cost of 10 units of B when $A = 20$?

3. Construct the marginal cost curve for industry-wide changes from the production function in Table 7–1, the costs in Table 7–4, and the information that the price of the variable service is related to the purchases of the industry by the equation, $p_v = \$3 + Q_v/500$ and there are 100 firms. The marginal costs in Table 7–4 are then valid when the price is $5, the purchases of Q_v are 1000, and the output of the industry is 8600.

4. (Due to A. C. Harberger.) Product X is produced by two factors of production, A and B. These factors must be used in fixed proportions, according to the recipe: $1A + 1B$ produces $1X$. The industry is competitive. Factor A has no use outside the industry, while factor B is so widely used outside the industry that the price of a unit of B is not influenced by variations in output in the X industry. The price of B is \$1. There are 1000 units of factor A, all of which are available at any price above \$0.50, none of which are available at a price below \$0.50. The demand curve for product X is $XP_x = \$2500$.

(a) What will be the equilibrium price and quantity of X?

(b) What will be the equilibrium price of factor A? of factor B?

(c) Suppose an excise tax of 20 per cent of the price to the consumer is imposed. What will be the price of X paid by the consumer? What will be the price received by the producer? How much X will be produced? What will be the price of factor A? of factor B?

(d) Suppose that a monopolist takes over industry X, and that he is assured that no entry will take place and no government will interfere with his operations, so long as he charges a single price for all the units of X he in fact delivers. What will be the price set by this monopolist? What will be the output of commodity X? What will be the price of factor A? of factor B?

chapter ten

The General Theory of Competitive Prices

Everyone knows that prices are set by supply and demand. A much smaller group, but one including careful readers of the preceding pages, knows what factors govern supply and demand. Our task is to gather these pieces of analysis and fit them into a general picture of the workings of competitive markets.

THE GENERAL PRINCIPLE

A competitive market must fulfill certain conditions if it is to be in equilibrium:

1. Each firm must be operating at the output which it deems most appropriate to the conditions of cost and demand.
2. The total quantity all firms wish to sell at the market price must equal the total quantity all buyers wish to purchase.

When these conditions are fulfilled, the price will be an equilibrium price—that is, it will have no tendency to change until supply or demand conditions change.

The first condition—an appropriate output of each firm—is in turn fulfilled when two conditions are met:

1. Each firm is in the industry which yields it largest profits.
2. Each firm is operating at the output where marginal cost equals price, which is the output which maximizes profits in this industry.

Quite clearly we are judging the "appropriateness" of an entrepreneur's decisions by whether they maximize his profits.

The extent to which the entrepreneurial behavior can be explained by efforts to maximize profits is a celebrated debating ground for economists.[1] We shall nevertheless use this assumption without extensive defense, and on two grounds. First, and most important, it yields a vast number of testable conclusions, and by and large these conclusions agree with observation. Second, no other well-defined goals have yet been developed and given empirical support.

These conditions of competitive equilibrium are readily translated into a diagram (Figure 10-1). For the firm the demand curve

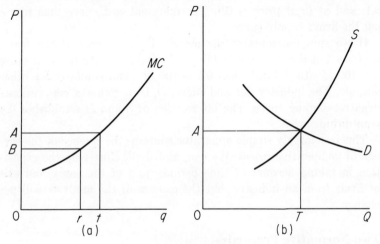

Figure 10-1

is a horizontal line, by our definition of competition that the firm be sufficiently small relative to the industry so variations in its output have a negligible influence on price. We may pause to notice that if our demand curve refers to this month (we shall soon look closely at the time dimensions), then the demand curve of the firm will be independent of next month's demand. Even if an unusually

---

[1] Even business men do not like this formulation. In one field study, when they were asked whether they maximized profits, they indignantly rejected the suggestion and pointed out that they were sincerely religious, public-spirited, and so on—as if these traits were inconsistent with profit-maximizing. But when the question was reformulated as: would a higher or lower price of the product yield larger profits?, the answer was, usually, no.

high price this month will lead to a reduction in industry demand next month, the individual firm cannot influence next month's price (say, by selling more cheaply now). Hence the demand curve of a competitive firm is independent of future conditions. Later we shall see that this is not true under monopoly.

The firm will operate at the output where its marginal cost curve intersects the demand curve. If we are examining (as we usually shall) forces that impinge on all firms in the industry, the marginal cost curve should be that which incorporates the effects of external economies—what we call the marginal cost for industry-wide changes (see pp. 166f.)[2] The firm operates at output $0t$ if price is $0A$, and at $0r$ if price is $0B$. The marginal cost curve thus traces out the firm's supply curve.

If we sum horizontally the marginal cost curves of the firms, we trace out the supply schedule of the industry (curve S). If there are 100 identical firms, then $0T = 100 \ 0t$, and similarly for other outputs. The industry demand curve, D, is of course a conventional negative-sloping curve. The intersection of S and D establishes the equilibrium price.

This becomingly simple apparatus contains the essence of the theory of competitive prices. We can, and shall, clutter up the exposition in taking account of time periods, and of the entry and exit of firms from an industry, but the essence of the analysis will not change.

Two Normative Properties

Competitive prices are widely admired: by customers, for they connote the absence of monopoly power; by lawyers, since the antitrust laws are designed to achieve competition; and by economists. The economic advantages of a competitive price are two.

First, the division of output among firms is efficient in the sense that with no other division would the same output be so cheap to produce. Consider two firms which were not in competitive equilibrium (Figure 10-2). Firm 1 is operating at output $0b$, firm 2

---

[2] If a force were to impinge on only this one firm (say a tax on only this firm, or only this firm introducing a technological improvement) we should of course use the marginal cost curve for single firm changes in output.

at output $0d$. Clearly competitive equilibrium is lacking because the firms are not selling at the same price. If we reduced the output of firm 1 by ab, its costs would fall by $abmn$. If we increased the output of firm 2 by cd ($= ab$), its costs would rise by $cdsr$. Clearly the costs of firm 1 would fall by more than those of firm 2 rose, so total costs of the two firms would decline for the given total

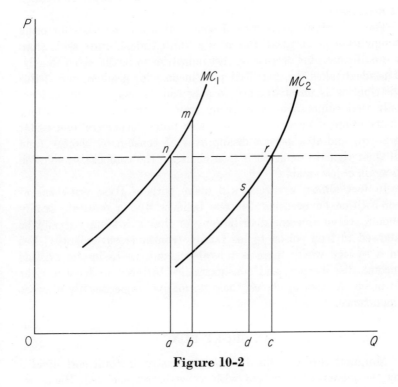

Figure 10-2

output. In competitive equilibrium marginal costs of all firms are equal, and thus no reduction in total costs would be possible by reshuffling output among firms.

Second, the output of the industry is "correct." The price is such that marginal cost equals price. The price is, for each consumer, the measure of the importance of an increment of the commodity—a demand price of $2 is implicitly a statement by each consumer that a marginal unit of this commodity yields $2 of utility.[3] The marginal cost is the value (= alternative cost) of the resources necessary to produce a marginal unit. If price exceeded marginal cost (as it will be shown to do under monopoly), then consumers would gain by expanding output: a product worth about $2 is obtained by sacrificing the smaller alternative product (= marginal cost).[4] The gain from expanding output would persist until price had fallen to marginal cost.

These felicitous properties of competition are the basis for using competition as an ideal. But it is a limited ideal, quite aside from a qualification for decreasing cost industries to be discussed shortly. The ideal takes the distribution of income for granted, and if this distribution is unsatisfactory to a person, he may accept as ideal only that competitive equilibrium which rules with a satisfactory distribution of income. The ideal also takes consumers' desires for granted, and if a person disapproves of consumers' choices (and of their right to make their own choices), the competitive solution is again objectionable.

In fact almost everyone will make both of these criticisms of competition on occasion. No one believes that a destitute family should starve (income distribution) or that a consumer should be allowed to feed poison to his family (consumer sovereignty). Yet in a society where there is tolerable acquiescence in the existing income distribution, and consumers are believed to have a right to much freedom of choice, these normative properties are of great importance.

THE LONG AND THE SHORT RUN

Marginal cost is defined as the increment in total cost divided by the increment in output with which it is associated. Hence we shall have as many marginal costs for a given increment of output

---

[3] Recall that at equilibrium,

$$\frac{P_a}{P_b} = \frac{MU_a}{MU_b},$$

and if we call all commodities other than A money income (B), so $P_b = 1$ (the price of a dollar is 1 dollar),

$$P_a = \frac{MU_a}{MU_{\text{income}}}.$$

[4] We say "about $2" because as output expands, the demand price falls, and with continuous demand curves even a one-unit increase in output leads to a small fall in price—perhaps from $2.00 to $1.99999.

as there are relevant ways of producing this increment. If the firm operates its plant overtime its marginal costs will be governed by the additional wages, materials, power, and so forth. If the firm expands its plant, marginal costs will also include interest on the additional investment and appropriate depreciation charges.[5] If a new plant is constructed, marginal cost may include the salary of a new superintendent, etc.

The firm will normally handle short run fluctuations in output by varying its rate of operation of the existing plant (and by holding inventories). Investments in durable assets will be made on the basis of more persistent changes in output. We call the short run the period within which the firm does not make important changes in its more durable factors ("plant"), and the long run the period within which the size (and existence) of plants is freely variable. Clearly the short run is of no interest if a firm can quickly increase and decrease all inputs, and it is basically an empirical judgment that in general there will be important resources which cannot be worn out or built in (say) a year. The long run may also be longer for contractions than for expansions, or vice-versa.

The short-run marginal cost curve of a firm will rise more rapidly than the long-run marginal cost, because the law of diminishing returns will hold more strongly, the more inputs are held constant. Both curves (for single firm changes) must rise with output in the effective region if competition is to exist—if marginal cost fell with output but selling price did not (and it does not under competition), profits would increase indefinitely with increases in output and the firm would acquire a significant control over price. But marginal cost curves for industry-wide changes, which incorporate effects of external economies, may either rise or fall with output.

The Firm and the Industry

The industry's long-run supply curve, like its short-run curve, is the sum of the marginal cost curves of the firms in the industry. Its slope will therefore be governed by two factors:

[5] If the additional plant were to be used for only one year (even though it might last 10 years with care), the appropriate depreciation rate is 100 per cent. If the additional output is to be produced indefinitely, only a fraction $(1/10$ by the now unpopular straight-line depreciation formula; $10/(1 + \cdots + 10) = 10/55$ by the sum-of-digit formula) should be charged off the first year.

1. The slope of the long-run marginal cost curve of each firm (for industry-wide changes).

2. The price at which firms enter or leave the industry.

We have nothing to add on the first score: the firm will operate somewhere on its long-run marginal cost curve.[6]

The price above which firms will enter the industry, or below which they will leave, can be different for every firm (existing or potential) in the economy. It will take a higher price of aluminum pots and pans to attract a firm from cotton textiles than a firm from aluminum toys because the former firm's familiarity with the basic technology is less. It may take a lower price of trucks to attract a firm from agricultural implements than one from the hand tool industries because the large capital requirements are easier for the former firm to meet. It will take a higher price to attract a bachelor than a married couple into the corner grocery industry, because the latter has a captive labor supply.

The number and versatility of existing firms is so large, relative to the number in any one industry, that one would generally expect the number of entrants to increase rapidly as the price of the industry's product rose. Only if the industry employed specialized resources (say, a special kind of land) or if (what is ruled out under competition) there are barriers to entry would one generally expect numbers of entrants to be unresponsive to price in the long run.

The empirical evidence suggests that in fact a large part of the increases in output of a growing industry come from the existing firms.[7] Our geometry tells us that the existing firms will produce this additional output only if the long-run marginal costs of existing firms do not rise with output. This line of analysis therefore suggests that the long-run marginal costs in most industries (for single-firm changes) are relatively flat.

---

[6] One minor point may be noted. If the marginal cost curve for industry-wide changes falls with output, the firm will still operate where this marginal cost equals price. The individual firm never has a choice of where to operate on the curve for industry-wide changes, but the curve for single firm output changes leads to this output. The accompanying graph illustrates the point.

[7] For manufacturing industries some evidence is given in my *Capital and Rates of Return in Manufacturing Industries* (New York: National Bureau of Economic Research, 1963), pp. 31–34.

The Quicksilver Character of
Competitive Industries

A large amount of effort is devoted to assisting or burdening competitive industries. The assistance may be a protective tariff, a subsidy, or some free governmental service. The burden may be a tax, a minimum wage, or a compulsory industrial safety device. Usually it is believed that the firms in the industry will reap the gain or bear the burden of the measure, at least in part. This belief is usually correct, but only temporarily.

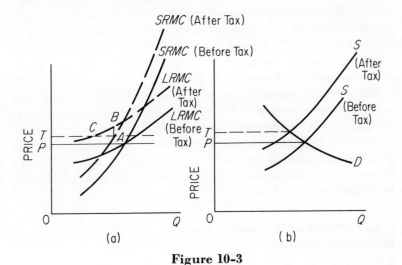

Figure 10-3

Consider a firm with the long- and short-run costs displayed in panel A of Figure 10-3, and selling its product at price $0P$. If a tax is now imposed on each firm, its costs may rise as indicated. The price will rise by a smaller amount than the tax if the demand is not completely inelastic (see panel B). Marginal losses of AB per unit of output will be incurred by the firms. With the passage of time resources will leave the industry because they can earn an amount elsewhere equal to their long-run marginal cost to this industry. Eventually the short-run marginal cost curves (and with them, their sum, the industry's short-run supply curve) will shift to the left enough to raise price to long-run marginal cost. The contraction of output of a plant will be to some output larger than TC, because price will rise above $0T$ as the number of firms declines. The firms will again be earning a competitive rate of return. The analysis of a subsidy is completely symmetrical.

Only short-run gains or losses, therefore, can be given to the firms in a competitive industry. These gains may of course be large: if durable assets without alternative uses have on average a remaining life of 6 years, a firm may gain 3 or 4 years' return if the policy prevents the contraction of the industry,[8] or if it takes 3 years to build a new plant, extra gains may persist this long.

Even these temporary gains or losses will not be incurred, however, if the developments are fully anticipated. If the tax is anticipated, investment will have fallen appropriately by the time it is imposed. Similarly, if a tariff is expected, the industry's investment will have risen to where only a competitive rate of return is obtained when the tariff is imposed.

There is one group who may reap permanent gains or losses from policies designed to help or burden an industry: the owners of specialized resources. They will not have alternative uses for their resources, so their returns will vary directly with industry output. Thus the permanent beneficiaries of a subsidy on zinc will be the owners of zinc mines; the permanent losers from rent ceilings will be landowners.

Is the Output of Decreasing Cost Industries Optimal?

We have said that a competitive industry has an optimal output—when marginal cost equals price, resources are satisfying marginal demands in this industry as important as these same resources could satisfy elsewhere. Decreasing cost industries, however, pose a special problem.

Consider the long run cost curves for single-firm changes, LMC_1 and LAC_1 in Figure 10-4. Let us begin with a price of $10, and an output of the firm of 1,000 units per week. Average costs are $9.60, and the "profit" of $1,000 \times \$0.40 = \$400$ is the payment to the en-

---

[8] The duration of the short-run gains will depend upon how much the industry would have to contract, as well as how fast it would contract, in the absence of the favoring legislation.

trepreneur for his scarce services.[9] Total costs of production are
$1,000 \times 9.60 = \$9,600$.

If now demand increases and price rises, the firm's output will
rise to (say) 1,400 units. Since this is a decreasing cost industry,
some inputs fall in price and the cost curves for single firm changes

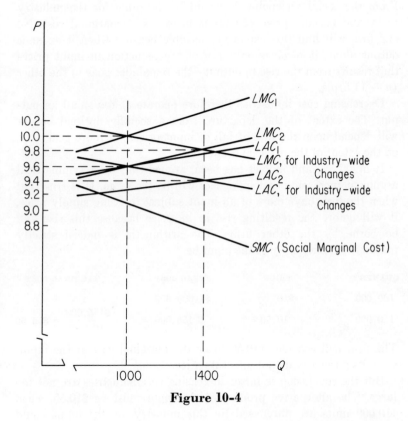

Figure 10-4

shift downward to LAC_2 and LMC_2. The price in the new equilibrium, we assume, is \$9.80 and the average costs \$9.40. (The long-
run marginal cost for industry-wide changes is also presented as
the locus of intersections of the various marginal costs with de-

---

[9] If this type of entrepreneurial service were not scarce, there would be
sufficiently many firms in the industry, each operating at 1,000, that marginal
and average cost would be equal.

mand.) Total costs are now $1,400 \times 9.40 = \$13,160$. Hence the marginal cost of output (for industry-wide changes) is

$$\frac{\$13,160 - \$9,600}{1400 - 1000} = \$8.90.$$

From the social viewpoint, it would be desirable for the industry to expand because price ($9.80) is in excess of marginal cost. No one firm will find this expansion feasible because when it expands output alone, it receives only $1/n$ of the reduction in input prices that results from the rise in output—the remainder goes to the other $(n-1)$ firms.

Decreasing cost industries therefore operate at too small an output. The extent of the departure from a socially optimal output will depend upon the rate of fall of input prices; or more generally, on the extent of the external economies.

It might be, and in fact has been, argued that by a symmetrical argument increasing cost industries will be too large. It is true that when the firm buys more of an input subject to rising supply price, it will ignore the resulting rise in its price because this rise will be borne by the other firms. The arithmetic is indeed strictly parallel: let the supply of the input be

QUANTITY	PRICE	TOTAL COST	MARGINAL COST
100,000	$10	$1,000,000	
110,000	10.50	1,155,000	$\dfrac{\$155,000}{10,000} = \$15.50$

The firm will consider $10.50 to be the marginal cost of the input, since its purchases do not affect its price.

But the conclusion is false: increasing cost industries are not too large. The alternative product of the input must be $10.50, when 110,000 units are purchased by this industry, or the input could not be obtained at this price. The extra $5 is a rent accruing to the suppliers of the input who had previously received only $10.[10] No product is foregone as a result of this price increase—it is a transfer payment, ultimately from consumers of the product to owners of the input. The difference between the decreasing and increasing cost industries is this: the price increases of inputs do not

---

[10] Their receipts rise by $100,000 \times \$0.50 = \$50,000$ and $\$50,000/10,000 = \$5$.

represent foregone products, whereas the price decreases of inputs represent economies in their production on a larger scale.

An Exercise in Analysis

The apparatus of competitive price theory is the staff of life for the economist: he uses it much more often than any other part of his knowledge, and it is the basis upon which most of his fancier knowledge is erected. A thorough command of the apparatus comes only from using it frequently, but we must be content here with a partial analysis of a general problem, the effects of protection of agriculture in an industrial society.

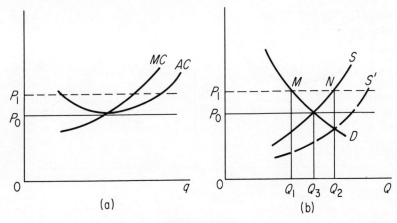

Figure 10-5

Agricultural industries, both in the United States and elsewhere, are often given assistance by price support programs. A governmental agency (the Commodity Credit Corporation is our leading instrument) will lend at designated prices against the product on what are called nonrecourse loans (loans which permit no assessment on the farmer if the agency fails to recover the full amount of the loan). The program is presumably initiated when the industry is earning less than the rate of return in other industries. Hence the initial position for a firm and the industry are something like the situation portrayed in Figure 10-5, A and B, with price p_0. The support price is set at p_1, and it obviously serves to increase output and diminish purchases, and to increase consumer expenditures if demand is inelastic. In fact the increase in producers' receipts will be the sum of

Increase in consumer expenditures, $Q_1 p_1 - Q_3 p_0$,
Governmental loans, $(Q_2 - Q_1) p_1$.

In each period of time (say, crop year) the governmental stocks will rise by $(Q_2 - Q_1)$, assuming there is no entry of new firms or expansion of existing firms,[11] and that costs of production do not change for a farm. If technological progress lowers costs and shifts the industry supply curve to S', of course the governmental

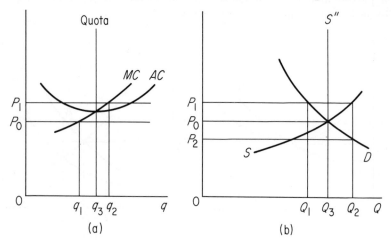

Figure 10-6

stocks increase more rapidly. Eventually there will be complaints at the growth of the governmental stocks (whether for reasons of expense or the outrage of some primitive ethical code), and production controls will be imposed. The controls may be direct output quotas for individual farms, or more commonly—because of the short-run fluctuation of yields due to weather changes—quotas on the acreage devoted to the product.[12] The situation is now illustrated by Figure 10-6, where Q_3 is the sum of the quotas of all

[11] The latter assumption is especially unrealistic, but is made to simplify the discussion.

[12] Since one input is being fixed, but others are free, the farmer will substitute other inputs (fertilizer, better seed), so output will not fall in proportion to the reduction in acreage.

farms. The annual increase in governmental stocks now decreases to $(Q_3 - Q_1)$. There is no saving to consumers, but governmental expenditures fall by $(Q_2 - Q_3)p_1$.

Let us accept without question the desirability of giving the producers the increase in income here achieved. This income increase for a typical farmer is $q_3(p_1 - p_0)$ *minus* the additional costs of growing the larger quantity $(q_3 - q_1)$, which is the area bounded by p_0, q_3, and MC in Figure 10-6A. The objections to giving this increased income in this manner are

1. Producers are using an unnecessarily large amount of resources to produce the output:

(a) Marginal costs will inevitably vary among firms—violating the optimum property discussed earlier.

(b). If an input is controlled, the substitution of other inputs will lead to the violation of another optimum condition: that inputs be used in such proportions that their marginal products are proportional to their social costs. Here too much fertilizer, and not enough land, will be used.

2. A portion of the output is unnecessary, and is measured by governmental purchases. Storage costs should be added.

3. The price is above marginal cost (even accepting the combination of inputs used) so consumers would gain by an expansion of purchases.[13]

The first two components represent resources wasted; the third represents the consumer loss due to an inappropriate composition of output.

The same increase in income could be given to the farmers by other devices:

1. Output quotas could be made sufficiently small to raise prices and reduce costs the desired amounts. Then component 2 of waste would be eliminated; the other components of waste would rise.

[13] They would gain roughly the amount indicated by the shaded area in the accompanying figure. The increase in output $(Q_3 - Q_1)$ would require resources which would produce roughly $p_0(Q_3 - Q_1)$ worth of product elsewhere, which must be foregone. Notice that this is a measure of the utility gain to consumers; the money gain (if demand is inelastic) represents only a transfer from farmers.

190 *The General Theory of Competitive Prices*

Query: would the price still be p_1?[14]

2. The government guarantees each producer a price p_1 but the market could be allowed to become free, so the price would fall to p_2 (Figure 10-6B). This scheme would eliminate the first two components of waste, but retain the third (with price below marginal cost).

Query: how much should the guaranteed price be to keep farmers' incomes constant?[15]

3. Prices and output could be freed, and a direct subsidy paid. Then all components of waste would be eliminated.

Query: is the subsidy now larger or smaller than in case 2?[16]

We should notice that this third policy, and in fact all policies, raise other economic (to say nothing of political) questions. Each policy implies a different income distribution, immediately for farmers and consumers, ultimately for everyone through the implicit taxation necessary to finance the policies. The quota systems will benefit landowners who possess quotas, but not tenant farmers. The direct subsidy system (policy 3) and the quota systems must face explicitly the problem of dividing the benefits among farmers; the subsidized price system (policy 2) need not. All systems except the subsidy system will yield larger benefits to farmers as technology improves (and cost curves fall), which may be a factor in the opposition of farm groups to the direct subsidy plan.

RECOMMENDED READINGS

Knight, F. H., "Cost of Production and Price Over Long and Short Periods," *Journal of Political Economy,* **29** (1921), 304–35; reprinted in *The Ethics of Competition* (New York: Harper & Brothers, 1935).

[14] To keep the questions tolerably manageable, assume that the cost curves stay put, that is, there is no substitution of other inputs for land. Assume also that we are interested in "profits"; if some of the farmer's wage and interest income must be separated out of the cost curves, the geometry becomes complex. Then a farmer's receipts fall by $p_1(q_3 - q_1)$ at price p_1, and costs fall only by the area bounded by p_0, q_3, and MC in Figure 10-6. Hence price must rise above p_1 to maintain his profits.

[15] The rise in income from expanding output to q_2 would exceed the rise in costs (since MC is less than p_1), so the price would fall below p_1 if profits were maintained.

[16] The subsidy is smaller. The costs of the extra produce ($q_2 - q_3$) which could be sold only at a price less than marginal cost, need not be incurred.

Marshall, A., *Principles of Economics,* London: Macmillan, 1922, Bk. V, Chs. 1–5.
Wicksteed, P. H., *The Commonsense of Political Economy,* London: George Rutledge & Sons, 1934, Vol. II, Bk. 3.

PROBLEMS

1. A general problem in pricing. (This is a summary of a problem constructed by the late Henry Simons, in *Economics 201: Materials and Problems for Class Discussion,* University of Chicago, n.d.)

An industry consisting of 1,000 firms produces a standardized product. Each firm owns and operates one plant, and no other size of plant can be built. The variable costs of each firm are identical and are given in the adjoining table; the fixed costs of each firm are $100.

OUTPUT	TOTAL VARIABLE COST	OUTPUT	TOTAL VARIABLE COST
1	$10	13	$101
2	19	14	113
3	27	15	126
4	34	16	140
5	40	17	155
6	45	18	171
7	50	19	188
8	56	20	206
9	63	21	225
10	71	22	245
11	80	23	266
12	90	24	288

The industry demand curve is $pq = \$255,000$. Calculate the marginal and average costs of a firm, and the demand schedule of the industry for prices from $10 to $20. (See p. 238 for the cost equation.)

PART I

(a) Draw the supply curve—that is, the sum of the marginal cost curves—and demand curve of the industry on the same graph (Figure 1). Read off the equilibrium price and quantity. Prove that the answer is correct by comparing quantities supplied and demanded at (1) a price $1 higher, (2) a price $1 lower.

(b) Draw the cost and demand curves of the individual firm on the same graph (Figure 2). Accompany these graphs with detailed textual explanation of their construction.

PART II

Congress now unexpectedly imposes a tax of $4 per unit on the manufacture of this commodity. The tax becomes effective immediately and remains in effect indefinitely. Assume (1) no changes in the economic system other than those attributable to the tax; and (2) none of the changes due to the tax has any effect on the prices of productive services used by this industry.

(a) Draw the new supply curve and the demand curve of the industry (Figure 3). Read off the new equilibrium price.

(b) Draw the new cost curves and demand curve of the individual firm (Figure 4). Explain the details of the construction of these graphs.

(c) Why can the price not remain as low as $15?

(d) Why can the price not rise to and remain at $19?

(e) Precisely what would happen if the price remained for a time at $16?

(f) At precisely what level would the price become temporarily stable? What does it mean to say this is an equilibrium level?

(g) Suppose the short-run equilibrium price to be $17. How would you answer the query: "I don't see why every firm should produce 15 units per day when the price is $17. It would make just as much if it produced only 14, for the 15 unit adds just as much to expenses as it adds to revenues." Precisely what would happen if some firms produced 14 units per day and others 15 units?

(h) Would short-run equilibrium be reached at a higher or lower price (and with larger or smaller output) if the elasticity of demand were lower (less than unity)? If it were higher (greater than unity)?

(i) What would happen if demand had an elasticity of zero? An elasticity of infinity?

PART III

As Figure 4 will reveal, the new minimum average cost is $19. The short-run equilibrium price is $17; hence this industry becomes unattractive as an investment, relative to other industries. As plants are worn out, therefore, they will not be replaced; plants will be junked sooner; and even maintenance will be reduced. To simplify the problem, we assume: (1) each plant has a life of 1000 weeks; (2) the plants in the industry are staggered so that, at the time the tax was imposed, there is one plant 1 week old, one plant 2 weeks old, and so on; and (3) at the time the tax was imposed, 20 plants were so near completion that it was impossible to divert them to other uses. These are completed at one-week intervals. Hence, for 20 weeks the price will stay at $17, and then rise gradually as entrepreneurs fail to replace worn-out plants.

(a) What will the situation be at the end of the twenty-fifth week? (Answer in terms of "greater than" or "less than.")

(b) When 120 weeks have passed (900 plants left) will the price be above or below $18?

(c) How many weeks must pass (how many plants must be scrapped) before the price rises to $18?

(d) Will the output per plant increase or decrease as the number of plants declines?

(e) When 220 weeks have passed (800 plants left), will the price be above or below $19?

(f) How many plants must be scrapped before the price rises precisely to $19?

(g) What would the price be if the number of plants declined to 750? What would be the output per plant? What would happen to the number of plants?

(h) What happens to the short-run supply curve of the industry as the number of plants diminishes. Draw, on the same graph (Figure 5), the supply curve when there are 1000 firms and 800 firms. Compute elasticities of supply for these two curves at a given price.

(i) How could the process of adjustment, and the final equilibrium, be different (1) if the elasticity of demand were greater than unity; and (2) if the elasticity of demand were less than unity? (The significant points are price, output per plant immediately after the tax is imposed, and number of plants and total output at the new long-run equilibrium.)

2. *The same problem with multiple products.* Assume that the cost schedule in the foregoing table is for outputs of commodity X, and that for every unit of X, one unit of Y is necessarily produced. The demand curve for X is $pq = \$170,000$, and the demand curve for Y is

$$p = \$22 - \frac{q}{1000}.$$

PART I

(a) Verify that the industry is in equilibrium. The marginal costs of X and Y cannot be calculated separately (p. 162), so the supply curve of the industry refers to the equal quantities of X and Y forthcoming at any price. Hence draw the demand curves for X and Y and add them *vertically* to get the price per unit of X plus Y.

(b) Then, for the individual firm, draw the demand curves for X and Y and their sum against the costs, to find profits.

PART II

A permanent decrease in the demand for X now takes place unexpectedly. The new demand curve is $pq = \$100,000$.

(a) Find the new prices of X and Y and the loss per firm.

(b) What would be the effect on short-run prices of a more elastic demand for X? For Y?

PART III

Make the same assumptions about plant life and the rate of entry and exit of firms as in Problem 1.

(a) What will the prices of X and Y be when there are only 900 firms in the industry? What will losses per firm be?

(b) What is the number of firms consistent with the price of X plus the price Y equal to \$15? Is this the long-run equilibrium?

(c) If a technical change now permitted the proportions between X and Y to be variable within considerable limits, would you expect the price of X to rise relative to that of Y?

chapter eleven

The Theory of Monopoly

Let us now make an abrupt transition from the industry of many firms to that of one firm. This firm may owe its sheltered existence to a patent, the fact that it is much more efficient than any small rival, or to other circumstances which we shall discuss in the next chapter.

MONOPOLY PRICE

A monopolist is no less desirous of profits than a competitive firm, and is in a somewhat better position to achieve them. The monopolist will by definition face the industry demand curve, and take conscious account of the influence of his output on price. When he increases his output, the resulting fall in price will be borne by himself alone—not, as under competition, almost exclusively by rivals. Marginal revenue is therefore less than price, and is in fact given by the equation,

$$\text{marginal revenue} = p\left(1 + \frac{1}{\eta}\right),$$

where η is the elasticity of demand. It follows immediately that since no monopolist will willingly operate where marginal revenue is negative, he will never willingly operate where demand is inelastic.

Maximum profits are obtained when an increment of output adds as much to revenue as to cost, that is, at the output where marginal revenue equals marginal cost. We illustrate this principle in Figure 11-1, where output will be $0M$ and price MT.

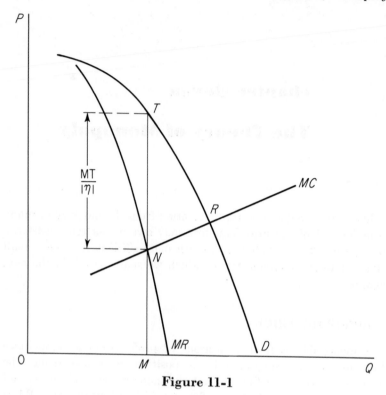

Figure 11-1

Monopoly and National Income

The Earl of Lauderdale criticized those writers who said that a nation's wealth was the sum of the wealth of its citizens:

The common sense of mankind would revolt at a proposal for augmenting the wealth of a nation, by creating a scarcity of any commodity generally useful and necessary to man. For example, let us suppose a country possessing abundance of the necessaries and conveniencies of life, and universally accommodated with the purest streams of water—what opinion would be entertained of the understanding of a man, who, as the means of increasing the wealth of such a country, should propose to create a scarcity of water . . . ? It is certain, however, that such a projector would, by this means, succeed in increasing the mass of individual riches.[1]

[1] *An Inquiry into the Nature and Origin of Public Wealth* (Edinburgh: A. Constable, 1804), pp. 43–44.

Forming a monopoly of water and selling it, however, would lead to a reduction in national income, the noble Earl to the contrary.

The reply is superficially easy: the income of the monopolist would rise, but the (real) income of others who must now pay for water would fall. Yet this sounds like a simple transfer of command over the community's output, which would leave aggregate income unchanged. The reduction of real income would occur because wants previously satisfied no longer were satisfied, with no corresponding increase in output elsewhere (in fact a reduction, if resources are necessary to bottle and guard the water). If we constructed a price index to deflate money incomes, it would compare the cost of the bundle of goods produced before monopoly with its cost afterward, and the rise in this price index would imply a fall in real income.

The cost and demand curves need not be the same for a product if it is monopolized as they would be if a competitive industry produced it; in fact they will probably differ (more on this shortly). But if the cost and demand conditions were the same, we could measure the misallocation of resources which results with monopoly from Figure 11-1. At the margin, resources necessary to produce a unit of the product have a marginal cost, and hence an alternative product, of MN. In this industry however, they produce a product which consumers value at MT. Hence if output were expanded one unit, the product added here would exceed the product foregone elsewhere, and aggregate income would rise by NT. As additional units were produced, additional but declining gains would be achieved until marginal cost equalled price. The approximate triangle NTR measures the rise in income that would be achieved if output were to increase to the competitive level.

THE MONOPOLY DEMAND CURVE

The demand curve of a monopolist must have a negative slope. If a firm is the only producer of a commodity, and consumers display normal demand characteristics, the firm can sell more at a lower price. Only if there is at least one other producer of the identical commodity (oligopoly) will the monopolist's demand curve be horizontal over a significant range of outputs.

The slope of the demand curve will in general depend upon how good the substitutes for the monopolized good are, and how many substitutes there are. The producer of any commodity is limited in his price-making power by the availability of other products which are close substitutes for it. Hence monopoly can arise (in the absence of collusion among producers) only if the product of the firm is substantially different from the products of all other firms—that is, if the cross-elasticity of demand for the output of this firm with respect to the price of each other firm is small. We should therefore say that the maker of any one brand of furniture is not a monopolist because, if he raises his prices, consumers will shift to other brands. Whether the maker of nylon is a monopolist depends upon the extent to which consumers will shift to silk or rayon if the price of nylon rises relative to the prices of silk and rayon. The telephone company is definitely a monopoly because telegrams, letters, bridge parties, and messengers are poor substitutes. If there are only a few producers of the good substitutes, we call the market structure oligopolistic.

This raises the question of when the substitutes are good or poor. Suppose there is only one grocery store at point A, but a road runs through A, and there are identical rivals on this road at B and C, and the cross-elasticity of demand for groceries at A with respect to prices at B or C is 0.05. Then we would say that A is a monopolist: he can raise his price 20 per cent and lose only 2 per cent of his customers to B and C (although he would lose customers also to other products).[2] Suppose now that 50 roads run through A, with two rivals like B and C on each road. Then there are 100 rivals, and with a 20 per cent rise in the price at A, sales at each of these other stores will rise 1 per cent—that is, the quantity demanded at A will vanish. Hence the power of a firm to set prices depends upon both the closeness of substitutes and the number of substitutes; many producers of poor substitutes may limit the firm as much as a few good substitutes.

Although there is no impropriety in calling a firm a monopoly if its demand curve has an elasticity of -100, there is also little purpose in doing so. The theory of monopoly will only tell us why this firm's price exceeds the competitive level by about 1 per cent $[= p(\frac{1}{100})]$, and this order of magnitude is not very interesting in

---

[2] If the various firms are of equal size, then η_{ap_b} may be taken as about equal to η_{bp_a}. Hence a 20 per cent rise in p_a will lead to roughly a 1 per cent rise in purchases at both B and C, and thus to a fall of only 2 per cent in purchases at A. See mathematical note 10 in Appendix B.

a world where the best measurements of marginal cost have more than a 1 per cent error. In general we shall wish to think of monopoly as involving demand curves which are not extremely elastic.

The monopolist's demand curve will depend upon the conventional determinants: the prices of substitutes and complements, incomes, and tastes. Incomes are beyond his control, but the prices of complements and substitutes are frequently capable of being influenced.

The entrance of the automobile companies into the finance business may illustrate the influencing of complementary prices. The purchase of an automobile depends upon the cost of credit as well as upon the price of the automobile, and in fact for buyers on credit the relationship is additive (down payments aside): the same increase in sales can be achieved by reducing the price of the car, or the cost of credit, by $10. If credit is supplied competitively, there is no profit in reducing its price further, but if it is supplied on monopolistic terms (by dealers), a reduction in price will benefit automobile producers. Of course it may be asked why a monopoly in financing automobile sales would not attract others besides the automobile manufacturers. The answer may be that entry is much easier for the manufacturers than for others, since they can compel the use of their credit facilities by their dealers as part of the franchise,[3] or the answer may be that the manufacturers simply were the first to be attracted by the gains. Indeed the main effects of the entry of the automobile finance companies would be (1) to redistribute profits between manufacturers and dealers, and (2) probably to lower credit costs to buyers of automobiles.[4] When the typical savings and loan association extends a mortgage, it writes the property insurance policy through an affiliated agency, which is a related instance of the exploitation of complementary demands.[5]

[3] Commercial banks did eventually enter into this line of finance.

[4] That the entry will not lead merely to a redistribution of monopoly profits from financing can be shown as follows. For a dealer the rate of return on selling cars will be at the competitive rate (assuming the automobile firm is not engaged also in philanthropy), but his rate of return on financing activities where *he* has monopoly power will be above the competitive level. Hence he will sacrifice auto sales to obtain more than a competitive rate of return from sales of finance, whereas the manufacturer will prefer an output mixture with more cars and less financing revenue.

[5] If the insurance agency business is competitive, the profits from this combination presumably come from the avoidance of selling costs.

Advertising

We could have discussed advertising earlier, for it will occur also under competition. Under competition, the main tasks of a seller are to inform potential buyers of his existence, his line of goods, and his prices. Since both sellers and buyers change over time (due to birth, death, migration), since people forget information once acquired, and since new products appear, the existence of sellers must be continually advertised. Price information poses heavy burdens: a store selling a thousand items would have to advertise perhaps 10,000 prices a year if it wished to remind people of its prices and notify them of changes.

This informational function of advertising must be emphasized because of a popular and erroneous belief that advertising consists chiefly of nonrational (emotional and repetitive) appeals. Even the seller of aluminum ingots or 2,000 horsepower engines advertises (and makes extensive use of solicitation through salesmen), although he is dealing only with more or less hard-headed businessmen.

What is true is that under competition the individual firm will not attempt to increase the desire for the product. Even if $1 of advertising would increase total sales of apples by $5, a single farmer would obtain only a tiny fraction of the industry's return, so only a cooperative advertising program would be feasible. A monopolist, on the other hand, would obtain the full returns from the advertising and hence undertake it.

Advertising, and selling activity generally, will be pursued like any other productive activities, until the expected returns and costs of various media are equated at the margin. It is commonly believed that advertising may first yield increasing, and then decreasing, returns—where we measure the marginal return of a dollar of advertising by the increase in receipts, holding output constant.

The return from a given advertisement will accrue gradually over time. Let us assume that the correct amount of advertising for a firm is $100,000 a year, and that it will reach 20 per cent of potential customers, who number 200,000. Moreover, assume that each year 5 per cent of the customers die or move away (and are replaced by births or immigrants), or forget the product once they have learned of it.

1. In the first year, $0.20 \times 200,000$, or 40,000 customers are informed.
2. In the second year,

$0.95 \times 40,000$ old customers are still informed	= 38,000
New customers are $0.05 \times 200,000 = 10,000$	
Previously uninformed customers = $0.95 \times 160,000$ = 152,000	
$0.20 \times 162,000$ uninformed customers	= 32,400
Total informed	= 70,400

3. In the third year,

$0.95 \times 70,400$ old customers are still informed	= 66,880
New customers are again 10,000	
Previously uninformed customers = $0.95 \times$ (200,000 − 70,400), or 123,120	
(or, more simply, there are $200,000 - 66,880 =$ 133,120 uninformed customers)	
$0.20 \times 133,120$ uninformed customers	= 26,624
Total informed	= 93,504

This process can be continued, to yield the set of numbers of informed customers given in Table 11–1.[6] In eventual equilibrium, each year 10,000 new customers enter the market to replace those who leave, and 5 per cent of 166,667 informed customers (= 8,333) leave or forget the product. The number of uninformed customers is 41,667, made up of:

10,000 new customers, who replace
      8,333 previously informed customers,
      1,667 (= $0.05 \times 33,333$) previously uninformed customers,
31,667 (= $0.95 \times 33,333$) previously uninformed customers.

The accumulated advertising capital consists of the value of being known by 166,667 customers, and depreciates at the rate of 5 per cent a year. Since this depreciation is exactly offset by new advertising costing \$100,000, the capital value of the advertising is $20 \times \$100,000$ or \$2 million.

[6] See my "The Economics of Information," *Journal of Political Economy* (June 1961).

If customers turn over or forget quickly, of course the depreciation rate will be higher and the capital value will be smaller. But under these conditions larger amounts of advertising will be necessary to reach any given number of customers—so hotels catering to tourists will advertise more than apartment houses.

The effect of advertising on the elasticity of demand for the product is still a matter of conjecture. The primary purpose of advertising is of course to shift the demand curve to the right and upward. It is often said that the monopolist wishes a less elastic demand because he may then raise the price without a large reduction in

Table 11–1

Number of Customers Informed by a Given Rate of Advertising

YEAR	NUMBER
1	40,000
2	70,400
3	93,504
4	111,063
—	—
Eventually	166,667

sales. This presumably means that he prefers D_1' to D_2 (Figure 11-2); if so, it is false. Beyond output T (the monopolist may wish to operate beyond T to maximize profits) D_2 is a more profitable demand curve because a given quantity can be sold for a higher price. For the statement to be valid, one must restate it: the monopolist prefers a higher inelastic demand curve (D_3) to a lower elastic demand curve (D_2). This is indeed true, but it is also true if the words "elastic" and "inelastic" are interchanged or deleted.

Future Effects of Present Prices

We noted that a firm in a competitive industry must ignore the effects of the industry's price on future sales because it could not influence the price. A monopolist cannot ignore such future influences, and as a result the distinction between the long run and the short run loses much of its relevance in a regime of monopoly.

Suppose, to be concrete, that the demand curve of a monopolist this year is given by

$$q_t = 100 - p_t,$$

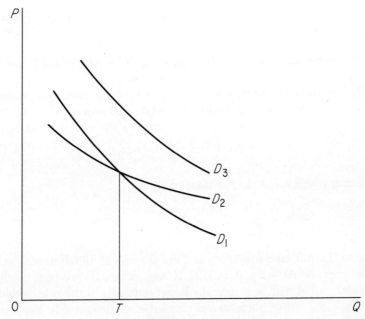

Figure 11-2

but that the demand curve next year is given by

$$q_{t+1} = 100 - p_{t+1} + \tfrac{1}{2}(30 - p_t).$$

This demand curve tells us that one more unit can be sold next year for every two dollars by which the price falls short of $30 this year. If consumers have delayed responses to prices, as we argued above (Chapter 3, p. 26), this sort of demand function is highly plausible.

The marginal revenue of output in the present year will then have two components:

1. The current marginal revenue, which may be calculated:

$$p_t = 100 - q_t,$$

$$\text{Revenue}_t = q_t(100 - q_t),$$

$MR_t =$ Revenue from $(q_t + 1)$ units *minus* revenue from q_t units,

$$= (q_t + 1)(100 - [q_t + 1]) - q_t(100 - q_t)$$

$$= 99 - 2q_t.$$

2. The future marginal revenue from current output (we ignore discounting):

$$\text{Revenue}_{t+1} = q_{t+1}\{100 - q_{t+1} + \tfrac{1}{2}(30 - [100 - q_t])\}$$

MR_{t+1} = Revenue next period if $(q_t + 1)$ units sold now *minus* revenue next period if q_t units sold now,

$$= q_{t+1}\left(\frac{q_t + 1}{2}\right) - q_{t+1}\frac{q_t}{2},$$

ignoring terms which do not involve q_t, or

$$= \frac{q_{t+1}}{2}.$$

Hence the full marginal revenue from the sale of an additional unit this year is $99 - 2q_t + q_{t+1}/2$. Hence marginal revenue in the present period will be larger, the larger output is in the next period.

The same sort of phenomenon may arise on the cost side. Suppose, for example, a reduced output in the present period will lead to laying off men, and there is a substantial cost in rehiring. Then the full reduction in costs from a decline in current output will be less than the saving in wages by the amount of prospective rehiring costs.

These effects of the future will almost invariably be to increase the elasticity of current demand and cost curves. The rational monopolist must recognize the fact that people learn from experience, and that present acts therefore have future consequences. Yet this is often implicitly denied. Thus it is said that large buyers sometimes demand goods on unremunerative terms from small, competitive suppliers on threat of taking all their business elsewhere. As a single act this is possible, and quite possibly profitable, because it will pay the supplier to sell at a price above variable costs in the short run. But in the long run such suppliers will disappear if they do not earn a competitive rate of return. A monopolist (called a monopsonist in this buying role) who plays this game will therefore end up paying more than the competitive price, since suppliers would demand the equivalent of an insurance premium against such capricious behavior.

THE MONOPOLIST'S COST CURVES: MONOPSONY

The firm which is the only buyer of a productive service (a monopsonist) has the same power to control price in buying that a monopolist has in selling. The buyer will face a rising supply price (as a rule) and this supply price represents the average cost of

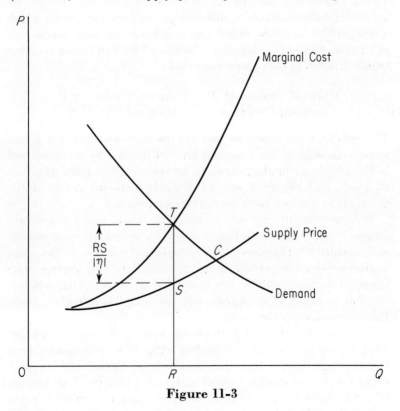

Figure 11-3

the productive service to him. The marginal cost will bear the usual relationship it has to an average, so $MC = p(1 + 1/\eta)$ where now η is the elasticity of supply. If we postulate also a demand curve by the monopsonist (it is analyzed in Chapter 14), he will buy that quantity which equates marginal cost and demand price.

We illustrate this monopsony situation in Figure 11-3. The quantity purchased will be $0R$, and the price paid to the suppliers RS.

The triangular shape, STC, will be a measure of the social loss arising because the resources are producing more valuable products here than in their alternative uses. The analogy to monopoly pricing is complete, and it is true in general that the formal analysis of monopoly power in buying is symmetrical with that of monopoly power in selling.

If a monopolist has any power on the buying side, he will be led to combine resources in different proportions from those which a competitive industry would use, and hence his cost curves will differ from those of a competitive industry.[7] He will in fact combine inputs A and B in such proportions that

$$\frac{\text{Marginal Product of } A}{\text{Marginal Cost of } A} = \frac{\text{Marginal Product of } B}{\text{Marginal Cost of } B}.$$

This condition for minimum cost has the same meaning that it had under competition: the marginal product divided by marginal cost is the additional product obtained by spending one more dollar on an input, and clearly if one input yields more per dollar at the margin than another, costs are not being minimized.

The monopsonist will substitute inputs whose prices rise slowly (whose supplies are elastic) for those whose prices rise more rapidly with quantity.[8] Therefore if his production function is the same as that which a competitive industry would have,[9] his average costs for given outputs would be less than those of the competitive industry. But as Figure 11-3 suggests, this "economy" is actually a waste from the economy's viewpoint.

Care must be taken, by both monopsonists and students, to know what supply curve they are dealing with. If a monopsonist buys from a competitive industry, in the short run the industry's supply curve (= sum of marginal costs) will have a positive slope because of diminishing returns. If a monopsonist should calculate a curve marginal to the firms' marginal costs, on average he will buy at

[7] Of course the comparison is with competitive cost curves for industry-wide changes—the only kind of cost curve a monopolist has.

[8] The marginal cost of a productive service to a monopsonist is $p(1 + [1/\eta_s])$, where p is the price of the service and η_s is its elasticity of supply. The monopsonist therefore uses relatively more of resources with more elastic supplies.

[9] In general it will differ because of economies or diseconomies of company size.

such prices as will impose losses on suppliers and in the long run enough firms will depart to force remunerative prices on him. Hence he has only short run monopsonistic power in this situation, and should use it only if he plans to contract his own scale. If the competitive industry's long-run supply curve rises because of rising input prices, however, he will take account of his indirect influence on input prices by calculating a marginal cost of the industry's product which is marginal to the industry's supply curve.

BILATERAL MONOPOLY

Bilateral monopoly arises when a monopolistic seller deals with a monopsonistic buyer. It would be pleasant to mention several important examples of this market structure, but its theory will serve to explain why it is seldom encountered (except in labor markets).

Suppose a monopolist has the marginal cost curve C (Figure 11-4). Then at fixed prices he would supply quantities indicated by this curve so it may be termed the average cost curve to the buyer, and then C' is the marginal cost of the commodity to the buyer. The monopsonist's marginal revenue product curve is R, and since he would purchase quantities on this curve for fixed prices, it is the average revenue curve to the seller, and R' is the marginal revenue curve to the seller. The monopolist would maximize profits by operating at output $0A$, and price AB, where his marginal cost (C) equals his marginal revenue (R'). The monopsonist would maximize profits by operating at output $0G$ and price GD, for here his marginal cost (C') equals his marginal revenue product (R). The objectives are inconsistent, so price under bilateral monopoly is said to be indeterminate.

Indeterminacy has a special meaning: the conditions of cost and demand are not sufficient to determine the price and quantity. Obviously if we look back at any year, there will have been a definite quantity and a definite price, but they will have been determined by factors outside the traditional theory: skill in negotiation; public opinion; coin flipping; a wise marriage. To say that a situation is indeterminate is a refined way of saying that it is not fully understood.

Joint profits of the two firms would be combined if they did not seek to exploit one another—that is, if they were content to exploit their suppliers and buyers. If R is the curve of marginal revenue for the buyer, and C is the curve of marginal cost for the seller, total profits of the two firms combined would be larger at output $0F$ than at any other.

One method that might be used to reach this output is an all-or-none contract: the quantity $0F$ could be specified, although the

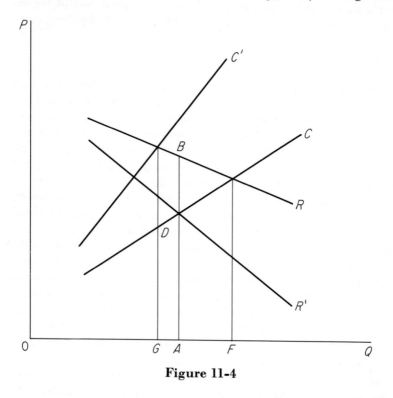

Figure 11-4

price would still be indeterminate. The objection to this solution is that cost and demand conditions fluctuate over time, so it would usually be undesirable for either firm to commit itself long in advance to its rate of production or purchase. Since the profits of the two firms are larger if they can operate where marginal cost equals marginal revenue, there is a strong incentive for them to combine. The difficulty in naming interesting examples of bilateral monopoly arises because it is an unstable form of organization.

PRICE DISCRIMINATION

We tentatively defined price discrimination as the sale of the same commodity at two or more prices. On this strict definition, price discrimination is a relatively uncommon phenomenon. The essence of discrimination is to separate buyers into two or more classes whose elasticities of demand differ appreciably, and this usually requires that the product sold to the various classes differ in time, place, or appearance to keep buyers from shifting. The purest cases of discrimination are found where the commodity is intrinsically untransferable (a service, like medical care) or can be prevented from being transferred by contract (as when buyers of aluminum for cable contracted not to use it otherwise).

The scope of the theory may be enlarged by defining discrimination as the sale of two or more similar goods at prices which are in different ratios to marginal cost. If a book in hard covers sells for $6 and in a paperback version for $2, there is presumably discrimination since the binding costs are not sufficient to explain the difference in prices.[10]

Price differences do not necessarily indicate discrimination. Banks charge small borrowers a higher interest rate than large borrowers of equal financial reliability because the costs of the small loan are larger per dollar of loan. Wholesalers get lower prices than retailers if on the average the wholesalers buy in larger lots, pay more promptly, and so on. Conversely, price equality does not demonstrate the absence of discrimination. If a college charges the same tuition for a large elementary class taught by an instructor, and a small advanced class taught by an expensive professor, it

---

[10] Our definition of discrimination turns upon the inequality,

$$\frac{p_1}{MC_1} \neq \frac{p_2}{MC_2}.$$

Some economists prefer the slightly different definition: prices are discriminatory if the difference in price is not equal to the difference in marginal cost, or

$$p_1 - MC_1 \neq p_2 - MC_2,$$

The proportionality definition has the merit of separating a monopolist's behavior into two parts: (1) the simple restriction of output such that price is greater than marginal cost; and (2) the misallocation of given goods among buyers, which is zero if prices are *proportional* to marginal costs.

is clearly discriminating. However, if it charges the same tuition for two classes whose costs per student differ by say $5, we should not call it discrimination because it would undoubtedly cost more than $5 to have separate fees for the two classes.

Conditions for Discrimination

The basic requirements for price discrimination are that there are two or more identifiable classes of buyers whose elasticities of demand for the product differ appreciably, and that they can be separated at a reasonable cost.

The demands of different buyers will be governed by the factors discussed in Chapter 3. Their elasticities may vary with

1. Income, as in the demand for medical care.
2. Availability of substitutes, as in the use of aluminum for cans facing great competition from tin plate and glass whereas aluminum in aircraft does not have good substitutes.
3. As a special case of substitutes, there may be rivals in one market (say, foreign) but not in the other (domestic).
4. Tastes, as when some buyers are eager to get early access to the commodity (a first run movie).

The form of discrimination is often more subtle than these examples might suggest. It has been common, for example, to lease rather than sell certain kinds of machinery, although the practice is declining somewhat due to antitrust convictions. When shoe machinery was leased, the basic charge was so many cents per pair of shoes processed—for example, 0.5¢ per pair for heel loading and attaching.[11] If use is not the chief cause of a machine's retirement, and it has more often been obsolescence, costs clearly are not twice as high for a machine which produces twice as many shoes, so discrimination is being practiced. The use of output as a basis for pricing is then a simple method of measuring the urgencies of desire of different manufacturers for the machine.

The tie-in sale may offer a still more indirect method of discriminating among customers. If the use of a machine is correlated with some other commodity—salt tablets for a dispensing machine, cards for a tabulating machine—the machine may be leased on a

---

[11] See Carl Kaysen, *United States* v. *United States Shoe Machinery Company* (Cambridge, Mass.: Harvard University Press, 1956), p. 322.

time basis and the user compelled to buy the related material from the lessor, who uses this material as a metering device to measure urgency of demand. For this explanation to hold, of course, the metering device must be sold at a non-competitive price.

Discriminatory Pricing

The monopolist will fail to maximize the receipts from the sale of a given quantity of his product unless the marginal revenue in each separable market is equal. For example, suppose he sells a given aggregate quantity in two markets at $10. If the demand elasticities are -2 and -3 the respective marginal revenues are $5 and $6.67, and the transfer of a unit from the former to the latter market will raise receipts by $1.67. In addition, the common marginal revenue must equal marginal cost.

The determination of prices may be illustrated graphically (Figure 11-5). Let the demand curves in two separable markets be D_1 and D_2, with corresponding marginal revenues MR_1 and MR_2. Then if the marginal revenue curves are added horizontally to get MR_t, we obtain the curve of aggregate quantities that can be sold at given marginal revenues. Output will be set where total marginal revenue equals marginal cost, or $0C$. This output will be sold in the two markets at prices P_1 and P_2, for at these prices marginal revenues are equal.

This analysis holds only if the markets are independent—that is, if the demand curve in one market does not depend upon the price set in the other market. This is seldom the case. Often there is some direct movement of consumers between markets: if first run movies get more expensive relative to second runs, some people will shift from the former to the latter. Often the movement is indirect. For example, if a railroad has no competition at point A but other transportation rivals at point B, we should expect demand for railroad transportation to be less elastic at the former point. Yet if the firms at A and B are in the same industry and selling in the same markets, in the long run the branch of the industry at A will decline if high rates are charged.

The theory of discrimination is only a special case of the theory of monopolies selling multiple products, and when the markets are not independent it is then necessary to treat the products sold in the various markets as fair substitutes for one another and employ

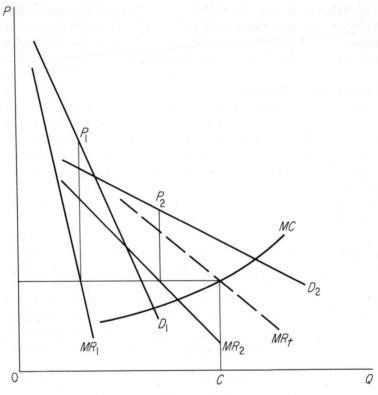

Figure 11-5

the theory of multiple products. That theory says simply that the monopolist will maximize profits if he equates the marginal revenue and marginal cost of each product. If the products are related in demand, however, one must calculate a "corrected" marginal revenue that takes account of the effect of the price of one product on the sales of others. For example, if product A has the demand schedule:

PRICE	QUANTITY	RECEIPTS
$10	100	$1,000
9	200	1,800

the crude marginal revenue is $800/100 = \$8$. But if this reduction in the price of A decreases the sales of a substitute product B, also sold by the monopolist, from 500 to 400 units at a unit profit of $3, then the net gain of receipts is only $500 and the marginal revenue of A is only $5.

Discrimination as a Condition for Existence

Although discriminatory prices are an inefficient method of allocating a commodity among individuals, they do yield a larger

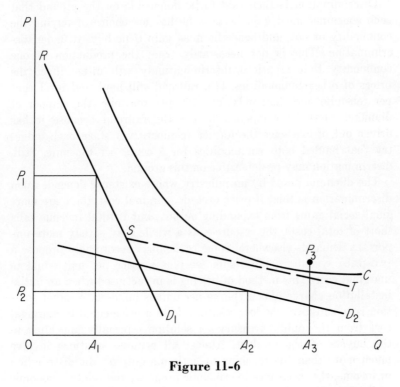

Figure 11-6

revenue than a single price system. Situations may therefore exist in which costs of production cannot be covered by receipts unless discrimination is practiced.

Consider, for example, a community with two classes of consumers, with the respective demand curves for a commodity, D_1 and D_2 (Figure 11-6). Adding these demand curves, the total demand curve is RST. The average cost of producing the commodity is C. Without discrimination, there is no output at which price is so great as average cost. With discrimination, a quantity A_1 can be sold at price P_1, another quantity A_2 at price P_2, and the total quantity $(A_1 + A_2 = A_3)$ sells for an average price of P_3, which exceeds its cost. This is, in a simplified form, the defense of price discrimination among commodities by railroads. In less extreme cases the output may be considerably larger (and also considerably smaller) with discrimination than without discrimination.[12]

Discrimination is then said to be defensible on the ground that each consumer must gain because he has his choice of buying the commodity or not, and hence he must gain if he buys it under discrimination. This is not necessarily true: the production of one commodity that is priced discriminatingly will often affect the prices of other commodities. If a railroad will haul coal for 1 cent per ton-mile and diamonds for $100 per ton-mile, the shipper of diamonds may be compelled to use the railroad because it has driven out of existence the former (competitive) stagecoach industry that hauled both commodities for 5 cents per ton-mile. Still, discrimination may be defensible on this ground.

The dilemma posed by an industry whose existence depends upon discrimination is this: if price exceeds marginal cost, there are marginal social gains from expanding output; but if total revenue falls short of total costs, the resources as a whole may satisfy more important demands elsewhere. Some economists accordingly propose a two-price system: a lump sum fee plus a price per unit equal to marginal cost. This method of pricing is in fact used when an initial installation charge plus a charge per unit is imposed. Another solution is to subsidize the loss resulting from a price equal to marginal cost from the public treasury—a solution especially appealing to the buyers of the product. Almost all genuine solutions involve much more than the reaching of optimum output: the distribution of income, the incentives to economic progress, and related economic and political questions are inevitably introduced.

RECOMMENDED READINGS

Henderson, A. M., "The Pricing of Public Utility Undertakings," *Manchester School*, **25** (1947), 223–50.

[12] There is no simple rule on the effect of discrimination on output; see J. Robinson, *The Economics of Imperfect Competition* (London: Macmillan, 1933), pp. 188–95.

Hicks, J. R., "The Theory of Monopoly," *Econometrica,* **3** (1935), 1–20. Reprinted in *Readings in Price Theory.*

Hotelling, Harold, "Stability in Competition," *Economic Journal,* **39** (1929), 41–57; reprinted in *Readings in Price Theory.*

PROBLEMS

1. If the marginal cost of a monopolist were, $MC = 60 - 3q\,(q < 21)$ and his demand curve were $p = 50 - q$, where would he operate? Deduce the condition for stable equilibrium.

2. Under discrimination the demand curve of a monopolist is made up of two parts:

$$p = 160 - 8q \text{ and } p = 80 - \frac{q}{2}.$$

Plot these demand curves, and the marginal cost curve, $MC = 4 + q$. Determine prices in the two markets and total profits; compare with price and profit with nondiscriminating monopoly.

3. Calculate the short-run marginal cost of a monopsonist, given the production function of Table 7–1 and the supply curve of the variable service: $p = \$6 - q/10$ (for $q < 50$).

4. A monopolist has a set of buyers, each of whom has the demand function,

$$p = 100 - q$$

and the monopolist has constant marginal costs = \$10. He charges a fixed license fee which each buyer must pay in order to purchase the product, and also charges for each unit.

(a) What license fee will be set if there is no income effect upon the demand for the commodity? (Hint: the maximum fee is the consumer surplus.)

(b) What fee will be set if the quantity a consumer buys falls 1 unit (at any price) for each \$10 of the fixed fee?

5. The marginal reduction in price from reading one more advertisement, or seeing one more dealer, is (on average) a diminishing function of the number examined.

(a) Will rich people pay higher or lower prices than poor people?

(b) Will people read more ads on kitchen stoves or on toasters?

(c) Will a store advertise each price? Each price change? If not, which?

chapter twelve

Oligopoly and Barriers to Entry

The industry consisting of two firms is called duopoly; the industry with a few firms is called oligopoly. The theory of price formation with oligopoly is, and for more than a century has been, one of the less successful areas of economic analysis, in spite of the fact that almost every major economist has thought about the problem, and a large number have written on it. The difficulties of the theory will first be discussed, and then we shall pass on to the perhaps more important problem of why there are few firms in certain industries.

THE OLIGOPOLY PROBLEM

Suppose two firms each own a mineral spring whose water is much esteemed by customers. There are no costs of production—the consumer comes to the well and fills a jug. This is the original formulation of the problem, as given by Cournot in 1838. If the firms combine, they will sell at the monopoly price (where marginal revenue equals marginal cost, here zero) and maximize their combined profits.

This could be viewed as a solution of the duopoly problem, with one proviso. How the profits of the monopoly are divided between the two owners of the springs is not explained, and indeed it is indeterminate. Either man can hold out for the 99.9 per cent of the profit, on threat of selling at marginal cost (here zero) or even less, if his demand is not met. But presumably some division will finally be agreed upon, because the two men together can do better by combining than by independent action.

Cournot put this solution aside, without explaining why he did not relish it. Modern economists have usually followed Cournot in rejecting the monopoly solution. Their rejection is based upon two grounds:

1. The collusive solution appears to have no natural stopping point—why should not 3, or 30, or 300 firms collude on the same logic?

2. Almost every economist believes that an industry with 2 (and certainly with 5) firms behaves differently from a monopoly.

The basis for this belief will be returned to shortly.

Cournot proceeded to analyse the problem on the assumption that each firm acts independently, in the sense that each firm assumes that the rival's output is not affected by his changes in output. The analysis then proceeds as follows: let the demand curve be $p = 100 - q$, and retain the condition of no cost.

1. Let A set *any* output, say 40, which fetches a price of 60. The final solution will be independent of this output.

2. Then B will take A's output as given, and seek the output that maximizes B's profits. In panel A of Figure 12-1 the output of B is found to be 30. The price in the market is $100 - (30 + 40) = 30$.

3. Then A sets his output to maximize profits, on the assumption that B's output will be 30. A's output is found (panel B) to be 35, and the market price is $100 - (30 + 35) = 35$.

4. It is now B's turn. Panel C tells us that B's output will now be 32.5, and the price 32.5.

5. A in turn sets an output of 33.75, with a price of 33.75 (Panel D).

Since this is an infinite series, it would require an undue amount of time and space to follow the remaining steps, but it is fairly obvious that the final solution will be for each duopolist to produce $33\frac{1}{3}$ units, with a market price of $33\frac{1}{3}$. The monopoly price would of course be 50. In this straight-line-demand-and-no-cost-case, the price will be $100/(n + 1)$, if there are n firms.

The objections to Cournot's solution are two. First, neither duopolist seems to learn from experience, although even introspec-

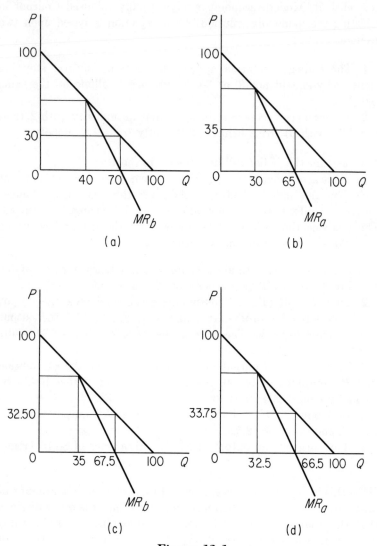

Figure 12-1

tion should suffice to teach that his output changes affect his rival. If he did, he would take these effects into account in fixing his own output. Second, and in some ways much more important, the basic assumption is completely arbitrary. Why not assume that the rival will match his output?[1] Or that the rival will follow price cuts after one week? In general there is no rational basis to the firms' conduct in the sense of selecting a form of behavior that is calculated to maximize profits—except in the monopoly solution, which economists have been unwilling to accept.

Just how good is the evidence that duopolists do not achieve the monopoly solution? The answer must be rather imprecise because no one has ever analyzed the evidence, which consists almost exclusively of individual historical incidents. One systematic statistical study suggested that in the case of radio commercials, the elasticity of advertising rates with respect to number of stations was −0.07—that is, a 25 per cent increase in the number of stations (from 4 to 5, or 12 to 15) reduced advertising rates by about 2 per cent.[2]

A collusive system encounters two main problems. First, agreement is difficult to reach if the transactions in which the firms deal are highly heterogeneous. When an industry does custom work, for example, each transaction may be unique, so "the" monopoly price is difficult to determine. But heterogeneity is typical: buyers differ in the quantities they purchase (with large effects on costs), in the amount of service they demand, in their promptness of payment, and so on. If the firms standardize qualities, lot sizes, service terms, credit terms, and the like, these difficulties can be reduced—but it will reduce profits to standardize where buyers wish variety. Furthermore an intricate formal classification becomes "cumbersome," meaning that it tends to hinder adaptation to the changes which shifting economic and technological conditions call for.

Second, an agreement must be policed. Even a whole-hearted colluder—and few are whole-hearted—cannot control all of his salesmen. Since there are many indirect ways of cutting prices, there will usually be some chiseling, as it is fondly termed—indeed the

---

[1] This market sharing assumption, it should be noted, leads to the monopoly price; see Problem 1 of this chapter.
[2] See my "A Theory of Oligopoly," *Journal of Political Economy* (February 1963).

difficulty of detecting chiseling makes it sensible for each firm to engage in some chiseling on the realistic assumption that his rivals are doing it. This chiseling will be harder to detect, the fewer and larger the buyers.

The costs of forming agreements and especially of policing them are a major reason for departures from the monopoly solution. These costs will be larger,

1. The more numerous the firms. The costs would probably be prohibitive for 20 firms of equal size.

2. The more complex the industry's product structure, including in this term the differences among buyers in demand elasticities (and hence possibilities of price discrimination), types and quantities of products bought, and so forth. Unfortunately there is no objective criterion of the complexity of product structure, but clearly a custom work industry (say, erecting refineries) has much more complex structure than an industry producing a few well-defined major products (say, petroleum refining).

3. The more rapid the changes in demand and supply conditions. These changes call for new agreements, and complicate the task of policing since they add opportunities for chiseling (for example, predating an order).

The number of rivals is clearly of great importance in determining the extent of collusion. Not only does an increase in the number directly increase the difficulty of collusion but also it usually seems to increase the complexity of the price structure (especially if the new firm's location changes the geographical pattern of prices) and constitutes one important source of changes in supply conditions.

The very persistence of oligopoly (or monopoly) must be sought in barriers to entry if the industry earns more than a competitive rate of return. We turn now to these barriers.

BARRIERS TO ENTRY

Barriers to entry arise because of economies of scale, or differences in productive factors, or legal control of entry. We distinguish two types of economies of scale—those peculiar to the industry, and those due to absolute size.

Economies of Scale Within an Industry

If there are economies of scale throughout the region of possible industry outputs, only one or a few firms may be able to exist in the industry. For example, let the (long-run) industry demand curve be D_1 and half the industry demand curve be D_2, in Figure 12-2. With homogeneous products a monopolist can sell at various prices the quantities indicated by D_1, and each of two duopolists can sell the quantities indicated by D_2. If the average alternative

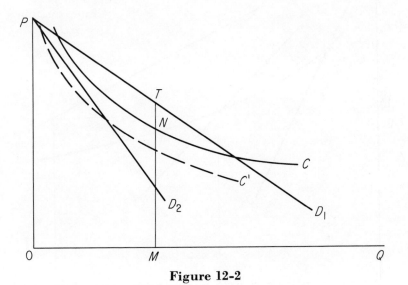

Figure 12-2

cost curve is C, a monopolist can operate at output $0M$ and make profits of NT per unit, but if a second firm with identical costs enters, neither can sell any quantity at a price equal to or greater than the average cost of production. If the average cost curve is C', two firms may exist in the industry, but not three. Under these conditions, monopoly or oligopoly will not be eliminated by the entrance of rivals, and monopoly profits will persist until technology or demand changes.

But if the demand is larger, or much less elastic than average cost, the economies of scale may not prevent the entrance of a con-

siderable number of rivals. Again let the demand curve of the industry be D_1 and half the demand curve D_2, and one-quarter of the
demand curve D_4, as in Figure 12-3. Let the average cost curve
of one firm be C. Then with two or four firms there are outputs
for each firm at which price exceeds average cost, and the number

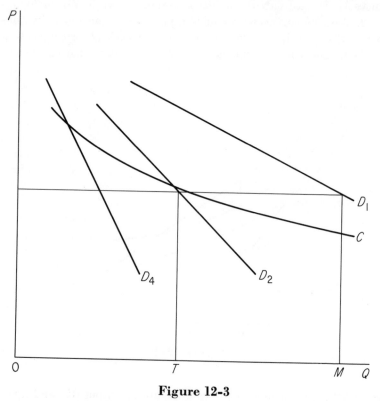

Figure 12-3

of firms may increase.[3] This situation is illustrated in the retailing
of food. There are no great economies from operating a large store
rather than a small one, and consumers attach some value to a
conveniently located store. Hence in sparsely settled sections the
stores will be smaller and more numerous relative to consumers.
No appreciable monopoly profits are to be expected in this case,

[3] In neither this case nor that described in Figure 12-2 *must* additional
firms enter: a single firm can set a sufficiently low price to make any output
of a rival unprofitable, while still making some monopoly profits.

nor will prices be much above the (competitive) levels in densely populated sections.

The importance of economies of scale in creating concentrated industry structures varies widely from field to field. In the local public utilities (water, gas and electricity, telephone) it is decisive. In the manufacturing sector there are few industries in which the minimum efficient size of firm is as much as 5 per cent of the industry's output and concentration must be explained on other grounds.

Economies of Scale for Capital

In the period before corporations were the typical form of business organization (roughly, from 2000 B.C. to 1885 A.D.), the amount of equity funds an enterprise possessed was given by the personal distribution of wealth and the possibilities of using partnerships. There were, accordingly, few enterprises that could have equity investments of the magnitude of 100 or 500 times the average size of personal wealth.

Equity funds can of course be augmented by borrowed funds, but since the equity funds provide the guarantee of repayment of debt, lenders will charge higher rates the larger the proportion of the funds of an enterprise they supply. The borrowing capacity of a firm, at a given interest rate, will depend also upon the nature of its business: an industry with relatively stable earnings (electric utilities, for example) can borrow much more at given interest rates than one with uncertain earnings (prospecting for crude oil).

The corporation has weakened the connection between firm size and personal wealth because it eliminates the major handicap of large partnerships, the liability of each for the debts of all. But even with limited liability investors seldom flock to new ventures in large numbers: an enterprise must have a history of sustained success before it can raise large sums by the sale of common stock.

There will therefore be only a small number of enterprises that can enter industries in which relatively vast amounts of capital are necessary to efficient operation. If the number is small relative to the profitable opportunities for such large ventures, the rate of return on large equity funds will exceed that on small funds. This is commonly alleged, at least implicitly: it has often been said that high rates of return in automobiles, cigarettes, certain chemicals, and other industries have persisted over long periods because no new firms could raise the capital necessary to enter on an efficient scale. The evidence, however, is not persuasive.[4]

In addition to this problem of scarcity of large amounts of equity funds, there is a popular belief that smaller amounts of capital (either borrowed or equity) frequently cannot be obtained by enterprises which could use them to earn much more than market rates, taking risks into account. A variety of industrial practices have been attributed to this "imperfection of the capital market."[5]

The most famous is the predatory price war. It is part of American folklore that the old Standard Oil Company cut prices below costs in selected markets and forced its rivals into selling out at bargain prices. If this be true, it would be an effective technique only if the small rivals could not raise capital to finance the price war: if they could, there would be no sense in even trying the technique. The historical evidence does not support this folklore; Standard Oil usually bought out rivals at attractive prices.[6]

There is no poverty of instances of able men who could not raise the capital for a wise investment—William C. Durant could not

[4] In the period 1954–57, for example, we may take the 200 largest manufacturing firms (*Fortune*, 1956) and classify them roughly into so-called 3-digit industries. The industries in which the large firms have the largest fractions of industry assets are given below, together with the average rates of return in these industries during the period.

INDUSTRY	NUMBER OF GIANT FIRMS	SHARE OF INDUSTRY ASSETS (%)	INDUSTRY RATE OF RETURN, 1954–57 (%)
Tires and tubes	5	100	5.47
Petroleum refining	23	99	6.53
Motor vehicles	12	86	9.48
Miscellaneous tobacco (cigarettes)	5	86	7.60
Industrial chemicals	17	81	8.07
Tin cans	2	75	6.20
Iron and steel	16	75	7.11
Glass	4	73	10.39
Communications equipment	6	61	5.14
Pottery, cut stone, etc.	5	58	5.81
Office and store machinery	3	55	6.96
Soap, perfumes	2	54	8.16
Generating apparatus, lamps, and so on	4	53	7.10
Pulp and paper	12	50	7.79

The matching of industries with companies poses numerous minor problems. The general lack of association of rates of return (taken from my *Capital and Rates of Return in Manufacturing Industries*) and the share of the giants in an industry is obvious.

[5] The most important example comes later: the inability of men to borrow funds for academic training that would be highly remunerative; see p. 265.

[6] See John S. McGee, "Predatory Price Cutting," *Journal of Law and Economics*, **1** (1958).

raise $2 million to buy Ford's company in 1909; it could have been a lovely investment. But the demonstration of important imperfections in the capital market cannot be made by selective hindsight. If the expected rates of return on investment, given the probabilities of success as they appear ex ante do not differ among industries and areas, the market is not imperfect—it simply has imperfect knowledge of the future. The efficiency of the capital markets is still a relatively unexplored subject in economics, and we leave its status as a barrier to entry in doubt.

Superior Resources

Occasionally superior qualities of natural resources occur in such small quantities that a major barrier to the expansion of the industry is provided by the unavailability of other good sources. Among the most famous cases are diamonds, nitrates, potash, radium, bauxite, nickel, and sulfur. The situation is an unusual one, however: almost always subsequent discoveries have been made of deposits of comparable or even higher quality—in fact this is true of each item in the above list.

But a rising supply price of a resource, even a steeply rising supply price, will not lead to an oligopolistic organization of the industry unless the individual firms have economies, or at least no appreciable diseconomies, of scale. The extractive industries have been organized as compulsory cartels more often than as small number oligopolies.

One unnatural resource, the entrepreneur, occasionally reaches such heights of ability as to become the dominant producer even in a major industry. Henry Ford is, of course, the premier American example of such a man: without any advantages other than ability he lifted his company to where it produced over half the output of a great industry. A considerable number of less famous men have achieved comparable positions in smaller industries. The resulting concentration of control is intrinsically unstable: captains of industry have been no more successful than kings or dictators in discovering a method of breeding heirs of outstanding ability.

Franchises and Patents

In some industries entry is controlled by franchise. A certificate of convenience and necessity, or its equivalent, is necessary to open a bank, build a pipeline, start an airline, broadcast radio or television, or produce gas and electricity. Often these fields would have few firms in any market because of economies of scale, and public utilities were once defined as "natural" monopolies (industries that could not be competitive). But franchises have been granted very restrictively not only in fields where there was obviously room for more firms (banking, pipelines, radio) but also in fields where competition was highly effective (motor trucking, taxis). The effectiveness of these entry controls will be greater if they are applied to the individual plant (as New York City taxis, where a franchise is worth more than $20,000) than if they are applied only to the firm (a regulated motor carrier can have as many trucks as it wishes). There is no special problem of explanation for these restrictions: as an ancient Scottish philosopher almost remarked, businessmen and legislators seldom have a picnic except at the consumer's expense.

The patent is a grant for a period of 17 years to the exclusive right to a process or product. The basis for the grant lies in the fact that the production and testing of new knowledge is expensive but copying it is cheap. Without patent protection, an enterprise would invest in research only on such a scale that the expected returns to the firm because of a head start or secrecy would equal cost at the margin, whereas from the economy's viewpoint the marginal cost of research should equal its marginal social product (including gains to all other firms). This basis is obviously formally valid, but does not guide us in determining the types and amounts of rewards necessary to bring marginal private and social products together. All one can say for the 17-year period is that it was not inconsistent with the amount of invention we have had in the past.

An inventor will normally license everyone in a competitive industry to use the patent simply because this is the most profitable way to exploit it. If the patent holder did not license and instead sought to displace the competitive industry, diseconomies of scale would usually thwart the desire or lead to much smaller net returns.

When the patent covers a new product it is more likely to lead to monopoly or oligopoly. Among one-time American monopolies based upon patents one may mention aluminum, ethyl gasoline, rayon, cellophane, scotch tape, and sulphur extraction (Frasch process). Even when an inventor devises a new product, however, it has usually been possible for others to find alternative routes to the same end, and patents have not played a major role in bringing about industrial concentration.

The Pace of Entry

If the discussion of entry barriers suggests that there are effective permanent obstacles to entry in many industries, it is misleading. No really profitable monopoly or oligopoly has ever lasted a mere 100 years: rivals find their way into the field or devise an alternative product to attract away the customers. Of course this does not call for excessive sympathy for the monopolist: if he can retain his position for nine years, earning $1 million of monopoly profits a year, the present value of this annuity (at 8 per cent) is half of the value of a perpetual annuity of equal amount. Nine years in hand are worth nine hundred in a distant bush.

Once we take explicit account of the fact that entry is basically a question of rate, we should take account of two other devices to retard entry. One is secrecy: if one can conceal the profitability of his situation, entry will be slower. The second is related: if one does not seize the entire profits that could be obtained in the absence of entry, entry itself may be retarded, because the prospective entrant is better able to judge existing profits than maximum possible profits. This is the rationale of the traditional belief that potential competition is a significant limitation òn the power of a monopolist or group of oligopolists. Whether potential competition serves this function to any important degree depends upon how the potential entrants are affected by changes in current profits.

The intelligent prospective entrant will rank industries, let us assume, by their current rates of return and the probable rates of growth of demand over time. The monopolist can reduce the attractiveness of his field by selling at lower prices, but in general he cannot or will not retard the rate of growth of demand. If the rate of growth of demand is large (say equal to one-half or more of the interest rate), it will dominate the rate of entry; in the converse case the current profit rate will be dominant and there is more room for the policy of moderate pricing to discourage entry.[7]

[7] See mathematical note 11 in Appendix B.

RECOMMENDED READINGS

Bain, J. S., *Barriers to New Competition,* Cambridge, Mass.: Harvard University Press, 1956.

Fellner, W., *Competition Among the Few,* New York: Knopf, 1950.

Hurwicz, L., "The Theory of Economic Behavior." Reprinted in *Readings in Price Theory.*

Modigliani, F., "New Developments on the Oligopoly Front," *Journal of Political Economy* (June 1958).

Stigler, G., "A Theory of Delivered Price Systems," *American Economic Review,* **39** (1949), 1143–59.

Stigler, G., "The Kinky Oligopoly Demand Curve and Rigid Prices." Reprinted in *Readings in Price Theory.*

Sweezy, P., "Demand under Conditions of Oligopoly." Reprinted in *Readings in Price Theory.*

PROBLEMS

1. Each duopolist expects to have 50 per cent of the sales at any price (market-sharing). Determine price and output for the Cournot case of a demand curve, $p = 100 - q$, and no production costs. What will happen if the duopolist's expectations are for shares adding up to 110 per cent of the total?

2. (The Dominant Firm) Suppose a firm with a large share of the industry's output decides to act monopolistically on the assumption that numerous small competitors act competitively. Then at any price these competitors will sell quantities such that marginal cost equals price, and the remainder will be the quantity demanded of the dominant firm. [See my "Notes on the Theory of Duopoly," *Journal of Political Economy,* **48** (1940), 521–541.] Now an example:

$p = 200 - q$ is market demand,

$MC = \dfrac{q}{2} + 1$ is sum of the marginal cost curves of the minor firms,

$MC = q - 15$ is the marginal cost curve of the dominant firm.

Determine price, output, and profits of the dominant firm.

3. The following are famous solutions in the theory of duopoly. Solve and appraise their significance.

(a) The two firms have constant marginal costs of \$10; market demand is $p = 100 - q$. *A* is first a monopolist; then *B* enters and sells an amount which maximizes his profits on the assumption that A will not change his output; then A does likewise; and so on. [Cournot]

(b) The same costs and demand. A is again a monopolist; then B enters and sets a price on the assumption that A will not change his price; then A does likewise; and so on. [Bertrand]

(c) Same as (b), except that the maximum output of each firm is 40. Hence take into account the possibility of one firm increasing its profits by raising its price when the other firm is sold out. [Edgeworth][8]

4. An oligopoly theory that reappears from time to time emphasizes the threat of potential entry. As a result, the oligopolists (presumably acting in collusion) set a price such that if an entrant appeared, there would be no rate of output at which he could make more than a competitive rate of return. Illustrate the argument graphically.

[8] See mathematical note 12 in Appendix B.

chapter thirteen

Cartels and Mergers

If a large number of producers wish to escape the rigors of competition, they must do so by forming an agreement to act together (called a cartel, after their German name) or by actually merging into one firm.

The distinction between a cartel and an outright merger is only one of degree. There are all degrees of scope and duration in the agreements firms may make. The loosest form—a set of verbal promises to abide by a price or market division—is called a gentleman's agreement, although the participants seldom are, or long do. More formal arrangements are customary, and two examples may be mentioned.

The first cartel successfully convicted under the Sherman Antitrust Act (1890) is our first example. Six firms making cast-iron pipe dominated this industry in 35 Southern and Western states and in Indian Territory. They founded a combination in late 1894, which later took the following form. Certain cities were reserved for each company, and in these cities the other companies entered higher bids on all contracts to give an appearance of rivalry. In nonreserved cities, prices were fixed by a central committee and each company offered a "bonus," say of $2 to $9 a ton, to the committee for the contract. The highest bidder received the right to make the official bid (the rivals again quoting higher prices) and the "bonuses" were periodically divided among the firms in proportion to assigned capacities.

We may note that although this method of allocation of contracts was ingenious, it made for friction among the colluders. Bonuses could be bid up by firms which were not interested in getting a particular contract simply to increase the bonus distributions, so the division of industry profits could be altered continuously. Less frequent determinations of the division of gains is expedient, if the collusion is to be stable. Aside from this objection, the plan had the merit of giving each contract to the firm whose cost plus freight was smallest for the given contract, so the division of business among the firms was efficient.

The German cartels in industries such as cement and steel displayed a more formal organization.[1] Each firm was assigned a quota, based sometimes on historical production (iron), sometimes on "capacity" estimates by impartial experts (cement). Firms exceeding quotas (which included use within the company, in the industries with vertical integration) sometimes paid penalties and firms falling short of quotas received grants, but in other industries (steel) the quotas could be sold. A joint selling agency was used in some industries, and in others customers were assigned to each producer. There were usually prohibitions on assisting new entrants in any manner. Prices were set by the cartel. These cartels were substantially free of legal restraints and displayed a greater durability than the illegal American conspiracies.

When the cartel agreement is legally enforceable, and provides for a joint sales agency, it differs in only minor respects from a full merger. The chief economic differences, in fact, are only two: the cartel contract is not perpetual (as a merger is); and if independent firms continue to operate the plants in a cartel, any economies or diseconomies of scale are avoided. Essentially the same economic theory therefore applies to both cartels and mergers for monopoly. There are, of course, many mergers wholly irrelevant to monopoly, and they will be discussed subsequently.

THE THEORY OF CARTELS AND MERGERS FOR MONOPOLY

Assume that there are n competitive firms in an industry, in short- (and long-) run equilibrium. The situation of a typical firm and the industry are portrayed in Figure 13-1. The price is p_0, the

---

[1] See the numerous reports of the *Commission to Investigate Conditions of Production and Distribution in the German Economy* (in German, 1930). The present legal situation of cartels varies greatly among European nations.

output of a firm $0m$, and the output of the industry $0M$ ($= n$ times $0m$). A cartel is now formed, and each firm is assigned a quota of $1/n$ times total output. In effect, then, each firm faces a demand curve equal to $1/n$ of the industry demand curve. Provided the quotas are obeyed by all firms, they will each produce the same output. Therefore when a firm increases output by one unit, total output is rising by n units. Price now depends upon the output of the firm, so we may draw a demand curve, d ($= 1/n$ times D),

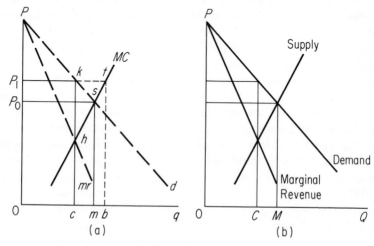

Figure 13-1

and a corresponding marginal revenue curve, mr. Profits are maximized by the price, p_1.

The merger analysis is strictly equivalent. Draw the marginal curve MR for the industry, and treat the supply curve (which is the sum of the marginal cost curves) as the marginal cost curve of the combined enterprise. Again a price of p_1 is set. If there are diseconomies of scale, the supply curve will shift upward and the analysis differs in details from the cartel case.

It is evident that since d must go through point s, the short-run result is a rise in profits. (A corresponding statement holds for mergers unless there are large diseconomies of scale.) At least four problems are encountered, however, which destroy this idyllic extortion.

The Recalcitrant Firm

Suppose $(n-1)$ firms join the cartel, but one firm remains outside. So far as the members of the cartel are concerned, the situation is not very different. Each gets a quota of $1/(n-1)$ of total sales by the cartel. The firm remaining outside the cartel is not large enough to have much influence on price, so it will sell approximately $0b$ if the price is about $0p_1$. Hence the output of each member of the cartel at this price would be $(0C-0b)/(n-1)$, which is only slightly less than $0c$ if the number of firms is fairly large. If we were inclined to get the exact new price we could do so by an extension of these remarks: subtract the amount supplied by the outsider (given by his marginal cost curve) at every price from the market demand, to get the cartel demand. Divide this by $(n-1)$ to get the cartel member's demand curve. Then find the output (and price) at which marginal revenue equals marginal cost.

If the cartel members are not much influenced by the recalcitrant firm, its owner is much altered in circumstances. He obtains a profit of hkt in excess of that of a cartel member, per unit of time. After all he is getting the full benefit of the higher price without paying any of the cost by way of reduced output. In labor union language he is a free rider.

And this is the first difficulty in forming a cartel. Every firm would prefer to be the outsider, and yet if enough stay outside the cartel becomes futile: a large group of free riders will find that the streetcar won't run. In general the cartel becomes feasible only if the number of firms is not very large, and (what is then usually the case) a few firms are so large relative to the industry that they cannot individually abstain from the cartel or it will not be formed.

Different Costs

If two cartel members with different marginal cost curves receive equal quotas, a second set of problems arise. We illustrate them with Figure 13-2. Firm B would prefer a lower price than firm A would $(P_a > P_b)$. Moreover, profits of the cartel are not being maximized at any price: minimum costs require that marginal costs be equal for each company. This condition will be met only if the quotas of A and B are in the proportion $0r/0s$.

This problem is customarily solved by allowing the sale of quotas by one cartel member to another. But in public cartels (such as the American tobacco allotment scheme or the Texas Railroad Commission's prorating of output of oil wells) the quotas are not fully transferable, and an inefficiency additional to monopoly itself is introduced.

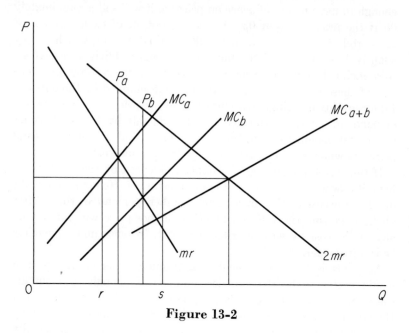

Figure 13-2

Investment Rivalry

The cartel system described through Figure 13-1 is a short run solution. There are incentives to individual firms to engage in rivalry by way of investment. Suppose the quota of a firm is based upon some sort of "capacity" measure—say, barrels of oil that a plant can refine, or tons of iron a blast furnace can produce (in each case under "normal" operations). The individual firm may then find that revenue is approximately proportional to its quota, but long run marginal costs are less than price. It will then have an incentive to enlarge its plant and add to its quota.

We illustrate this temptation by Figure 13-3. The firm was originally at $0c$, with a plant whose costs are given by SMC. If the firm increases its "capacity" by 1/3, it will be allowed to sell $0t$ ($= 4/3\ 0c$). The long-run marginal cost curve (C) for a firm which must have an oversize plant to justify its quota will lie above the long-run marginal cost curve (LMC), which in turn lies above SMC at output $0c$.[2] Nevertheless, the firm's profits rise by the cross-hatched area.

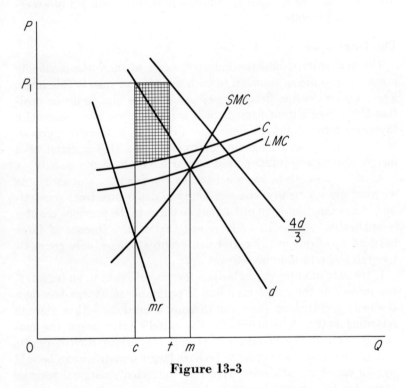

Figure 13-3

And this is the story of cartels' lives. When this rivalry does not take the form of investment, some other form achieves the same result. Thus some states have had laws that no one could sell liquor, or gasoline, or some other commodity at less than a designated price (or mark-up). A firm will then seek additional patronage by advertising more, giving better service, or some such device. As a result,

---

[2] LMC is above SMC if (as postulated in Figure 13-1) the original competitive position was one of long-run equilibrium, because then long- and short-run marginal costs were equal at output $0m$.

the cost curves shift upward, and in long-run equilibrium, the long-run marginal cost eventually equals price.

The theory of cartels, we have said, is closely related to that of mergers. The merger will certainly have the problem of the firm that refuses to join. The merger will escape our latter two problems, however: each plant can be run at the output such that marginal costs are equal for all plants, and total investment will not be excessive, as with cartels.

The Interloper

The new entrant into the industry, eager to share the monopoly profits, is a problem common to both merger and cartel. This interloper, as the existing firms caressingly describe him, is in the position of the recalcitrant firm: he will not join unless given unusually favorable terms (quota, or purchase price). It is, therefore, crucial to the stability and long-run profitability of either a cartel or a merger that new entrants do not appear too often or too quickly.

At this point, then, we are back to the conditions of entry, as we must always be in discussing long run departures from competition. Since the discussion of barriers to entry in the previous chapter is applicable, we shall merely repeat that in the absence of large barriers, the firms in the cartel will eventually earn only competitive rates of return on investment.

If the rate of entry depends upon the rate of profit in an industry, the merger or the cartel may find it profitable to charge less than the price dictated by short-run demand conditions with a view to retarding entry. A reduction in the cartel's price below the monopoly level in the present period will (1) reduce current profits and (2) increase future profits because larger quantities can be sold by the cartel at each price. Hence a "corrected" marginal revenue curve for the present period will be more elastic than the uncorrected curve. Industries forming cartels or monopolistic mergers almost invariably suffer declining market shares over time, and presumably the rate of decline is dependent upon the pricing policy.

MERGERS FOR OTHER PURPOSES

A comprehensive census of mergers would reveal a vast number that have no real relevance to the question of monopoly. When a farmer buys (or leases) additional land, this is obviously a merger. When two lawyers form a partnership, this is a merger. When the local lumber dealer buys a service station this is a merger. Clearly none of these mergers may have the slightest relevance to monopoly.

Perhaps the largest part of these mergers—and an equally numerous stream of dissolutions (or negative mergers)—are incidents of the investment programs of individuals. As such they are not different from the merging of ownership of two stock certificates, each for 100 shares of a given corporation.

The vertical merger, in which a firm acquires a supplier or a customer, has already been discussed implicitly (p. 169) as a phenomenon associated with the size of the market. There is a deepseated suspicion of vertical mergers in American antitrust law, on the ground that such a merger forecloses part of the market for rivals—for example, if a shoe manufacturer acquires a chain of shoe stores, rivals will no longer be able to sell to them. This suspicion is in general illogical, since the ability of rivals to sell shoes will be impaired only if the retail chain had monopolistic powers in the retail market.[3]

There are, in fact, only three reasons associated with imperfect competition for vertical integration. The first is to practice price discrimination: a monopolist in the production of aluminum, for example, usually could not discriminate in the price ·of aluminum ingots for different products emerging from fabrication unless he was also the fabricator. The second reason for vertical integration, more difficult to document, is the desire to put an obstacle in the way of prospective entrants: if a new steel company had to enter the iron ore as well as the steel industry, presumably entry would be retarded.[4] The third noncompetitive reason for vertical integration is to eliminate monopoly: if a cartel set noncompetitive prices on supplies, backward integration by buyers would be a suitable way to get the supplies cheaper. Such integration would of course be unnecessary if the cartel were intelligent enough to recognize that it could not exclude entry by large customers, for then it would

---

[3] Of course one can buy a monopolistic seller or buyer, but only at a price which includes the capitalized value of any monopoly gains.

[4] The European cartels frequently had exclusive dealing contracts with suppliers and distributors, or granted "loyalty discounts" (based on aggregate purchases from the cartel) to this end.

not attempt to get noncompetitive prices from such customers. People without monopolistic power should not exercise it.

RECOMMENDED READINGS

Patinkin, D., "Multiple-Plant Firms, Cartels, and Imperfect Competition," *Quarterly Journal of Economics*, **66** (February 1947), 173–205.
Stigler, G. J., "Monopoly and Oligopoly by Merger," *Proceedings, American Economic Association* (May 1950).

PROBLEMS

1. Each firm in an industry has the cost curves given in Problem 1 of Chapter 10 (p. 191). The industry demand curve is $p = 25 - q/170$. Marginal costs of a firm are $MC = q - 2$ and total costs are

$$C = \frac{(q-1)(q-2)}{2} + 135.$$

(These equations reproduce the table on page 191 for $q \geqq 7$; note that MC is not a derivative of C because finite changes are employed.)

(a) Verify that the industry is in competitive equilibrium with 100 firms.

(b) If all the firms join in a cartel, what price will be set? What will profits per firm be?

(c) If all the firms except one join a cartel, what will the price be? What will be the profits per member firm, and per outsider firm?

(d) What will price be after 10 additional firms enter the industry and join the cartel with equal quotas?

(e) How many firms must enter before profits are eliminated?

(f) What will happen to price and profits if now the cartel is abolished?

2. The same basic problem applies to mergers. Now let there be 20 firms and the industry demand curve, $p = 25 - Q/34$. Will it be profitable to form a merger of the firms if (fixed) costs of each plant rise 10 per cent because of internal diseconomies of scale?

chapter fourteen

The Demand for Productive Services

The apparatus of price theory we have been discussing is formally just as applicable to markets for productive services as it is to markets for intermediate or finished goods. After we establish the determinants of the demand for productive services in the present chapter, we shall not be much concerned with manipulating supply and demand curves, for there are no new principles involved. Instead we shall examine the determinants of the supply curves of labor and specific productive goods. Capital in general will be treated in Chapter 17.

DEMAND UNDER COMPETITION

The firm will hire each productive service in such quantity as to maximize its profits. Profits will be maximized when the amount added to the revenue of the firm by an additional unit of the productive service equals the amount it adds to costs. Under competition a firm does not exert an appreciable effect on the prices of the productive services it buys, so the amount a unit of the productive service adds to costs is equal to its price. The amount added to receipts is the marginal physical product multiplied by the price of the product (since the output of the firm also exerts little influence on the price of the product). These relationships are illustrated numerically in Table 14–1. The marginal physical product times price (called the value of the marginal product) diminishes as the quantity of the productive service increases because the marginal physical product diminishes and the price of the product is constant.

Table 14-1

QUANTITY OF A	QUANTITY OF PRODUCT	PRICE OF PRODUCT	RECEIPTS OF FIRM	MARGINAL PHYSICAL PRODUCT	VALUE OF MARGINAL PRODUCT
20	6810	$0.60	$4086		
21	6865	0.60	4119	55	$33
22	6915	0.60	4149	50	30
23	6960	0.60	4176	45	27
24	7000	0.60	4200	40	24

The value of the marginal product is the demand price for a productive service if the *quantities* of the other productive services are held constant. Demand curves, however, usually refer to demand prices when the *prices* of other productive services are held constant. We shall show the difference between these two demand prices graphically (Figure 14-1). Let MP_1 be the curve of the value of the marginal product of a productive service A when the quantity of the other productive service B is 100. If now the price of A falls from OR to OS, the quantity of A demanded will rise from RC to SD if B is held at 100. But the entrepreneur will not hold B at this level for, if the price of B has not changed, the minimum cost condition,

$$\frac{\text{marginal physical product of } A}{\text{price of } A} = \frac{\text{marginal physical product of } B}{\text{price of } B}$$

no longer holds. The increase in the quantity of A (from RC to SD) will increase the marginal product of given quantities of B, so the quantity of B will be increased to (say) 125 to minimize costs.[1] This larger quantity of B will raise the marginal value product of A, and a new marginal product curve, MP_2 results. Hence at price OS, the quantity of A demanded rises to SF. If we join points such as C and F, we trace out the demand curve of the firm for A, the price of B (and that of the product) being held constant. The demand curve will be more elastic than the curve of the value of the marginal product.[2]

[1] It is possible with A and B substitutes, for the marginal product of B to be reduced if the quantity of A rises. Then the entrepreneur will reduce the quantity of B and this will in turn increase the marginal product of A.
[2] See mathematical note 13 in Appendix B.

The demand curve of the industry is the sum of the demand curves of the industry's firms, but, as with supply curves, we must notice that things constant to one firm need not be constant to the industry. If the price of a productive service falls, and all firms expand output, the price of the industry's product must necessarily

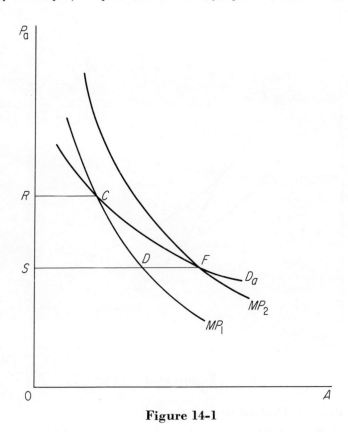

Figure 14-1

fall. We therefore distinguish between the demand curve of a firm when the price of the productive service varies only for this firm, and the demand curve when the price varies for all firms. Thus, let D_{10} be the demand curve of a firm for a productive service when the price of the product is \$10 (Figure 14-2). If the price of the productive service falls from OR to OS for all firms, output of the industry will rise enough to reduce the price to (say) \$9.

Then the demand curve of the firm will fall to D_9, and it will take ST of the productive service at this price. If we connect points like M and T, we trace out the demand curve (D) of the firm for industry-wide price changes, and it is this type of demand curve that we may add to get the industry demand curve.

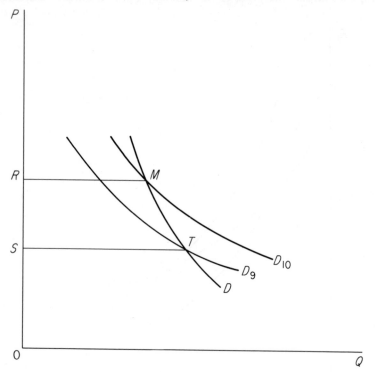

Figure 14-2

The Rules of Derived Demand

Since the demand for productive services is created by the need to produce a product for sale, the demand for the services is said to be a derived demand. The elasticity of this derived demand for a productive service is governed by four conditions, and three rules of derived demand have accordingly been proposed.[3]

---

[3] See A. Marshall, *Principles of Economics,* (London: Macmillan, 1922), Book V, Ch. 6; also the papers by Bronfenbrenner and Hicks, *Oxford Economic Papers* (October 1961). See mathematical note 14 in Appendix B.

RULE 1: The demand for a service is more elastic, the more readily other services may be substituted for it.

The measure of substitutability commonly used is the relative change in the ratio of the quantity of the productive service in question to the quantity of some other productive service, divided by the relative change in their price ratio.[4] It is self-evident that high substitutability entails a large substitution of other services for one whose relative price has risen. Since aluminum and copper wire are both efficient for conducting electricity, each will have an elastic demand in the neighborhood of the ratio of the price of aluminum to that of copper of 2 to 1 (taking account of their weights and conductivity).

RULE 2: The elasticity of demand for a productive service will be larger, the larger the elasticity of demand for the final product.

The logic of this rule is also direct: the more elastic the demand for the product, the more output will fall for a given rise in cost (and price) due to a rise in the price of one productive service.

RULE 3: The demand for a productive service will be more elastic, the more elastic is the supply of the other productive services.

When the price of one productive service rises, the increase can be borne either by buyers of the final product (who pay more) or by suppliers of other productive services (who receive less). The more elastic the supply of these other services, the less possible it is to reduce their price with a given reduction in their quantities. Hence the greater must be the reduction in the use of the productive service whose price has risen, if price is to equal marginal cost.

There is a fourth rule, which will appear more obvious to most people than any of the foregoing: the smaller the fraction of total cost the payments to a productive service are, the less elastic will

---

[4] This is the elasticity of substitution, formally defined as

$$\frac{\dfrac{\Delta(a/b)}{a/b}}{\dfrac{\Delta p_b/p_a}{p_b/p_a}},$$

where changes in (a/b) are compared with changes in (p_b/p_a) to keep the elasticity positive.

be its demand. If doorbells double in price (say from \$1 to \$2), the cost of building a house will also rise by \$1, or say 0.005 per cent. Since few people will be discouraged from buying a house by this rise, the demand for doorbells will be quite inelastic. There is some truth in the rule,[5] but its basic limitation may be suggested as follows. Suppose we classify the carpenters who build a house into Polish, German, Irish, and so on. Since the wages of any one group of national origin will be a small fraction of total cost—if it is not, we shall subclassify carpenters by village of origin—can we not say that the elasticity of demand for Irish carpenters is smaller than the elasticity of demand for all carpenters? Indeed we can say this, since freedom of speech includes freedom to speak error. The substitutes of course become better as we subclassify carpenters and the substitution effect leads to an increase in the elasticity of demand. This is usually the case, or we would be able by mere subclassification to make all derived demands inelastic.

It follows from the theory of cost curves that the elasticity of demand for an input will be greater in the long run than in the short run. In the short run the quantities of all resources are not freely variable, so the full effect of a price change on the proportions in which inputs are combined will not be achieved. There are really at least two long runs to take into account for a complete analysis: the industry purchasing the input whose price changes will require time to make a full substitution in favor of or against the input, and the buyers of the commodity in turn require time to make a full adjustment to the resulting change in the price of the industry's product.

DEMAND UNDER MONOPOLY

The demand price for a productive service will be equal to the increment of revenue that the firm derives from the use of one more unit of the service. Under competition this increment of revenue is called the value of the marginal product, for it equals the marginal physical product of the service times the price of the product.

---

[5] It is not generally valid, however, unless the elasticity of demand is larger than the elasticity of substitution; see footnote 3 for details.

If a laborer adds 20 units of product per day, and the product sells for $0.50 per unit, the value of his marginal product is $10.

Under monopoly the firm must take account of the fact that the increment of product lowers the price of all units of output, so only the marginal revenue of the increment of output is received. The increment of value, which is called the marginal revenue product, is therefore the marginal physical product times the marginal revenue.[6]

The fact that the demand price of a monopolist equals the marginal revenue product of a productive service is the reason monopoly leads to a misallocation of resources. Suppose this marginal revenue product is $10, which will also be the value of the marginal product in competitive industries. Then the value of the marginal product in the monopolistic industry will be greater than $10,[7] and aggregate output would be increased by shifting resources from competitive industries to the monopolistic industry.

Two of the rules of derived demand carry over from the competitive to the monopolistic case with little change. The demand for a productive service will be more elastic the better the substitutes for it, and the demand will be more elastic, the greater the elasticity of the marginal revenue curve. The rule that the elasticity of demand for a productive service will be greater, the greater the elasticity of supply of the other factors, however, raises a problem: if the supply of any service is not infinitely elastic to a monopolist, then he can also exert influence on its price and becomes a monopsonist (see p. 206). He will accordingly take account of this influence, and hire such services only up to the quantity where their marginal cost equals their marginal revenue product, so the rule must be restated: the demand for a productive service will be more elastic, the more elastic the marginal costs of the other services.

[6] When the quantity of the productive service rises by Δa, revenue rises by

$$\Delta R = (p + \Delta p)(q + \Delta q) - pq$$
$$= p\Delta q + q\Delta p, \text{ approximately.}$$

$$\frac{\Delta R}{\Delta a} = \frac{\Delta q}{\Delta a}\left(p + q\frac{\Delta p}{\Delta q}\right)$$

$$= \frac{\Delta q}{\Delta a} p\left(1 + \frac{1}{\eta_D}\right) = \text{Marginal physical product} \times \text{Marginal revenue.}$$

[7] It will be equal to $10 divided by $(1 + 1/\eta)$, or $12.50 if $\eta = -5$.

RECOMMENDED READINGS

Bronfenbrenner, M., and J. R. Hicks, *Oxford Economic Papers* (October 1961).

Marshall, A., *Principles of Economics*, London: Macmillan, 1922, Bk. V, Ch. 6.

PROBLEMS

1. If there are fixed coefficients of production so a unit of product always requires n units of productive service A, and the supplies of other productive services are infinitely elastic, prove that the elasticity of demand for A is K times the elasticity of demand for the product. (K is the amount spent on A as a fraction of total value of the product.)

2. Explain how the demand for gasoline would be affected by each of the following:

(a) A tax on bus tickets.

(b) Growing traffic congestion in a city.

(c) A tax on horsepower of automobile engines.

(d) A subsidy on lubricating oil produced in fixed proportion with gasoline.

3. Let each of 60 firms have the marginal product for a factor A, $MP_a = 30 - Q_c/10$. Let the quantities of the other factors be fixed in the short run and derive the industry demand curve for the factor, given the demand curve for the product, $p = 20 - q/1000$. (Note that the prices of the other factors are not held constant, as in the usual demand curve.)

chapter fifteen

Rents and Quasi-Rents

As recently as a century ago, the treatises on political economy still devoted much space to land—to its unusual properties, to the various forms of tenure which were used in various places, and to the formidable barrier to economic growth that a fixed supply of land constitutes. Thereafter, as agriculture rapidly declined in relative importance, it declined also in the attention it received in economics.

The interest of rent theory for general economics is nevertheless substantial. Any productive factor in inelastic supply receives a return that partakes in some measure of a rent. Almost every piece of capital goods—a building, a machine, a tool—may have an inelastic supply in the short run, and then its return is called a quasi-rent because of this similarity to the rent of land in the classical theory.

THE CLASSICAL THEORY

Let us assume, with David Ricardo, that the supply of land is absolutely fixed in supply, and that the country is a closed economy (no international trade). Then clearly the supply curve of land (or of lands, if they differ in significant respects, including locations) is a vertical line to the industry using land, and rent will be equal to the value of the marginal product of land. If the demand declines, rents will decline; if the demand rises, rents will rise. We may therefore say that rent is not a cost, but is determined by price—which is obvious enough when one reflects that we have lumped all uses of land together: then naturally land has no alternative uses.

247

The classical economists (who get this name from, of all people, Karl Marx) reached this result with another apparatus that is of some interest. They combined other inputs into a dose of "capital-and-labor" and postulated a schedule of diminishing marginal products of capital-and-labor on each quality of land. A typical set of schedules would look like Table 15–1.

Table 15–1

Marginal Product from Various Agricultural Lands

DOSES OF CAPITAL-AND-LABOR	QUALITY OF LAND					
	A	B	C	D	E	F
1	140	135	120	110	100	90
2	150	140	120	100	95	
3	160	135	115	90		
4	150	125	110			
5	140	110	105			
6	125	105	100			
7	110	100	95			
8	100	95				
9	96					

The land of the lowest quality that will yield a product equal to the cost of a first dose of capital-and-labor is called the extensive margin. This would be land E if the cost of capital-and-labor were 100 bushels; it would be D if the cost were 110 bushels. The last dose which is just remunerative on any type of land is called the intensive margin; at a cost of 100 bushels, on C land this would be the sixth dose, on A land, the eighth dose.

Rent is here the surplus over what the capital-and-labor costs. With competition the variable input receives its marginal product; in other words, the farmer will use variable inputs until their cost equals the value of their marginal product. If a dose of capital-and-labor costs 100 bushels, the A farmer will hire 8 units. His rent, which equals the sum of the marginal products $[140 + 150 + \cdots + 110 + 100 = 1075]$ minus the input bill $[8 \times 100 = 800]$, is 275, the maximum obtainable. We could also measure rent directly by the marginal productivity technique:

varying the amount of land, hold the number of doses of capital-and-labor constant. The result would be the same.[1]

One aspect of this proof that rent is not a cost is a source of misgivings: we lumped together all the uses of land, so by definition there are no alternative uses for land. Would not the same definitional trick turn wages into noncosts? Ricardo's answer, previously unpublished, is: but men must be paid enough to live and reproduce themselves, whereas the land will remain no matter how men behave. Only if we could add to the demand for labor the demand not to be born and live could we say there are no alternatives. A very good reply, but not wholly satisfactory. Some land also has the alternative of death: one may cultivate in such a manner that the fertility of a soil is destroyed. It is not so easy, however, to destroy location (for example, a central metropolitan location).

There are nonproduction (consumption) uses for all resources, however, and these compete for resources. Just as the alternative to labor is leisure, so the alternative to a commercial use of land is a personal use—a flower garden, a large parking lot for the wife, a putting green. What is true, again, is that the consumption uses of land take only a tiny fraction of land, whereas the consumption uses of a man's time are large. A large change in the demand for land could not be met in any significant degree by decreasing these nonproductive uses of land.

So it seems, again, that land is a little different: its aggregate supply is not highly elastic even in the long run. It is different, however, only in respects that do not matter much. Almost all real economic questions involve a particular use of land—growing wheat or trees, residential subdivisions, national parks, superhighways, and so on. Then the alternative uses of the land are significant, and one must recognize these costs (and, from another viewpoint, the substantial elasticity of supply of land).

Tobacco Quotas and Pure Rents

The tobacco acreage restriction program provides an interesting example of a pure classical rent problem. Some 500,000 farms have

[1] This is intuitively plausible. If we withdraw a unit of (say) D land, the product declines by 210 bushels. The 2 units of capital-and-labor can produce 200 elsewhere, so the net decline of output is 10—which is the rent of D land. More generally, look at the discussion of Euler's Theorem, p. 151.

allotments of acreage to grow tobacco, ranging from a fraction of an acre to hundreds of acres. These allotments are based primarily upon previous acreage in tobacco, and new allotments are almost unobtainable. If tobacco is grown on land without an allotment, the farmer must pay a tax of 75 per cent of the gross value (output times previous year's price).

The supply curve of tobacco land thus has three branches:

1. If the price of tobacco falls below the price at which more can be earned in other crops, the supply of tobacco land vanishes.

2. The supply is vertical in the ordinary range of prices.

3. If the price of tobacco rose to where 25 per cent of the receipts yielded a larger return than other uses of land, the supply of land would become immense.

We illustrate this curve in Figure 15-1.

Since allotments are in fixed supply, their annual value is set by the extra profit that may be earned by the cartel price implicit in the Department of Agriculture allotments. The capital value of an allotment is the present value of its expected flow of future profits—which obviously depends on tobacco prices, changes in allotments, and changes in taxes on tobacco not grown on allotment. This capital value was $1,600 to $2,500 per acre in 1957.[2]

Where tobacco farms are rented to tenants, the extra income due to the allotment goes to the landowner: tenants can earn no more in this line than in others under competition. When allotments are sold, the buyer pays such a price that he earns only the current rate of return on his investment: buyers of tobacco allotments can get no larger returns than buyers of other assets, under competition.

QUASI-RENTS

A quasi-rent is the return to a durable specific productive instrument. If the productive factor is durable, it will be used throughout its life provided it yields more than its scrap value. Since it is a

---

[2] See F. H. Maier, J. L. Hedrick, and W. L. Gibson, Jr., *The Sale Value of Flue-Cured Tobacco Allotments,* Agricultural Experiment Station, Virginia Polytechnic Institute, Technical Bulletin No. 148 (April 1960).

concrete productive instrument, say a house or machine tool, it is specialized to some degree, and cannot change into another form if the demand for its services falls.[3]

In the long run—in a period long enough to build new instruments or wear out old ones—the return to the instrument must equal the

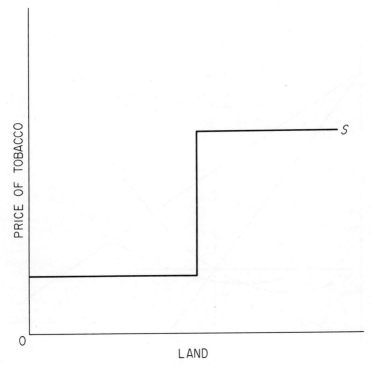

Figure 15-1

current rate of return on capital (with appropriate allowance for risk). If the machine's quasi-rents are less than interest plus depreciation, it will not be replaced; if the quasi-rents exceed interest plus depreciation more will be built until equilibrium is restored.

---

[3] If the future life of the instrument is shortened by using it in the present short run, this shortened life is a cost of current use, and is called the *user cost* of the instrument. The user cost must be covered by receipts to justify present use, but if it is covered, we reckon the gross returns inclusive of user cost as the quasi-rent.

The long-run *net* return on capital goods must yield the appropriate interest rate; their short-run *gross* return is a quasi-rent.

The graphical illustration of quasi-rents rests on the traditional short-run cost curves of the firm (Figure 15-2). The firm operates at output $0A$ under competition (with demand curve D_1), and the

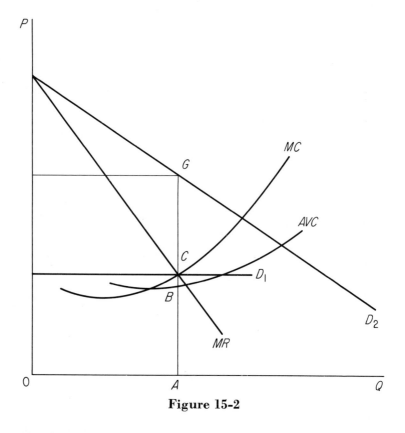

Figure 15-2

aggregate returns to nonvariable productive services are $0A \times BC$. Under monopoly conditions (with demand curve D_2) the aggregate quasi-rents are $0A \times BG$. These are quasi-rents inclusive of depreciation. If there are several capital goods involved, their separate quasi-rents would be determined by usual marginal productivity analysis.

The capital value of an existing capital good will be equal to the present value of its future quasi-rents. If the expected quasi-rents in year t are R_t, and the interest rate is i, the value of the good is

$$V = R_1 + \frac{R_2}{(1 + i)} + \frac{R_3}{(1 + i)^2} + \cdots + \frac{R_n}{(1 + i)^{n-1}} + \frac{S}{(1 + i)^n},$$

if it has an expected life of n years and a salvage value of S.

If we ask why the quasi-rents derived from a particular productive instrument over its entire life failed to return the original cost of the instrument plus the appropriate interest on this investment, the answer will always be: because of mistaken expectations at the time the investment was made. The entrepreneur must predict the future course of the supply and demand for the services of the instrument, at the time it is built. If the pace of technical advance is greater than he predicts, or the demand for the industry's output less, the quasi-rents will not return the investment plus the expected rate of return. There will probably be an asymmetry on the other side: if quasi-rents are larger than were expected, new instruments will be added until these extra quasi-rents are eliminated, so the extra gains will have a shorter duration than the unexpected losses. The asymmetry arises, of course, because one can build a machine or plant much more quickly than he can sensibly wear them out.

Since errors in prediction are inevitable, the entrepreneur must take account of them in his investment decisions. The more specialized he makes a machine, the more likely it is that its quasi-rents will not be what he expected, because the demand for a less specialized machine will be more stable than that for a specialized machine. Similarly, the less durable the machine, the sooner the investment can be disentangled if it proves to be unwise. We therefore expect to find the most specialized and durable instruments in the industries with the most stable demands and technologies.

AN APPLICATION OF RENT THEORY

The superhighways that are being built from the periphery to the center of American cities offer a variety of interesting problems for rent theory. Let us consider only the question: what is the magnitude and distribution of benefits?

To keep the problem concrete and simple, we shall study a city in a plane, with all laborers working daily in the central business district. A super highway is now built out to the periphery in one direction. It reduces the time required to drive to work by half for those living adjacent to it, and appropriately less for those who live near it. We can draw contour lines showing equal travel times to the central city before (with concentric circles) and after the highway is built (Figure 15-3).[4]

The cost of traveling to work is the sum of automobile costs and time and strain of driving. One hour of driving has been estimated to be worth perhaps $1.50 to the driver, and the automobile costs are perhaps $2.00 per hour. If the driver makes 240 round trips a year, the travel costs become $840 a year. As between two lots previously one hour from the city, that on the highway will have about $300 or $400 lower commuting costs per year,[5] and the value of that lot will be greater by the capitalized value of this sum, or perhaps $5,000.

If the population's demand for residential land was inelastic, the highway would lead to a reduction in aggregate residential land values, for the effective supply of residential land has risen (by almost half the diamond shape in Figure 15-3). But whatever the elasticity of demand for residential land, a new pattern of land values would emerge, and it would be governed (exclusively, in our simplified model) by the structure of transportation costs.

Since land becomes cheaper, the more distant it is from the city

[4] For those people living off the highway, the driving time from distance d (measured along a radius) will be one-half the former time plus the time necessary to cross over to the highway on an arc. If the angle between the radius on which they are located and the highway is θ, this circular distance to the highway is $d\theta$, so the boundary of the area benefitted by the highway is given by $d\theta + d/2 = d$, or $\theta = \frac{1}{2}$ (about $28°$). Within the benefitted area ($\theta < \frac{1}{2}$), the equal driving time contours (d') are given by solving $d'\theta + d'/2 = d$, or $d'/d = 2/(2\theta + 1)$. The area of the new territory within the 60-minute zone is found (by integration) to be about one-sixth of the initial largest circle.

[5] The $840 figure, and any based upon it, must be scaled down because there are on average perhaps 1.8 persons in each commuting car.

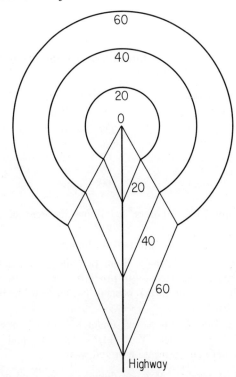

Figure 15-3

center, but building costs decline much less, if at all, as one moves out, land will be used in larger quantities relative to buildings. Hence the density of population will also decrease as the distance from the city center increases.

RECOMMENDED READINGS

Barnett, H. J., and O. C. Morse, *Scarcity and Growth,* Baltimore: Johns Hopkins University Press, 1963.

Lösch, August, *The Economics of Location,* New Haven, Conn.: Yale University Press, 1954.

Marshall, A., *Principles of Economics,* London: Macmillan, 1922, Bk. IV, Chs. 2, 3; Bk. V, Chs. 9–11.

Turvey, R., *The Economics of Real Property,* London: George Allen & Unwin, 1957.

PROBLEMS

1. Let there be 1,000 each of three types of farm, the marginal product schedules of which are as follows:

LABORERS	TYPE OF FARM		
	A	B	C
1	100	92	80
2	96	90	74
3	92	88	68
4	88	86	62
etc.	etc.	etc.	etc.

(a) If there are 7,000 laborers, determine the rent of each type of farm and the wage rate.

(b) Do the same when there are 14,000 laborers.

(c) Destroy one farm under condition (a), allocate its laborers to other farms, and measure the decrease in produce. The decrease (the marginal product of that type of farm) bears what relationship to the rent of that type of farm?

(d) A minimum-rent law is passed, under which no farm can be worked at a rent of less than 50. With 14,000 laborers, find the effect on aggregate product and aggregate rent and wages.

2. The marginal product of labor diminishes on a given farm as the number of laborers increases. Suppose that the total output of the farm is fixed, and that an improvement takes place in the methods of production. It may be of either type:

(a) The marginal product curve of labor is raised by a constant amount.

(b) The marginal product curve of labor is raised by a constant percentage. What will be the effect on rent in the two cases? Compare your answer with Marshall's (*Principles of Economics,* Appendix L).

3. Let the production function of tobacco be $Q = P^{2/3}L^{1/3}$ where P is labor and L is land. The demand for tobacco is $p = 100 - Q/100$. The price of labor is \$2 per unit; the rent of land in other crops is \$5 per unit.

(a) What will the price of tobacco be under competition? What will the quantities of labor and land be?

(b) Now reduce the land allotments by 10 per cent. What will happen to the price of tobacco? The value of an allotment of a unit of land?

chapter sixteen

Wage Theory

Labor is much the most important productive service—it receives four-fifths or more of total income even in an economy as well stocked with capital as the United States. Adam Smith said that the purpose of production was consumption; and because he said it, it is true. But it is almost as true that the conditions and nature of a man's work are a major part of his life.

This special significance of labor markets to its participants has led to many social controls, of which much the most important from the economic viewpoint is the prohibition of slavery. Even voluntary slavery—the making of enforceable contracts for the long term performance of labor services—is prohibited. The moral basis for this prohibition is beyond question, but it is worth noticing that like most desirable things, this prohibition has its costs. Since the worker cannot make enforceable long term contracts, he cannot shift the risks of unemployment to the employer. Since the worker cannot sell 10 years' services he may find it more difficult to borrow against future earnings, and therefore to equalize his income stream over time.

We shall concentrate attention chiefly upon relative wages in various occupations, but a few notes are added on population theory.

COMPETITIVE WAGE STRUCTURE

Competition tends to eliminate differences in rates of wages for similar workers in different occupations and geographical locations, for the worker who is in the job where wages are low will move to the higher paying job. This movement will raise wages in the market the workers are leaving, and lower them in the market the workers are entering.

Equilibrium will be reached in the occupational and geographical wage structure when the net advantages of all occupations open to the worker are equal. "Net advantages" embrace all the factors which attract or repel a worker, and the main content of the theory of competitive wage structure consists of the analysis of these factors. Aside from the wage rate itself, these components of "net advantages" are as follows.

Direct Occupational Expense

If a carpenter must provide his own tools, but an employee in a sash and door plant does not, the former must be compensated for the cost of his tools, in arriving at the comparative net advantages of the two occupations. Few questions are raised by this simple example,[1] but a host of subtle difficulties are raised by other cases—especially since the income tax allows one to deduct occupational expenses. Let us give just one example.

A professor buys books on the subject he teaches. Are they an occupational expense? Yes, since they are necessary to the work he does. Perhaps—but why doesn't he borrow them from the library? No, because he likes the subject and would buy at least some of them even if he were not a professor, say merely a college president. And what if he doesn't get around to reading the book? Should it then be charged to furnishings? These complications can in turn be made more complicated, but they should serve to suggest the shadowy boundaries separating occupational expenses from consumption expenditures.

Costs of Training

Suppose a young man of 17 just finishing high school is attracted by two occupations. In one (A) he will earn $3000 per year until age 65; in the other (B) he must first go to college for four years. How much should occupation B pay to offset the additional costs

[1] One is: why does not the employer pay directly for the carpenters' tools? The obvious answer is that a carpenter may work for many employers, but the provision of tools by workers is sometimes encountered in occupations in which workers do not change employers frequently. If a worker will use others' tools carelessly, it is to the benefit of both worker and employer to have the worker own the tools: the employer saves the costs of carelessness; the worker is better supplied with tools if their cost is less.

of training? These additional costs of training are two: the direct outlays for college (tuition, books, and so on); and the four year delay before his earnings begin. Living costs during college are not an additional cost because they are already covered by the income which will be earned if he enters A. He should go through the following arithmetic (assuming an interest rate of 8 per cent):

Occupation A

The present value of an annuity of $1 per year for 48 years is $12.1891, so the present value of lifetime earnings in A are $3000 \times \$12.1891 = \$36,567$.

Occupation B

1. The present value of an annuity of $1 per year for 4 years is $3.3121. If direct college costs are $1500 per year, the present value of these costs is $1500 \times \$3.3121 = \$4,968$.

2. The present value of an annuity of $1 per year for 44 years is $12.0771. When he leaves college, his lifetime earnings will have a present value of $\$S_B$ (his annual earnings) $\times 12.0771$. To discount this sum back four years to age 17, it must be multiplied by 0.7350.

The two occupations will therefore have equal present values of lifetime earnings if

$$S_B \times 12.0771 \times 0.7350 - \$4,968 = \$36,567$$

$$S_B = \$4679.$$

It may be noticed that the interest costs of the four year delay in receiving income in B account for most of the difference; elimination of direct school costs would reduce S_B only to $4,119.[2] Of course a lower interest rate would reduce the equilibrium difference.

To the investment in formal schooling we should also add the investment in acquiring knowledge and skill on the job. If for men of equal age and schooling one job will give experience in one year that increases future income by $20 a year (as compared to experience in the others), clearly it is a more attractive job, and hence in equilibrium earnings must be appropriately lower in this occupa-

---

[2] Since the various components of the difference are not additive, there is no simple way of breaking up the difference between the equilibrium earnings in A and B, but

1. The four year shorter working life in B leads to a present value per dollar of only $12.1891 - \$12.0771 = \$0.112$, or about 1 per cent less than in A.

2. The costs of training have a present value of $4,968, or about 14 per cent of the present value of earnings in A.

tion.[3] Even today in most economies the amount invested in acquiring training in the labor force far exceeds the amount invested in training through formal education.

The life pattern of earnings in an occupation invariably displays a rising and then falling section. The rising section is due to the increase in ability attributable to experience; the falling section is due to decreased competence and (since earnings depend upon amount of work as well as the wage rate) lesser amount (time or intensity) of work. The lengths of these segments will obviously depend upon the nature of the work, and the 1960 patterns given in Figure 16-1 display some of the variety we observe.

Instability of Employment

An occupation that offers steady employment will yield larger earnings, at the same wage rate, than one in which unemployment is at times substantial. If a postal clerk earns $4,000 a year, a similar occupation in which unemployment averaged 5 per cent would have to pay $4,000/0.95 = $4,211 to yield the same expected return. If the unemployment rate could be estimated accurately, and if men did not tend to stay unemployed longer when they received unemployment insurance, the premium for unemployment insurance would be $211 a year (plus costs of administration). The worker in the occupation with unemployment may be repelled by the uncertainties in employment and income, and demand an extra premium for undertaking them; we now turn to this question.

Uncertainty

Within an occupation there will be dispersion of earnings even for workers of the same age, training, and experience. Much of this difference will be due to differences in personal ability (a matter discussed in Chapter 18) but some will be due to other factors. Variations in unemployment have just been cited as one example, but others can be added: fluctuations in output due to weather (which affects many trades besides farming); fluctuations in amount of work due to business conditions; and so on. These forces will cause fluctuations over time in the average earnings for all members of the occupation.

---

[3] Earnings will be lower by the present value of the future income stream, which depends upon the age of the workers. If the age is 24, and 40 years of the additional earnings will be received after the year, at 8 per cent the present value is $221.

A second set of truly random forces will also operate. A factory may be closed by fire; only one salesman can get the huge order; personal injuries can hit haphazardly. These random factors have some tendency to cancel out over time, but they do not average

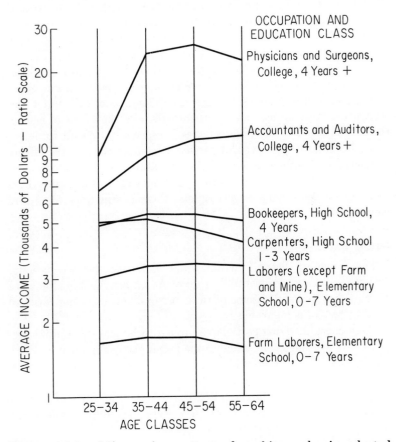

Figure 16-1. Life earning patterns for white males in selected occupations.

out completely in a human lifetime; if the standard deviation of the annual incomes in an occupation is $1,000, the standard deviation of a lifetime average is about $160,[4] so 2.5 per cent of the occu-

---

[4] The standard deviation of the mean is $\sigma/\sqrt{n}$, and n is taken here as 40 years. The standard deviation will be larger if, as is likely, there is some correlation of year-to-year fluctuations in earnings.

pation will have lifetime averages $320 above, and an equal number $320 below, the occupational average.[5]

Of two occupations with equal averages but unequal dispersions, which will be the more attractive? We may note one certain effect: the occupation with the greater dispersion will pay more in income taxes. A progressive income tax takes more from two incomes of $5,000 and $10,000 than it takes from two incomes of $7,500. This will make the occupation with the more stable incomes more attractive, since it is income after tax that workers will seek to equalize.

Putting this tax effect aside, there is no clear answer to our question. Some people believe in their good luck, and will prefer the occupation with larger prizes; others will take the opposite choice. How the market as a whole behaves is especially difficult to determine, because all observed dispersion is compounded of the effects of uncertainty and of differences in the ability of individuals, and dispersion due to the latter cause is not relevant to the choice. Fortunately our knowledge is incomplete; there is still work for future generations of economists.

Other Factors

The foregoing list of factors which influence the occupational structure of wages is essentially that of Adam Smith. Research since his time has quantified some of these factors, but it has not revealed many others of comparable size.

Differences in living costs have proved to be one substantial factor. Costs are consistently higher the larger the community in which one lives, so occupations which are concentrated in large cities must have higher average earnings than those concentrated in small cities. Thus it has been estimated that average incomes of lawyers would be 20 per cent lower if they were distributed among city sizes in the same proportion as population.[6]

Several other factors have been of comparable importance but of narrower scope. Prestige and social esteem are important in a few occupations, but more often the esteem attaches to those occu-

[5] This dispersion of individual earnings is independent of that due to fluctuations in average earnings of the occupation over time, which also may command a risk premium.

[6] M. Friedman and Simon Kuznets, *Income from Independent Professional Practice* (New York: National Bureau of Economic Research, 1945), p. 184.

pations in which earnings are large. Racial discrimination has had an important but declining influence.[7]

WAGES UNDER COMPETITION

The desire of workers to maximize the net advantages of work will lead them to jobs which yield the maximum sum of *net* monetary returns (that is, after deducting all differential costs) plus non-monetary returns (avoidance of risk, and so on). If all workers were of identical ability, we could be confident that the long-run supply curve of labor to any one occupation (and even more to any one locality) would be approximately horizontal. The only force that could be making for a rising supply price would be a rising cost of training, but we would rather expect training costs to fall as an industry grew and special training facilities (external economies) became feasible.

Since men are not of equal ability, and do not have identical preferences for types of work, it is possible that the expansion of an occupation will require men of lesser aptitude or liking for the work. This will be much more true of broad categories—construction workers, engineers—than it will be of specific occupations —carpenters, chemical engineers—because the specific occupation can draw workers from similar fields.

If there is a major expansion of demand for a large class of workers, as has occurred in the professional fields in the last hundred years, one would therefore expect some increase in the relative wages of this group. As men of lesser native ability entered physics or law or medicine, the cost of a unit of their services in these occupations would rise. The rise would be governed by the rise in training costs (and the higher costs of attracting men with stronger attachments to other work). Since the distribution of abilities is presumably more or less normal, with each small decrease in ability there will be a larger number of eligible workers, and the rise in wages should not be sharp. If we accept Adam Smith's view that there is little native difference between a porter and a philosopher, the rise of wages would be negligible. In actual fact, however, the earnings of professional classes have fallen relative to less-trained workers, for reasons we shall shortly discuss.

[7] See G. Becker, *The Economics of Discrimination* (Chicago: University of Chicago Press, 1957).

The long run in an occupation will have a length dependent chiefly upon the period of specialized training. If the number of lawyers has been stable and is now to expand, it will require three years before additional law school students can be graduated, and if the expansion is large it will take perhaps 5 or 10 years to restore lawyers' earnings to an equilibrium level.[8] Actually the period may be considerably shorter because lawyers are typical of most occupations in that many trained men practice law part time, if at all, and constitute an important source of supply if relative earnings rise in law.

The implications of these remarks are that the long run supply curve of an occupation will be highly elastic, and that the short run supply curve will be less elastic, the shorter the period and the more highly specialized the labor (as measured by its period of special training).

Hours of Labor. Even if the number of workers in an occupation is fixed, the amount of work they do will depend upon the hours of work. The efficiency of work will itself vary with hours, and there is some evidence that efficiency increases at first, but eventually diminishes so that at some level (varying with the work) the marginal product of another hour's work becomes negative. Whether this is at 50 hours or 100 hours a week is an open question.

For the individual worker earnings will vary either proportionately with hours, or in greater proportion if overtime is paid at a higher time rate. When the wage rate rises, he may wish to increase or decrease his hours of work. He will normally wish more leisure as his income rises, but the cost of an hour of leisure is the amount that he could earn, and with a rise in wage rates leisure has become more expensive.[9] Identifying these effects with income and

---

[8] Even then the structure of earnings as between inexperienced and experienced lawyers will not be in equilibrium. Equilibrium in the structure of earnings of experienced and inexperienced lawyers, however, must be defined in terms of the growth of the occupation: experienced lawyers will earn more relative to neophytes in a growing than in a stable occupation, because their number will be relatively smaller in the growing occupation.

[9] In an indifference curve analysis, let the axes be hours of leisure and money income. The budget line will have the slope of the wage rate, for it is defined by

$$\text{Money Income} = (24 - L) \text{ Wage Rate},$$

where L is hours of leisure. Even if leisure is a normal good, increases in wage rates can lead to larger or smaller amounts of leisure being consumed.

substitution, we may say that historically the dominant effect has been that of income: Hours have fallen by more than a third in the present century.

Often it has been said that in a modern industrial society the individual worker has no control over his hours of work, and indeed it is incongruous to visualize a worker strolling over to a foreman and saying, "I'm leaving the assembly line now, for I have just maximized utility." This is a pervasive problem in social life—it would be just as incongruous to order a ticket to the symphony orchestra concert in a town of 500 people.

The rigidity of social institutions, however, is easily exaggerated. There is much flexibility in hours in many occupations. Even within an occupation there are variations (teaching loads vary among colleges from 18 hours a week down to zero). If a majority of workers prefer longer or shorter hours, employers will find it profitable to cater to this demand because they can get better or cheaper workers by doing so. It will remain true that anyone whose tastes differ greatly from those of his fellows will be compelled to pay a substantial price (by way of choice of work) to behave differently.

NONCOMPETITIVE WAGES

There are two major noncompetitive factors which affect the wage structure, and we consider them in turn.

Opportunity and Wealth

John Stuart Mill created a doctrine of noncompeting groups in 1848:

So complete, indeed, has hitherto been the separation, so strongly marked the line of demarcation, between the different grades of labourers, as to be almost equivalent to an hereditary distinction of caste; each employment being chiefly recruited from the children of those already employed in it, or in employments of the same rank with it in social estimation, or from the children of persons who, if originally of a lower rank, have succeeded in raising themselves by their exertions. The liberal professions are mostly supplied by the sons of either the professional, or the idle classes: the more highly skilled manual employments are filled up from the sons of skilled artizans, or the class of tradesmen who rank with them: the lower classes of skilled employments are in a similar case; and unskilled labourers, with occasional exceptions, remain from father to son in their pristine condition. Consequently the wages of each class have hitherto been regulated by the increase of its own population, rather than of the general population of the country. If the professions are overstocked, it is because the class of society from which they have always mainly been supplied, has greatly increased in number, and because most of that class have numerous families, and bring up some at least of their sons to professions.[10]

The essence of this doctrine is that workers are not able to acquire the education and training necessary to enter the occupation much higher than those in which they were born. This vertical immobility is due to their inability to borrow the capital necessary to undergo the training required by the professional workers and skilled technicians. Even though the implicit rate of return on investment in such training is 20 or 30 per cent a year, it will persist if few families can afford to make the investment.

The extent of such departures in wages from complete equalization of net advantages may well have been very large even when Mill wrote, but data for that period are very poor. In 1910 we can give an example, which also serves to illustrate the method of finding the internal rate of return. College teachers earned an average of \$1,750 a year; urban public school teachers, \$700. Assume that the college teacher had four additional years of training, with expenditures on books, tuition, and so on, of \$200 a year. The present value of a public school teacher's income was

$$\frac{\$700}{i},$$

where i is the interest rate.[11] The present value of the college teacher's net income at the same age was

$$\frac{1750}{i(1+i)^4} - \frac{200([1+i]^4 - 1)}{i(1+i)^4}.$$

If we equate these two values, we find that public school teaching and college teaching were equally remunerative at an interest rate of 21.2 per cent a year.

---

[10] *Principles of Political Economy* (London: Longmans, Green & Co., Ashley Edition), p. 393.

[11] This is of course the value of a perpetual income of \$700. We could introduce the annuity values for limited working lives, but at a substantial cost in algebra—and the answer would not change much.

This is a rather high interest rate, judged by what (say) railroads paid in 1910 to get capital, and suggests that there were substantial limitations on peoples' ability to borrow funds for educational purposes. The estimated rate of interest is exaggerated to the extent that college teachers were more able, and possibly for other reasons,[12] but even with all adjustments the internal interest rate would probably be fairly high.

The great rise in family income, and the increased subsidization of schools, have reduced the importance of wealth as a requisite to education. Becker has found that the internal rate of return on a college education in 1950 had fallen to about 10 per cent, or to about 7 per cent after income taxes.[13] The doctrine of noncompeting groups still rules in many parts of the world, but has become almost obsolete here.

Unions

The major modern noncompetitive force on wages is the labor union. The labor union is for the labor market the equivalent of the cartel in the product market. Unions vary immensely in their effectiveness in raising wage rates. At one extreme, a few unions have probably reduced average wages slightly in the process of obtaining non-monetary returns for their members.[14] At the other extreme, unions have occasionally raised wages as much as 100 per cent above the competitive level but seldom has a differential of more than 25 per cent persisted for any length of time.[15]

The union faces problems in organizing a trade which are in principle much more difficult than those met in organizing a cartel. The number of workers is usually immensely larger than the number of firms, and the rate of turnover of workers in a craft is usually

[12] For example, college teachers were on average older, and their lifetime average salary would be in smaller proportion to that of public school teachers than 1,750/700.

[13] G. Becker, "Underinvestment in College Education?" *Proceedings of the American Economic Association* (May 1960).

[14] An example is the American Association of University Professors. To the extent that the A.A.U.P. has persuaded professors of the need for appointments on indefinite tenure (for life), which have certain costs to the employing institutions, they have substituted this security for larger money income.

[15] The basic work on the effects of unions on relative wage rates is H. Gregg Lewis, *Unionism and Relative Wages in the United States: An Empirical Inquiry* (Chicago: University of Chicago Press, 1963).

much higher than that of firms. In a legal environment as hostile to unions as the American law is to cartels, there would be no unions.

Even with a highly favorable legal environment, unions are now found chiefly in crafts and industries in which the labor market is relatively concentrated, either geographically or in terms of number of employers. Thus unions have usually been strong in mining and in fixed route transportation (especially railroads and airlines), both of which are geographically limited labor markets. The same explanation applies to the building trades, the clothing trades (New York), and printing (especially newspapers). The industrial unions are found chiefly in industries with few employers—automobiles, rubber products, primary metals, aircraft, and heavy electrical goods. In all these cases the union has not had to overcome the immense organizational task of organizing many small plants, or of having a large non-union sector of the industry whose competition would make substantial wage increases impossible.

Given control over the supply of labor, the extent to which a union can raise wage rates above the competitive level depends upon the elasticity of demand for the members' services. The rules of derived demand are fully applicable, so we should find that union effects on wage rates are larger,

1. The less elastic the demand for the product. The coal miners' unions could obtain higher wages before oil and gas became major rival fuels; the workers for Department of Defense contractors can get higher wages than those working for the commercial markets.

2. The poorer the substitutes for labor. For example, plasterers face the rivalry of plaster board so the demand for their services will be more elastic than that for plumbers. The chief long-run substitution for labor will of course come from capital equipment.

3. The less elastic the supply of other productive factors. The major instance of this rule is that existing capital goods are in inelastic supply in the short run, so union wages can rise substantially when an industry has much durable capital. In the long run most co-operating factors have elastic supplies, but mining land is an important exception.

Some illustrative estimates of the impact of unions on relative wages are reproduced in Tables 16–1 and 16–2. In these estimates

Table 16–1

Effects of Unions on Wages of Members Relative to Non-union Workers, Selected Occupations

OCCUPATION	YEAR	UNION EFFECT (AS PERCENTAGE OF NON-UNION WAGES)
Skilled building craftsmen	1939	25%
Common building labor	1939	5
Bituminous coal miners	1956–57	53
Motormen in local transit	1958	12
Barbers (large cities)	1954	19
Commercial airline pilots	1956	27
Seamen	1950's	20
Rubber tire workers	1936–38	14
Men's clothing manufacturing	1946–57	0

SOURCE: H. G. Lewis, *Unionism and Relative Wages in the United States: An Empirical Inquiry* (Chicago: University of Chicago Press, 1963), Chs. 3, 6.

Table 16–2

Effects of All Unions on Wages of Members Relative to Non-union Workers, 1923–59

PERIOD	AVERAGE EXTENT OF UNIONISM	EXCESS OF UNION WAGES OVER NON-UNION WAGES (AS PERCENTAGE OF NON-UNION WAGES)
1923–29	7–8%	15–20%
1931–33	7–8	more than 25
1939–41	18–20	10–20
1945–49	24–27	0–5
1957–59	27	10–15

SOURCE: Lewis, *Unionism and Relative Wages in the United States*, p. 193.

the measure of union effect is the excess of union wages over those of non-unionized workers of similar characteristics (age, sex, urbanization, training, and so on).[16] The tendency of collective bargaining to introduce short-run rigidities in wage contracts and hence for union wages to fall relative to non-union wages in periods of inflation, and to rise in periods of depression, is strongly evident in the economy-wide estimates.

[16] Since only relative wages are being studied, these effects are composed of (1) union wages higher than the competitive level, and (2) non-union wages lower than the competitive level, with weights of the proportions of the laborers in each class.

Members of the Rigor Club will have observed that nothing has been said about the objectives of union wage policy—no conventional maximizing goal has been invoked. None, in fact, has yet found general acceptance among economists. A maximum wage rate, which is presumably the goal of the individual worker, makes no sense for a union: this maximum would often be obtained when the absolute minimum number of workers was reached, and might involve a trifling membership.[17] The aggregate payroll of members of the union makes more sense as a short run goal,[18] but leaves open the question of how many members the union wishes—the very high wage rates of the United Mine Workers have been accompanied by a very drastic decline in the number of miners.

In fact the central problem of union wage demands is to determine the goal of union membership. The problem is formally analogous to that of a cartel in which a majority of the firms can vote to exclude any minority from an industry. The chief constraints on reducing numbers are (1) the majority of a given time does not wish to exclude itself, and may have an expected working life of 15 or 20 years; (2) often the union members wish to provide jobs for sons and sons-in-law; and (3) the larger the number of workers who are forced out of employment, the greater is the probability of their reappearance as non-union workers.

NOTES ON POPULATION

Since this book is by and for economists, we shall concentrate our discussion on the aspects of population change about which economists have something to say. They have a good deal less to say than they will in twenty years: population theory fell out of economics after the Malthusian theory was emphatically rejected by the experience of the nineteenth century in the western world, and only recently have economists returned to the subject.

Let us begin with the Malthusian theory, not only because it is the most famous of all population theories but also because it contains a portion of truth.

Thomas R. Malthus was led to his theory by an argument with

---

[17] The practice of featherbedding—requiring the employer to use more labor than he wishes for a given output—clearly substitutes more employment for higher wages.

[18] This goal is compatible with work-sharing, which unions often demand.

his father, who shared with Godwin the view that man would reach a state of perfection (which was not described as clearly as one might wish) if only evil and inept social institutions were abolished or amended. The son argued that there were deep natural reasons for the persistence of want and vice which would not be eliminated by any social reforms. It was a profitable argument: *An Essay on Population* (1798) became one of the most famous books in history, and has even been read by some people.

The essential Malthusian proposition was that labor has a constant supply price, governed by the conventional living standards of the working classes. Should the wage rate fall below this level, the operation of misery and vice would lead to a rise in death rates which in turn would eventually lead to a rise in wage rates to the conventional ("subsistence") level. Should the wage rate rise above this level, a decrease in deaths (and possibly earlier marriages, with a rise in birth rates) would eventually restore wages to the equilibrium level.

A rise in wage rates leads to a rise in population which in turn tends to lower wage rates, but suppose the demand for labor grew more rapidly than the supply? Not possible, said Malthus: the potential rate of growth of population far exceeds any conceivable rate of increase in the demand for labor.[19] In fact population could easily double every 25 years, as it had in the American colonies, but output could grow only "arithmetically," that is, by constant increments per unit of time. And the slightest knowledge of the laws of progressions, as he said, showed that the population series, 1, 2, 4, 8, 16, . . . would soon catch up with the potential output of the richest land, which would grow as (say) 25, 50, 75, 100, ...[20]

The error in the theory was double: population did not grow at an increasing rate as the standard of living rose in England, and the output of the economy did grow at a "geometrical" rate (on the order of 3 per cent a year).

---

[19] His own language differed: population would grow much more rapidly than the means of subsistence. But subsistence formed the demand (wages-fund) for labor.

[20] In fact, with these series, population = 2^n and output (measured in subsistence per head) = $25n$, the population outstrips the means of subsistence by the eighth generation—200 years for a society starting with a capacity for 25 times the initial population.

Yet there was the portion of truth. The cost of rearing children is surely *a* determinant of the patterns of birth rates we observe in a society, and so is the income derived from children's work.

Consider first costs. As between two families with equal real incomes, the cost of raising children will be less, the lower the relative costs of those goods and services which children consume relatively more of than adults. The money costs of rearing a child are, however, not easily determined. We can calculate the expenditures made directly on children, and by comparing expenditures on common items (housing, food) of families with the same incomes but differing family composition, we can also estimate the indirect costs of children. This latter component, however, will often be negative: thus families with an income of $5,000 spend less on recreation if they have two children than if they have none. Once one thinks of it, some such effect is inevitable: income is given, and as expenditures on children rise, other items (including savings) must fall. The cost of a child surely includes the value of the activities given up by the parents: the smaller amount of recreational activities, the lesser amount of travel, and so forth.

The expenditures on children (including or excluding foregone expenditures of parents) will rise with the income of parents, for two different reasons. The quality of the goods purchased for the child (room, food, clothing, education, medical care, and so on) will be better, the richer the parents—the child's standard of living will rise with that of the parents. The cost of a child with a given standard of living also rises with parental income: one large cost is the time of the parents, and this is more valuable the higher the (wage) income of the parents.

Consider then returns. The labor services of a child are of much greater value to a farm family than to a city family. Indeed children are a significant source of the labor force on farms. As late as 1950, for example, 44 per cent of the 16-year-old boys on farms were in the labor force, but only 24 per cent of urban boys were in the labor force. It is quite possible that on balance the returns from a child exceeded the costs for farmers until fairly recent times. The well-known excess of rural over urban birth rates is at least partly attributable to the differences in costs and returns.

Can we go a step farther and assert that the larger a family's income, the more children it will have? The historical evidence from the early nineteenth century until 1940 was emphatically against this modified Malthusian view: during a period of unprecedented rises in family income, average family size fell continuously. The cross-sectional studies also almost invariably show the poorest families having the most children. But the modest reversal of birth rates after 1940, and the suggestion of larger family size at highest incomes in some recent surveys, suggest the positive association. One explanation offered for these conflicting data is that effective knowledge of contraceptive devices is fairly recent and is possessed much more widely by the higher income classes, so observed family sizes may still depart from parental desires.

If the effect of income upon birth rates is in doubt, there is no doubt that higher incomes lead to lower death rates. The richer society avoids the consequences of malnutrition, acquires a larger medical service, and undertakes a large number of public health services (pure water systems, adequate sanitation, and so on). Large research efforts are devoted to special health hazards, as in the treatment of malaria, tuberculosis, and poliomyelitis. The decline of death rates in the last century and a half has been such as to increase life expectancy at birth to perhaps three times its level in ancient times and primitive modern communities.

RECOMMENDED READINGS

Becker, G., "An Economic Analysis of Fertility," in *Demographic and Economic Change in Developed Countries*, New York: National Bureau of Economic Research, 1960.

Hicks, J. R., *The Theory of Wages*, 2d ed., London: Macmillan, 1963.

Investment in Human Beings, Supplement to *Journal of Political Economy* (October, 1962).

Lewis, H. G., *Unionism and Relative Wages in the United States: An Empirical Inquiry*, Chicago: University of Chicago Press, 1963.

Marshall, A., *Principles of Economics*, London: Macmillan, 1922, Bk. VI, Ch. 3–5, 13.

Rees, A., *The Economics of Trade Unions*, Chicago: University of Chicago Press, 1962.

PROBLEMS

1. It is a view widely held among economic historians that the presence of a large amount of unsettled, tillable land was a "safety valve" up to 1890, because it provided unlimited employment alternatives. Assume that

there were no costs (and unimportant time lags) in any shift between industrial centers and frontier.

(a) Would the sudden loss of all unsettled land have affected wages, and if so, how?

(b) How would the presence of the "safety valve" affect the level of employment at any given time if industrial wage rates were (1) rigid (2) completely flexible?

(c) Would the workers have benefited more, during the period to 1890, if we had also possessed Canada?

2. Will a shift from a wage system which pays only for hours worked in a mine lead to different earnings than one based upon "portal-to-portal" pay?

3. So-called "truck" wage systems involve payment of wages to the worker in kind, usually at a store operated by the employer. Why would an employer institute this system of wage payment? Is it compatible with competition? [Compare G. Hilton, *Journal of Political Economy*, June 1957.]

4. Thornton's criticism of competitive wage determination (p. 10) can be dealt with now. Assume many identical firms and a common wage rate. One firm now cuts its wage offer to reduce its costs and selling price. Analyse the effects on wages and prices.

chapter seventeen

Capital and Interest

The tangible resources of an economy consist of its working population, or labor force, and its stock of useful things, which we call capital. On this all-inclusive definition, capital includes consumer goods (houses, furniture) as well as producer goods (plants, machines), even cash balances, and "natural" resources, such as land. A more formal definition of capital is: anything (other than a free human being) which yields valuable services over an appreciable period of time.

Capital, then, consists of all economic goods except people and perishables. People are excluded because they cannot be bought and sold—only their services can be traded. Perishables, such as a piece of pie or a band recital, are excluded because we do not wish capital to be a synonym for wealth—we wish to exclude commodities whose value simply equals that of their undiscounted services. A capital good, because it yields services over an appreciable time period, inevitably involves the appraisal of future as well as present services.

We can present the capital of a family or a firm or a nation by a gigantic inventory. It will contain commodities of great durability, like hydroelectric dams, and commodities of short life which are held as reserves, like stocks of coal. Such inventories have been made, at least for particular classes of capital goods: for example, American manufacturing corporations had total assets of $210 billion, or roughly $15,000 per worker, in 1958.

But capital can also be viewed as an accumulated fund of general productive power: as past income incorporated in particular physical forms, or as particular forms which will yield money income in the future. We can add the values of plants, and land, and houses, and inventories to obtain total wealth. The interest rate makes its appearance as the price of time, the price that allows us to compare next year's income with this year's income.

CONSUMPTION LOANS AND SAVINGS

Most capital is used by business firms for income-producing purposes, but it is convenient to begin the study of capital in a simple economy where capital is not productive. Let us assume that in this simple economy there is only one product: say, cocoanuts. They are grown on free land without the use of any capital equipment, and therefore labor is the only productive service. Since cocoanuts can be stored, however, we may still have saving and borrowing, which we shall now examine.

The choice between consuming this year's income (cocoanuts) this year or next year is an ordinary problem in consumer behavior, and can be analysed by the techniques presented in Chapter 4.

The consumer will have indifference curves relating consumption this year and each succeeding year. It is true that future consumption will be uncertain because future phenomena are uncertain: one may die before next year, or goods may be rationed, or new goods may appear, and so on. But one must make a forecast of uncertain events, and we shall assume that the consumer attaches a definite amount of utility to given amounts of consumption expenditure in future years.[1]

Let us consider only two years, although the analysis holds for any number. The indifference curves will have a conventional shape (see Figure 17-1). If the consumer has no accumulated wealth, he will have a budget line given by the present value of the two years' incomes,

$$\text{Present Value} = Y_1 + \frac{Y_2}{1 + i},$$

where i is the appropriate interest rate. At this stage in the analysis this interest rate is arbitrary, and can be positive, zero, or negative.

---

[1] The certainty of eventual death does not terminate this series of consumption expenditures, for a man attaches utility to the sums his heirs will consume. If he did not, the only insurance that men would buy would be annuities terminating at death.

For a given set of incomes, the budget line may be written,

$$Y_2 = (1 + i)(\text{Present Value} - Y_1),$$

so the slope of the budget line is $-(1 + i)$. If the initial incomes are Y_1 and Y_2 (which in our example is much smaller than Y_1), the individual will save S dollars this year, and spend $(Y_2 + S \times [1 + i])$ dollars next year, so S is his current saving. In the con-

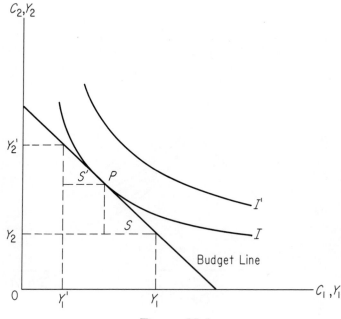

Figure 17-1

verse case, where Y'_2 is much larger than Y'_1, he will borrow S' this year, and consume $(Y_2 - S'[1 + i])$ next year.

If his income is equal in each year, how will he behave? In the absence of an interest rate, his incomes will lie along a 45° line (Figure 17-2). If he considered consumption in the two years to be symmetrical, the indifference curves (like I) would have slopes of -1 along the 45° line and equal amounts would be consumed each year. If the present consumption is preferred, the broken indifference curve (II) would have a slope numerically greater than 1,

and he would consume more this year than next. In this latter case
we would say that he has a positive time preference.

At any interest rate, and with any set of incomes (wages) in
the two years, an individual will wish to borrow or lend a specified
amount of cocoanuts. We may therefore construct a supply curve
(if he is a lender) or a demand curve (if he is a borrower). These

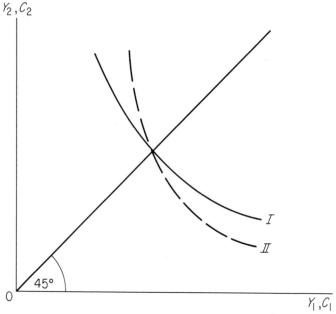

Figure 17-2

curves may be added together, to obtain the market supply and
demand and thus to determine the interest rate. The interest rate
can be positive or negative, as we illustrate in Figure 17-3.[2]

What factors determine whether a person will borrow or lend?
The foregoing analysis reveals two factors:

1. The pattern of income through time. If income is rising, the
consumer will normally wish to borrow in early years so that his
consumption will be more uniform through time. In terms of our

---

[2] No lender will pay more in interest to a borrower than it would cost
to store the cocoanuts for the year, however.

diagram, the larger Y_2 and the smaller Y_1, the larger the amount borrowed. Conversely, when income is falling, the consumer will save in early years for future consumption.

2. The interest rate. The higher the interest rate, the greater the cost of borrowing and the greater the return to lending. In terms

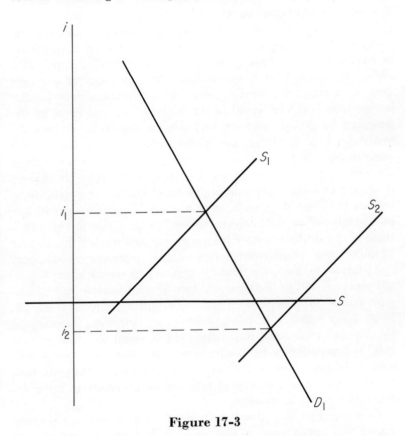

Figure 17-3

of our diagram, the higher the interest rate the steeper is the budget line, and the farther to the left will lie the tangency with an indifference curve.[3]

The absolute income of the consumer is often also introduced

[3] Strictly speaking, there is also a "wealth" effect in addition to this substitution effect: see Martin Bailey, "Saving and the Rate of Interest," *Journal of Political Economy*, **65** (1957), 279–305.

as a major factor, with the plausible expectation that richer people will save larger *fractions* of their income than poorer people. The large amount of statistical evidence that points in this direction has been shown to be a statistical illusion, however,[4] and the effect of income on saving is at best rather minor, if income is defined as a longer term average income of the family unit.

The tastes of people are a final factor of possibly major influence. Many economists have asserted that most people are "impatient" or have a "positive time preference" in the following sense: If a typical person had his choice of equal incomes this year and next year, or a larger income this year and a correspondingly smaller income next year,[5] he would prefer the latter pattern. Since by assumption we exclude all risks, and also all interest on savings, the preference is a simple myopia with respect to future needs. That some people are so constituted hardly seems disputable, but there are also extremely frugal people who seem to overvalue the future: it is said that the older families of Basel consider it profligate to live on the interest of one's capital—they believe one should live on the interest on the interest. No one has been able to prove that there is any strong tendency for the society as a whole either to over or under-value future consumption relative to present consumption.

At this state, then, the primary influence on saving in our cocoanut economy will be the time structure of wage income. In an economy with a stable population and stable national income, there will be as many people with falling incomes as with rising incomes and the supply and demand for savings will be equal at a zero interest rate. If population or per capita income is rising, more people will wish to borrow (because they expect rising incomes) than will wish to lend and a positive interest rate will be necessary to bring demand and supply to equality.

In a world of only two time periods, such as we have contemplated, if a family saves in one period, it dissaves an equal amount

---

[4] The explanation lies in the association of transitorily high or low incomes with transitorily high or low savings; see p. 35 above, and especially M. Friedman, *A Theory of the Consumption Function* (New York: National Bureau of Economic Research, 1957).

[5] Notice: we hold the total income of the two years constant. If interest were allowed on the first year's income, obviously everyone would prefer to receive both years' income now, and invest a portion to increase his aggregate income.

(after appropriate discounting) in the second period. Therefore the capital of a family equals its saving, or its total debt equals its net borrowing. Even in this case the equality is only superficial: capital is a stock, as of some instant of time, whereas savings are a flow per unit of time. Hence we must say that savings were N cocoanuts during a given period, and that capital was N cocoanuts at the end of the period.

Savings perform another function: they serve as a reserve for dealing with emergencies. The worker may become ill, or unemployed, and needs a reserve to carry him over this period. Or unusual expenses may arise. A highly negotiable reserve is therefore most useful. In a regime of uncertainty some savings will be made even in the absence of falling incomes, positive interest rates, or "time preference," simply to provide this reserve. In our simple economy, obviously the reserve must take the form of cocoanuts; in a modern society the function is served not only by money savings (a bank account or currency) but also by holding assets (a house, stocks) against which one can readily borrow.

We emerge, then with a savings function, in which the fraction of a family's income that is saved depends upon (1) the time pattern of the family's income, (2) the interest rate, (3) the extent of uncertainties against which reserves are to be held, and (4) individual "tastes" (family size, age, and so on). In addition, the *fraction* of income saved may vary with the absolute level of income, but apparently this dependence is weak at best. We note in passing that on average savings run at about one-tenth of national income in the United States, and that this annual increment of saving is on the order of 3 per cent of the existing capital stock.

INVESTMENT POSSIBILITIES

So far we have ignored any possibility of investment in our simple cocoanut economy. Let us now assume that it is possible to invest cocoanuts to yield a return (obviously in cocoanuts). For example, the laborers may go to school and learn more efficient methods to collect the cocoanuts, and the costs of attending school are paid in cocoanuts; here the investment is embodied in people. Or a machine of some sort is built to expedite the process of collection; here the investment is embodied in a tool.

It is in keeping with our general knowledge that the investment process is subject to diminishing returns. Whether the investment takes the form of machinery or (through training) increased skill of the worker, in our simplified economy, the enterprise will find that additional investment will yield diminishing rates of return. This diminishing return arises because of the diseconomies of scale for the individual firm, not because of diminishing returns to capital in the economy. (We shall discuss this latter problem below.)

In modern societies relatively little investment is undertaken directly by the individual saver—chiefly in consumer durable goods (homes, automobiles) and in small scale enterprises such as farming and retail trade. The great preponderance of investment is undertaken by specialized business enterprises or that most insatiable of all consumers, the state. Nevertheless we shall assume for a time that the individual consumer also makes investments. We do this chiefly out of deference for the precedent set by Irving Fisher, whom we are following in this area, but incidentally to save one diagram.

This individual has a variety of possible investment opportunities. On a farm, there is a whole array of machinery of varying productivity relative to cost, and in general each type of machine comes in different sizes and qualities. For the home builder (since this is also a form of investment), there are obvious possibilities of varying the size of the home, its attractiveness, its equipment and furnishings, and so forth.

If increments of investments are ranked in descending order of productivity, the yields in income next year for increments of investment this year will form an investment opportunity curve which is concave to the origin. That is to say: each additional equal increment of this year's income devoted to investment will yield a smaller increment of income next year.

If the interest rate at which one can borrow (and lend) is constant, the individual can borrow a dollar on promise to repay $(1 + i)$ dollars a year hence, so the budget line continues to have the slope $-(1 + i)$. The assumption of a constant interest rate, however, is implicitly a strong assumption: normally one would have to pay higher interest rates, the more he borrows, simply because the risk of default increases as the borrower's own equity becomes smaller relative to the loan. Our assumption of constant interest rates implies that there is no risk of default, and therefore that the outcome of investments is certain.

The equilibrium of the individual can now be presented in a single diagram (Figure 17-4). The investment opportunity curve VRF displays the combinations of incomes available in year 2 as one increases his investment (measured leftward from $0F$). The maxi-

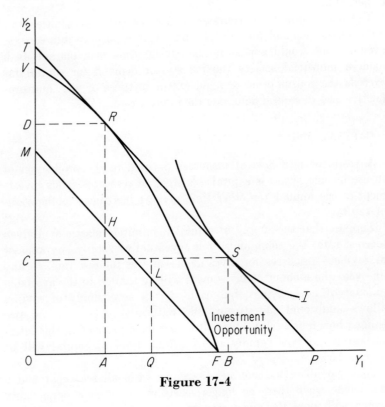

Figure 17-4

mum year two income is achieved where VRF exceeds the budget line FM by the maximum amount, or (what is equivalent) where a budget line TP, parallel to FM, is tangent to the investment opportunity curve. R is the optimum point, with investment AF, and returns beyond original investment plus interest of HR.

The consumer has a strong preference for income in year 1 relative to year 2, however, as the indifference curve is drawn. If the

individual's wage income in the two years is given by (say) point
L, the individual's budget line will be given by TP, which is the
budget line through L (or FM) plus the excess of returns over costs
on investment ($HR = MT$). The individual will require incomes
of AF (for investment) and $0B$ (for consumption) in period 1, so
he will borrow $AF + 0B - 0Q$, and repay this sum plus interest
in period 2.

The main point is, of course, that investment opportunities now
increase the demand for capital, and create a positive interest rate
even if none would appear in the consumption loan market. In a
modern industrial society the investment demand for capital far
exceeds the consumption demand except in times of war, and productive uses of capital dominate the interest rate.

CAPITAL AND INVESTMENT

Investment is a flow of resources devoted to the production of
future income, whereas capital is a stock of resources. Thus investment is the annual (or other time period) increment to the stock
of capital.

Suppose that the supply of capital is infinitely elastic at a given
interest rate: the community will (eventually) supply any amount
of savings—resources for investment—at this interest rate. In any
one year the amount of investment will be limited to the available
amount of new savings, but each year a new supply of savings
allows additional investment. We naturally seek to know two
things: how much capital will ultimately be demanded at this interest rate; and how rapidly this eventual level of capital will be
approached.

It is possible (but not necessary, as we shall see) that a day
will come when there no longer exists an investment opportunity
which will yield the given rate of return. The economy will presumably become stationary at this point: capital will only be
maintained. Moreover population must presumably have become
stationary, for continued population growth would surely create additional investment opportunities in both producer and consumer
capital goods. Hence only if a stationary economy eventually is
reached can we state that there is a definite schedule relating the
marginal product (rate of interest) of capital to its quantity.

The rate at which this stationary state is approached—the rate at which investment occurs—would presumably be governed by the availability of savings at the given interest rate. An attempt to maintain a higher level of investment would lead to a rise in interest rates which would ration capital demands to the most productive uses. But the annual investment is so small a part of the accumulated capital stock that we may infer that only a small rise in interest rates would be necessary to lead to a substantial curtailment of investment: the schedule of the marginal efficiency of investment, as it is called, would be fairly elastic.

In fact there may exist no equilibrium quantity of capital for a given interest rate, as we shall now see.

CAPITAL AND ITS RETURNS

The marginal returns to any productive service decrease as its quantity increases, by the law of diminishing returns. Capital is not necessarily subject to this law because, unlike all other productive resources, it takes on all forms, and therefore we cannot properly hold "other factors constant."

Consider the labor force. In a society which excludes enforceable long-run labor contracts, we nevertheless can invest in the quantity and quality of the labor force. Let us put aside the fact that a rise in births may come from rising wages. We may still increase the labor supply by appropriate investments in sanitation and public health measures, by industrial safety devices, and so on. We currently increase the quality of the labor force by immense annual investments in the formal education and on-the-job training of the labor force. It has been estimated, in fact, that the annual investment in labor skills in the United States substantially exceeds the investment in tangible capital goods. Although we can expect diminishing returns to capital when given workers are given more and more equipment, marginal returns will surely fall less rapidly when we increase the quantity and quality of the workers.

Or consider the natural resources—all the productive factors that the classical economists subsumed under "land." We no doubt will get diminishing returns from the more intensive cultivation of a given piece of land. But we can invest in methods of increasing the effective quantity or quality of land, just as we can for laborers.

Land can be improved by drainage, irrigation, and the like. Its accessibility can be increased by investments in transport systems. In the case of natural resources such as oil or coal we can invest in exploration for new deposits.

Finally, diminishing returns rests on a "given state of the arts"—a given level of technological knowledge. Yet investment in the discovery of new knowledge is still another way in which we may employ capital. The cultivation of "research and development" in recent decades has become so extensive that this type of investment is no longer likely to be overlooked or underestimated.

If labor and natural resources and the state of knowledge all change when capital increases, diminishing returns to capital are highly uncertain. In fact the theory of capital becomes a theory of general economic growth, and if the rate of saving from income is constant, an assertion of diminishing returns to capital is almost equivalent to an assertion of retardation in economic growth.

RECOMMENDED READINGS

Fisher, I., *The Theory of Interest,* New York: Macmillan, 1930.

Friedman, M., *Price Theory,* Chicago: Aldine, 1962.

Hirshleifer, J., "On the Theory of Optimal Investment Decision," *Journal of Political Economy* (August 1958).

Knight, F. H., "Diminishing Returns from Investment," *Journal of Political Economy* (March 1944).

Lutz, F., and V. Lutz, *The Theory of Investment of the Firm,* Princeton, N. J.: Princeton University Press, 1951.

PROBLEMS

1. An individual has wage incomes of $1,000 this year and $4,000 next year. His utility function is $U = C_0^{1/2} C_1^{1/2}$ where C_0 and C_1 are consumption in years 0 and 1. How much will he borrow in year 0 if the interest rate is 0? If it is 10 per cent?

2. The interest rate for loans for one year are 7 per cent at the beginning of 1900 and 5 per cent at the beginning of 1901. What will the interest rate be on loans for two years at the beginning of 1900?

3. The economy consists of an industry and the government. The industry borrows half its capital at 4 per cent (bonds) and raises the remainder at 8 per cent (stocks). The government can borrow at 4 per cent. Should

the government undertake investment projects which yield 4 per cent, or 6 per cent, or 8 per cent?

4. The determination of the interest rate under simplified conditions. (This example is due to Professor F. H. Knight.) Crusoe builds a tool in 25 days; it increases the productivity of his labor by 5 per cent and lasts 5 years (each year, for simplicity, has 300 days).

(a) What is the interest rate if the tool requires no repairs or maintenance and depreciation allowances do not yield interest?

(b) What is the interest rate if the tool requires 5 days of repairs a year and cannot be used during this time?

(c) What is the interest rate under the conditions of part (b) if depreciation allowances can also be invested to yield the current interest rate?

chapter eighteen

The Size Distribution
of Income

Although the size distribution of income—the distribution of households by size of income—has been the most important question of public policy over long periods and in many countries, it is, of all the major topics discussed in this book, the one that has been studied least. There are a thousand thousand criticisms and defenses of the income distributions of various societies, but they have emphasized moral and ethical factors. These factors *are* important, but so too are the economic aspects of the problem, and they will be our sole concern here.

The income of a household consists of its labor income and its property income. Of these the labor incomes are much the more important, accounting for something like four-fifths of national income.

LABOR INCOMES

The labor income of a household consists of the sum of the labor income of its members. Let us begin, however, at a still more basic level, the individual worker.

Earnings of the Individual

Suppose all men in an occupation to be strictly homogeneous: they have the same abilities, training, and experience (which is really training in a broad sense), and are therefore of equal age, and when employed work equally long with equal intensity. Their wages would still differ because of chance: luck in an older language, random fluctuation in a newer.

These components of luck are infinitely numerous but we may classify them into roughly three groups:

1. Personal factors—vicissitudes of health and accident.
2. Employer factors—vicissitudes of any one employer, both physical (fire, flood) and economic (bankruptcy).
3. Market factors—vicissitudes in finding new jobs, or getting the best rate of pay for given work.[1]

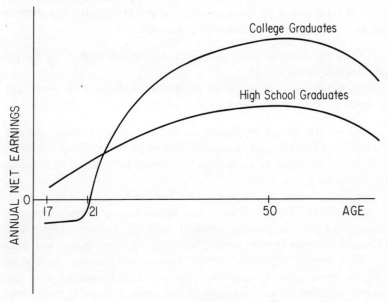

Figure 18-1

If we could find a group of identical workers, the differences in their earnings would measure these factors.

Let us now still keep the members of the occupation identical in abilities, and move them back to age 17, when they have just finished high school. Then let each young man be offered the choice of two kinds of future income streams (Figure 18-1). One stream begins immediately—he enters the labor force and begins to earn. The second stream assumes that he goes on to college: for 4 years

[1] On this last, see my "Information in the Labor Market," *Journal of Political Economy*, Supplement (October 1962).

it is negative (by the amount that his tuition, books, and so on, exceed part-time earnings), and then positive. Each stream rises after formal education is completed because men learn also by working, and then eventually declines after some age, as their energies and abilities decline.

These income streams can have the same discounted value on the day of graduation from high school,[2] and in competitive equilibrium the discounted values will indeed be equal. The life-time earnings, as represented by these present values, are identical. Yet there are now two additional sources of dispersion:

1. The variation in earnings among individuals with given formal education because of age.

2. The variation in earnings among individuals with given age because of formal education.

In fact we should not emphasize *formal* education, because one can learn also at work, and in most societies in the world much more training is obtained at work than in schools, if we measure training by its effect on earnings.[3]

We have reached an interesting conclusion. If the men in an occupation were of identical ability, and worked equal periods and with equal intensity, the present value of their life time earnings would be equal (chance factors aside), but their earnings in any one year or short period of years would display substantial dispersion. Chance factors would also be relatively less important over the entire working life, although there would not be complete cancellation.[4]

There would in fact be a larger dispersion, even under these assumed conditions of identity of worker's competence at age 17, than this analysis suggests. Some dispersion is essentially nominal, and if we could correct earnings for differences in costs of living and costs of working they would vanish. Examples are the higher wage

---

[2] Here we put aside the problem of borrowing to go to school, by assuming that loan funds are available at a given interest rate.

[3] See p. 259 above.

[4] Cancellation would be incomplete because of death and serious ailments (which we have put aside) and more generally because fluctuations in earnings in successive years will not be uncorrelated. The law of large numbers would ensure virtual elimination of chance from life-time earnings if the various events were independent.

rates in larger cities, where costs of living are higher,[5] and the higher wage rate of employees who use their own cars on company business if they are not compensated directly. These sources of nominal dispersion cannot be wholly eliminated at present (for example, there is no satisfactory index number of the cost of living in communities of different sizes), so they must be kept in mind in interpreting present day data.

Moreover, we must notice one final source of dispersion of earnings compatible with equal abilities. Men differ in their comparative desires for money and leisure, so one man will work 40 weeks, another 50, or one will work overtime when another does not. These choices will yield different money incomes but may represent equal streams of utility.

When we enlarge our view to compare different occupations—still retaining the assumption of equal abilities—most of the differences will still be of the kinds we have just discussed. For example, a college professor will earn more than a highschool teacher of equal ability because the former has invested for three or four years in getting a Ph.D. Similar remarks can be made about duration of work, on-job training, and size of community. But in addition we encounter two other sources of dispersion.

Some occupations have incomes which are much more stable over time than those of other occupations. The self-employed worker is much more subject to fluctuations in demand than the salaried worker, so the annual earnings of the former will be higher in good years and lower in poor years. Over a period of, say, five years, of course, most of this difference will be eliminated, but annual data will display large differences. In addition it is generally believed that these occupations with unstable incomes repel workers, so an additional premium must be paid for bearing these fluctuations.

We have not introduced the most obvious of the sources of inequality of earnings; differences in "ability." How much difference

---

[5] The higher cost of living in a larger city rests basically on the higher costs of land. Housing costs being higher, wage rates must be higher by compensating amounts (to maintain equality of real earnings with those of workers in smaller cities). Hence all personal services (medical care, haircuts, and the like) will also be more expensive in larger cities. The fact that enterprises in large cities can successfully compete with those in smaller cities despite the higher wage levels is due to the external economies obtainable in large economic centers.

there is in abilities of men, no one can say. In fact, ability is not measureable: it consists of more than strength, or I.Q., or creativity, or courage, or tenacity, or a liking for work, or personal charm, or handsome appearance, or unusual vocal cords. The only measure of ability we have, in fact, is the variation in earnings that remains after we have subtracted out the effects of education, age, community size, and other measurable factors.[6] But then we are mixing chance factors with ability, and in plain fact, no one knows how to separate this remaining dispersion into luck and ability. Individuals have the same difficulty: poor bridge players usually say they never get good cards.[7] Since able people congregate in certain occupations—physicists are on average more able than electricians—the aggregate effect of ability (and luck) on income is much greater than the effect within an occupation.

The list of factors making for differences in money income in any year is formidably long, but it is not complete. The differences in ability and luck aside, we have discussed only differences due to voluntary decisions of men, which would exist in fully competitive markets. In addition, any real society will exhibit dispersion because of the workings of several other forces.

First, there will be differences in returns due to monopoly power. If a labor union, or a cartel, succeeds in raising the incomes of its members above the competitive level, an additional source of dispersion will be created. We shall not attempt any direct estimate of the magnitude of such forces,[8] but for select groups earnings can be 20 or 50 per cent higher under favorable conditions than competition would allow.

Second, there are differences in earnings due to market imperfections, quite aside from monopoly. The following are characteristic:

1. It may be that the rate on investment in training is much higher than the going rate of interest for investments of comparable risk, and yet many people may not be able to borrow the funds to make this investment in themselves. We have indicated that this was probably an important source of dispersion at earlier times

---

[6] Since ability is surely positively correlated with education, and possibly with other factors we have enumerated, some of its effects will be attributed to these other factors.

[7] In 1,000 hands, the influence of the cards is negligible. If men lived 1,000 years, we could confidently ascribe their differences in earnings to ability.

[8] See the discussion in Chapter 16 of the effects of unions.

in the United States, and it is still an important source in many economies. We should also notice, however, that there is substantial over-investment in the training of many people, provided by parents acting on parental rather than economic motives.[9]

2. Imperfect foresight leads people to acquire training which proves to have a low value, as when a skilled craft is displaced by a technological advance. There are corresponding gains from unexpected increases in demand but they are of shorter duration since one can train additional specialists in a few years.

3. Discrimination against certain groups will lower their incomes—the conspicuous instances in history have of course been racial and religious groups.[10]

We do not add another phenomenon popular with detergent box orators, nepotism. If an able man bequeaths high office to an incompetent son, this is generally a bequest of property income disguised as wage income, and the son would be richer if the high office were filled with an able appointment and the additional income of the enterprise were paid to the son in dividends. Bequest is an influence on real wage income only when the job, rather than the control of the enterprise, is owned by a person.[11]

Some Approximate Magnitudes

We cannot measure each of these sources of dispersion with great accuracy but it is useful to make at least a few rough estimates. We shall employ two measures of dispersion:

1. *The Lorenz Curve.* Income recipients are ranked from lowest to highest, and against their cumulative number we plot their cumulative percentage of income received. This curve would be a line with a slope of 45° if all incomes were equal, for then K per cent of the recipients would receive K per cent of the aggregate earnings.[12] The coefficient of inequality for a Lorenz curve is the area

[9] A fond parent who invests $10,000 in a child's education with an internal rate of return of 1 per cent, would of course increase that child's money income if instead the $10,000 were invested in bonds and the child were given the income instead of the education.

[10] See, for example, the article on Jews in *Palgrave's Dictionary of Political Economy*.

[11] Such instances exist, of course, even outside politics. It used to be said that one could not become a professor in certain European countries unless he married the previous professor's daughter. The progress of economics in these countries was not always inconsistent with this hypothesis.

[12] See mathematical note 15 in Appendix B.

between the curve and the diagonal line (see Figure 18-2) divided by the area under the diagonal. It obviously has a maximum value of one (when the lowest 99.999 per cent receive no income) and a minimum value of zero (when all incomes are equal).

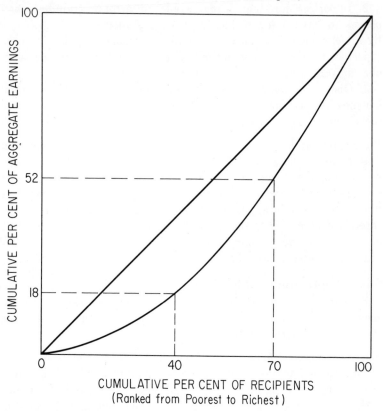

Figure 18-2.   Lorenz curve for hypothetical income distribution.

2. *The Standard Deviation and the Coefficient of Variation* (which is simply the standard deviation of a distribution of incomes divided by its mean).

The Lorenz curve is the more popular measure but the additive property of variances is a real advantage.[13]

---

[13] That is, if given incomes have two sources of dispersion, say age and education, measured by σ_1^2 and σ_2^2, the dispersion of incomes due to the joint action of both sources is:

$$\sigma^2_{1+2} = \sigma_1^2 + \sigma_2^2 + 2\sigma_1\sigma_2 r_{12}.$$

We can illustrate the magnitudes of the dispersions due to age and education from the earnings data in the 1960 Census. We choose salesmen, and the age-earnings and education-earnings relationships are given in Figures 18-3 and 18-4.[14] The two measures of dispersion may be applied to each relationship. The coefficients of variation[15] are:

$$\text{Age}: \frac{\sigma}{M} = \frac{\$1,011}{\$5,714} = 17.7\%,$$

$$\text{Education}: \frac{\sigma}{M} = \frac{\$1,001}{\$5,502} = 18.2\%,$$

and the Lorenz curves are given in Figures 18-5 and 18-6. Finally we can combine age and education, using a two-way classification of workers of various ages and levels of schooling. The coefficient of variation then becomes

$$\frac{\sigma}{M} = \frac{\$1,319}{\$5,717} = 23.1\%,$$

and the Lorenz curve is shown in Figure 18-7.

Dispersion or inequality has no natural scale by which we can say that a given number is large or small. Yet a guide is necessary to interpret a Lorenz curve or standard deviation. In the present case the natural basis for judging the amount of dispersion due to age or education is the total dispersion of earnings of all salesmen working full time. This underlying Lorenz curve has been

[14] These average relationships were calculated from a regression equation based on the 0.001 sample of the 1960 Census. The equation is:

$$W = -13,190.02 + 87.01X_1 + 319.29X_2 + 375.07X_3 - 3.83X_3{}^2 + 16.51X_4$$
$$ (12.41) \quad\quad (43.31) \quad\quad (46.46) \quad\quad (0.54) \quad\quad (9.53)$$
$$+ 1,498.88X_5 - 261.51X_6 + 1,342.02X_7.$$
$$(814.49) \quad\quad (358.69) \quad\quad (342.04)$$

$$(R^2 = 0.190; N = 1,802)$$

The variables are:
W = wages and salaries, 1959 (M = mean),
X_1 = weeks worked in 1959,
X_2 = years of school completed,
X_3 = age,
X_4 = hours worked during census week,
X_5 = race (1 = white, 0 = nonwhite),
X_6 = small city—population 50,000 or less (0 = no, 1 = yes),
X_7 = large city—population 250,000 or more (0 = no, 1 = yes).

[15] The coefficients of variation and Lorenz curves are determined by taking the wages at various ages or levels of schooling (Figures 18-3 and 18-4) and weighting them by the number of salesmen of each age or each level of schooling.

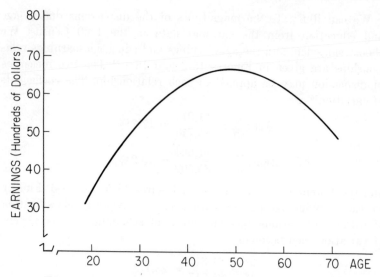

Figure 18-3.   Earnings of salesmen by age (1960).

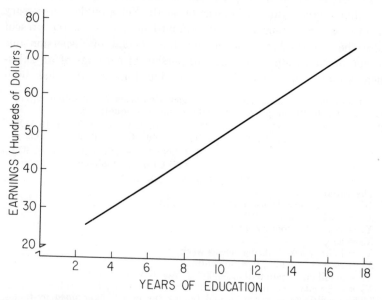

Figure 18-4.   Earnings of salesmen by years of education (1960).

drawn in Figure 18-8, and it can be calculated that the total coefficient of inequality is 0.287, and that of age-and-schooling 0.128.
These two variables account for 45 per cent of all inequality.

We could continue to add variables, such as weeks worked, size
of community, and race. Dispersion in weeks worked, in fact, has

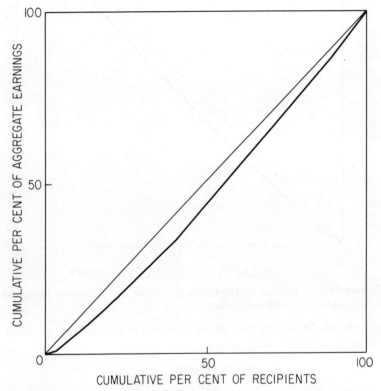

Figure 18-5. Lorenz distribution of earnings of salesmen identical
in all respects except age.

an important effect on dispersion and it it not presented quantitatively only because it calls for as much explanation as wage dispersion itself.

It may be instructive, instead, to present the measures of inequality for salesmen in comparison with that of all male workers.
Here again we include only those 18 and over who work full time

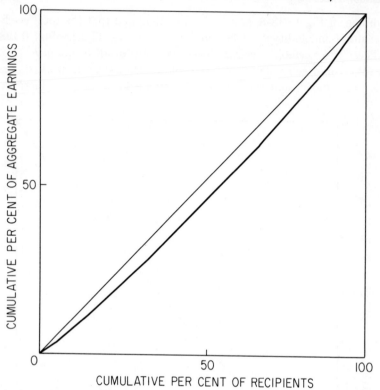

Figure 18-6. Lorenz distribution of earnings of salesmen identical in all respects except education.

(that is, 50–52 weeks) in 1959, so unemployment has been set aside. The coefficients of variation are:

$$\text{Salesmen} = \frac{\$3,609}{\$6,262} = 57.6\%,$$

$$\text{All workers} = \frac{\$3,142}{\$5,781} = 54.4\%.$$

The all-wage-earners Lorenz curve is also shown in Figure 18-9. The two groups have virtually identical degrees of inequality of income distribution.

Family Wage Income

Families display an astonishing variety of patterns in number of wage earners, but the dominant pattern in multiple earner fam-

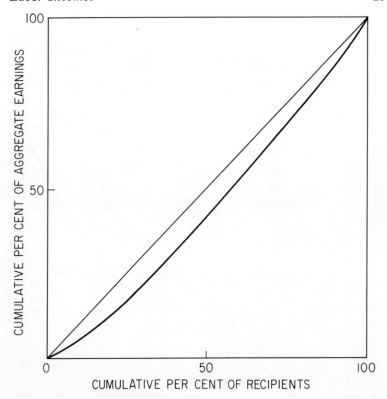

Figure 18-7. Lorenz distribution of earnings of salesmen identical in all respects except age and education.

ilies is of course for the husband and wife to work.[16] This is the only class of multiple earners we shall discuss.

Leisure is a so-called normal good—people consume more leisure as their income rises, prices remaining constant. We should there-

[16] The 1960 Census gives the following pattern of families (defined as two or more related persons):

FAMILY EARNER TYPE	NUMBER (1,000's)	1959 MEDIAN INCOME
None	4,840	$1,499
One	23,465	5,179
Husband	19,614	
Wife	1,318	
Single Family Head	2,530	
Multiple	16,825	7,013
Husband-Wife	11,172	
Other	5,653	

In addition 13.2 million unrelated individuals had a median income of $1,596.

fore expect fewer wives to work in the labor force as the incomes
of husbands rise. The facts are partially, but only partially, in
keeping with this expectation. If we compare different families at
a given time, it is generally true that the labor force participation
rate—a gracious phrase denoting the fraction of a given class of

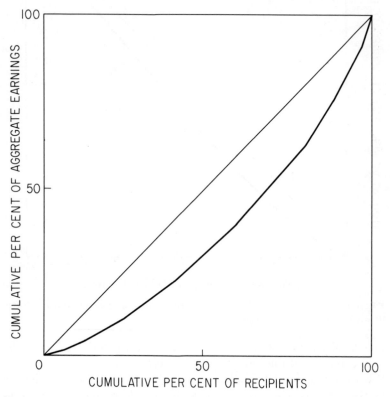

Figure 18-8. Lorenz distribution of all fully employed male
salesmen.

women who are in the labor force—varies inversely with the husband's earnings. We illustrate this characteristic finding from the
1960 Census (Table 18–1).

But this is only half the story. Over the last hundred years, the
share of women in the labor force has been rising rapidly while
average real earnings of both male and female workers have been

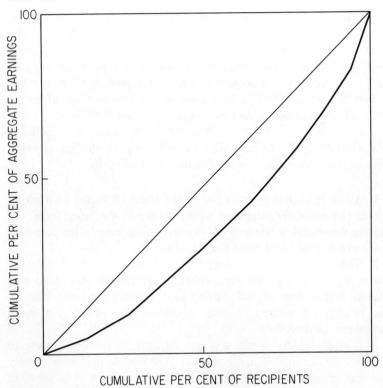

Figure 18-9. Lorenz distribution of all fully employed male wage earners.

rising about 2 per cent a year—over time the family appears to have bought less leisure for the wife. The reconciliation with the opposite finding in the cross-sectional data is to be found in the

Table 18-1

Labor Force Participation Rates of Wives in White, Non-farm Families with Husband Present

FAMILY TYPE	EARNINGS OF HUSBAND IN 1959, 1960, OR 1961					
	Under 1,000	*$1,000 2,000*	*2,000– 3,000*	*3,000– 5,000*	*5,000– 7,000*	*Over 7,000*
Children 6–17	53.9	49.2	49.3	47.0	39.2	28.2
Children Under 6	32.3	24.6	24.5	21.5	16.0	10.7

nature of the alternatives to work in the labor force. For a wife, the alternatives are in fact two: leisure; and work within the home. Leisure is undoubtedly a normal good, and if we could put aside work within the home, we would expect a rise in wage rates to lead to a reduction in women's labor force participation (as has in fact taken place with males) because the income effect of higher wage rates would dominate the substitution effect.[17]

The productive work of women within the home has modified this relationship.[18] The increasing labor force participation of wives with secularly rising incomes is due to three main forces:

1. A rise in real wages is a rise in the alternative cost of working within the home, as compared with working in the labor force and buying household services. This secular rise in wage rates therefore leads to a higher labor force participation.

2. The advances in technology have reduced the costs of purchasing many services previously performed within the household (including preparation of clothing and food, laundry services, cleaning, and so on), and hence increased the comparative efficiency of work for money income.[19]

3. Young children create a major demand for household services not cheaply obtainable in the market. The secular decline in family size has greatly increased the share of time women may serve in the labor force.

The presence of multiple earners affects the distribution of family income in various ways. If the labor force participation rate of wives were independent of that of husbands, the effect of their work would be to increase, and very substantially, the dispersion of family earnings. In fact, two relationships between wives' work and husband's earnings modify this. One force we have already noted:

[17] The cost of leisure is foregone earnings, so a rise in wage rates is a rise in the cost of leisure, which would lead to a decline in leisure if real income were held constant.

[18] For a fuller analysis, see J. Mincer, "Labor Force Participation of Married Women," in *Aspects of Labor Economics* (New York: National Bureau of Economic Research, 1962).

[19] The income tax has been a counter force: if a wife's earnings are taxed at a marginal rate of (say) 30 per cent, a wife must earn $100 in the market to purchase $70 worth of household services.

the lower the husband's income, the larger the share of wives who enter the labor force. In addition, when a family has a temporarily low income—perhaps because of ill health or unemployment of the husband—wives enter the labor force to offset this reduction: Mincer's studies indicate that there is a strong negative relationship between wives' labor force participation and transitory components of income. In fact he finds that the dispersion of earnings of family heads and of entire families are essentially equal.[20] The incomes of families with both husband and wife present had a coefficient of inequality of 0.327 for families with only husbands working in 1959, but there was slightly less inequality (0.309) among families in which both husband and wife worked.[21]

PROPERTY INCOME

The property income of a household has two main sources: current saving, and inheritance. These components will first be discussed separately, and then their comparative roles will be discussed.

Current Saving

Let us assume that all saving consists of temporary postponement of consumption, but that no savings survive at the death of the saver. This result can be achieved by investing the savings in annuities which terminate at death. Then in a society in which everyone had the same labor earnings and saved the same fraction each year for (say) 25 years, and then dissaved for 25 years, the distribution of property income would depend only on the age distribution of the population. People entering and leaving the labor force would have no property, and those at the terminus of the period of saving would have maximum property accumulation—and property incomes would be proportional to property if all investments yield the same rate of return.

[20] See "Labor Supply, Family Income, and Consumption," *Proceedings of American Economic Association* (May 1959), 574–83.
[21] These measures, based upon the 1960 Census, unfortunately include also property income. The coefficient for all families, regardless of number of workers, was 0.333.

We may calculate our measures of dispersion on these simple assumptions, for an equal number of people in every age class.[22]

	INTEREST RATE	
	5%	*10%*
Coefficient of Variation of Interest Income	58.6%	65.1%

The corresponding Lorenz curves are shown in Figure 18-10. It will be observed that these distributions have roughly the same dispersion as labor incomes within an occupation.

In the foregoing example, if we calculated the lifetime interest incomes of each person we would find them perfectly equal, so the substantial inequality we observe is due to the brevity of the time unit (one year) for which income was observed. For such long run phenomena, it would be more appropriate to compare wealth (the value of income streams) than income in any year. If we calculate the present value of the income from savings at (say) age 70 we would find that it was equal for all individuals.

If one goes to an even deeper concept of income, it is not clear that the distribution of "real" income is changed by savings. Suppose two men with identical wage earnings prospects embark upon lifetime savings programs, one saving 5 per cent of wage income, the other 10 per cent. If the choices were voluntary, we must conclude that the extra interest income foregone by the person saving 5 per cent was at least offset by the pleasure derived from earlier consumption. The lifetime distribution of "real income" or utility could be perfectly equal even though lifetime money incomes differed substantially.

[22] The calculations are based upon a table of which the following are sample entries:

		5%		10%	
AGE	CURRENT SAVINGS FROM EARNINGS	ACCUMULATED SAVINGS	INTEREST INCOME	ACCUMULATED SAVINGS	INTEREST INCOME
21	$100.00	$100.00	$5.00	$100.00	$10.00
22	100.00	205.00	10.25	210.00	21.00
45	100.00	4,772.71	238.64	9,834.69	983.47
46	0	5,011.35	250.57	10,818.16	1,081.82
47	0	4,906.35	245.32	10,708.15	1,070.82
60	0	2,953.46	147.67	7,740.51	774.05
65	0	1,804.69	90.23	5,189.93	518.99

The 5% return yields an annuity of $355.57 per year, and the 10% return $1,191.83 per year, starting at age 46.

Both the rate of accumulation of wealth and the property incomes drawn from wealth are much influenced by differences in rates of return on investments. If we make a single investment of $100 at rates of interest uniformly distributed from 2 per cent to 12 per cent, the Lorenz curves for accumulated sums after 5 and

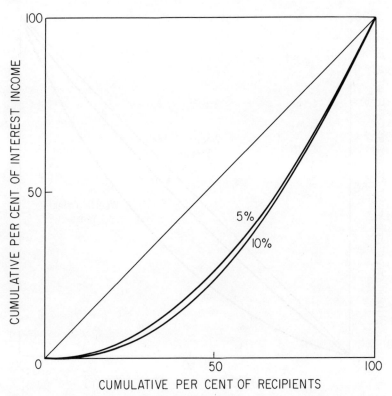

Figure 18-10. Lorenz distribution of interest income generated by life pattern of saving and dissaving in population with uniform annual savings (savings invested at 5 and 10%).

20 years are presented in Figure 18-11. The increase of inequality with the passage of time becomes remarkably great. Almost no work has been done by economists, unfortunately, on the extent of dispersion in rates of return over long periods, and the stability of these rates, for various investors. It is widely believed that higher interest rates are usually earned by the smaller investors in areas

where market credit facilities are poor, and if true this would argue that dispersion in interest rates offsets to a degree dispersion in wealth.

Of course the distribution of accumulated savings, and even more of property income, is more unequal than the foregoing argument

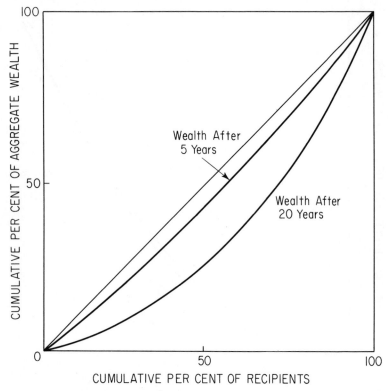

Figure 18-11. Lorenz distribution of accumulated wealth at interest rates varying from 2 to 12% (after 5 years and after 20 years).

would suggest. The labor incomes of individuals, the main source of current savings, have a range of the order of magnitude of 100 to 1 instead of the equality assumed above. We lump together interest, dividends, rents, and other property incomes: individually they will of course be less equally distributed than they are in the aggregate.

Inherited Wealth

Inherited wealth displays a much larger degree of inequality than any of the other income sources so far considered. Our argument that accumulated savings which are equal over long periods of time are very unequal in a given year holds with special force for inheri-

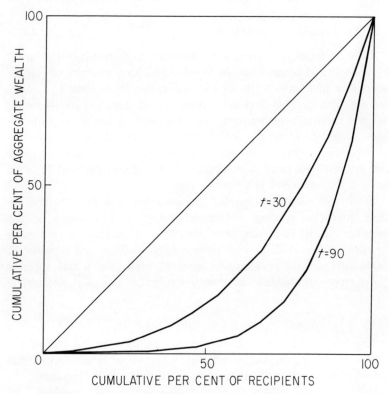

Figure 18-12. Lorenz distribution of accumulated wealth after *t* years with uniform rate of contribution.

tances: the time span becomes, not a part of a man's life, but part of the life of a family. We may illustrate this effect of the lengthening time span by the Lorenz curves in Figure 18-12. Each is based upon a uniform annual rate of saving and 8 per cent interest (reinvested). The coefficient of inequality rises from 0.47 to 0.71 as the period lengthens from 30 to 90 years.

The arithmetic of compound interest is inexorable, and if something did not interfere, ancient fortunes would be incredibly large.[23] That they are not—that not even a dynasty's wealth accumulates without end—is due to the heavy hand of chance. Sooner or later every accumulating fortune encounters one or both of the obstacles to unending growth:

1. A stupid or profligate heir;
2. An unstable environment.

Some societies have sought to preserve large fortunes (in land) by a system of bequest known as primogeniture, whereby the oldest male heir had only a life estate in the family fortune and could not diminish it. This device has more or less thwarted foolish heirs, but not rapacious governments or swarming armies. Some families have sought to avoid the losses that are inevitable in any one line of investment by diversification, but of course they then must allow the incompetent heirs to contribute to the diversification. It is an ancient fortune which is a century old.

From this viewpoint capital accumulation is a gamble, and we may invoke in analogy a famous theorem in probability on the gambler's ruin. If a man possessing A dollars plays a fair game of coin tossing with a rival possessing B dollars, and receives \$1 each time a head appears and loses \$1 each time a tail appears, the former's probability of eventual ruin (= loss of A dollars) is

$$\frac{B}{A+B},$$

which approaches unity if the "rival" consists of the rest of the world (so B is essentially infinite).[24] Sooner or later there occurs an adverse run of luck sufficient to destroy any finite fortune.

[23] For those who like such games, the following are the 1964 accumulations of \$1 invested at the death of the man in question:

MAN	1 %	5 %
Adam Smith (1790)	\$5.65	\$486.29
Caesar (44 B.C.)	471×10^6	33.645×10^{40}

The sum of $\$33.6 \times 10^{40}$ is essentially incomprehensible: Archimedes assumed that a grain of sand had a diameter less than 1/40 of a finger-breadth, and argued that a sphere the size of "the" universe would contain only 10^{51} grains. [*The Works of Archimedes*, ed. by T. L. Heath (New York: Dover), pp. 221–32.]

[24] The results are similar if the coin is not fair; see W. Feller, *An Introduction to Probability Theory and Its Applications*, 2nd ed. (New York: Wiley, 1957), pp. 292 ff.

The existence of heirs is also a determinant of the distribution of inherited wealth. The family line will eventually die out, or multiply to such an extent that the division of property by inheritance will diffuse the wealth. Indeed it is certain that one of these results will eventually take place—which one it will be depends upon the average number of children.[25] Lotka has shown that the probability that a family name will vanish (no male heirs) was about 0.48 in the first generation of children, and 0.82 ultimately, with American birth data of the 1920's, and that as an approximation, this latter probability equals the reciprocal of the average number of boys per family-generation.[26]

Inheritance and Saving

It is useful to form some notion of the comparative shares of inheritance and saving by living persons in the present accumulated wealth. It is useful because it will give us some estimate of the extent to which the distribution of property income will be affected by a highly progressive estate tax such as we now have.

The separation of the two sources, however, is very difficult. The procedure that has been used here is to estimate the accumulated savings of living persons, and compare this with total wealth, so inheritance is a residual. Even this crude approach involves extremely elaborate calculations, in which the following are the major steps:

1. Take as the basic group those living in 1960.
2. Find (from labor participation tables) the number at work at each date in the past—back to 1890.
3. Calculate their labor earnings, assuming they earn the average wage per worker in the economy.
4. Assume that they save 10 per cent of their labor income plus interest on savings.
5. Assume that once they retire from the labor force, they purchase an annuity with their accumulated savings.

The calculations are performed separately for males and females, at interest rates of 4 and 8 per cent, and with wage incomes corrected and uncorrected for price level changes.

[25] See Feller, *Probability*, pp. 224 ff.
[26] *Théorie analytique des associations biologiques,* II (Paris: Actualités Scientifiquies et Industrielles, 1939), pp. 123 ff.

The resulting wealth estimates are reported in Table 18–2. They are expressed as income received so as to be comparable to national income data. It will be observed that income on accumulated savings ranges from 26 to several hundred per cent of total property income. What can we say of the plausibility of the alternative assumptions which yield this wide array of results?

The "deflated" savings—savings of each year converted to 1960 prices—are the appropriate measure if savings are in fact put in real assets whose values rise with the general price level. Some savings take a fixed-income form (bonds, for example), but even here there are presumably offsetting gains, in the event of inflation, to borrowers.

Table 18–2

Share of Noninherited Wealth in Property Income, 1960*
(per cent)

INCOME TYPE	INTEREST RATE	
	4%	*8%*
1960 Dollars	40.9	242.9
Current Dollars	26.1	124.0

* Property income was $90.1 billion, the sum of rents, corporate income, net interest, and an arbitrarily estimated one-third of entrepreneurial income.

The interest rate, however, is a much more difficult number to establish. The rate we wish is of course the *realized* rate on all investments over long periods, not the rates promised by borrowers. The realized rate takes account of all failures of enterprises, in financial terms, and more basically all unsuccessful investments in physical terms. Since inherited wealth cannot be negative, our procedures suggest that the realized interest rate could not have been more than perhaps 6 per cent.

In short, inherited wealth may be a very modest share of present wealth or it may be a dominant share. Our analysis must remain uncertain with respect to level, but we can at least indicate the effects of certain obvious variables. The share of inherited wealth in a society will be lower

—the higher the rate of increase of wage income
—the longer the average working life of a person
—the higher the rate of saving from income
—the higher the yield of investment.

CONCLUSION

The strongly empirical tone of this chapter is of course due to the absence of a developed theory of the size distribution of income. But even these fragmentary calculations should support the following thesis: the distribution of income by size is influenced by most of the basic economic magnitudes of the economy (the rates of wages and of interest, the rate of growth of income, and so forth) and by many of the demographic characteristics of the population (age structure, family size, birth and death rates, and the like). A change in the degree of inequality of income can arise for reasons unrelated to the dispersion of earnings of individuals, or changes in their amounts or shares of property income. A fuller analysis would show, I believe, that educational and medical advances have probably had a larger influence upon the distribution of income than many public policies directed to changing the distribution.

RECOMMENDED READINGS

Friedman, M., "Choice, Chance, and the Personal Distribution of Income," *Journal of Political Economy,* **61** (1953), 277–290.

Kravis, I., *The Structure of Income,* Philadelphia: University of Pennsylvania, 1962.

PROBLEMS

1. The argument in the text implies that the distribution of earnings within an occupation will be more unequal,

   (a) The more unequal the ages of the workers.

   (b) The more unequal the formal educational training of the workers.

   (c) The more varied the sizes of communities in which they live.

Test these implications with the data on earnings in the population census.

2. The members of an occupation each have an average income of $5,000 but in any one year it exceeds or falls short of this average by a random amount. For (say) 25 individuals, calculate incomes in one year and an average of two years, where the random component is determined by coin flipping. More precisely, in each year the income of an individual exceeds $5,000 by $300 for each consecutive heads, and falls short by $300 for each consecutive tails. Plot the Lorenz curves and calculate the coefficient of inequality.

3. Why is the distribution of interest and dividend income much more unequal than that of rental income?

appendix A

Fundamental Quantitative Relationships

The study of quantitative economic phenomena requires certain tools of analysis. For some purposes arithmetic is adequate, but there are several objections to complete reliance on numerical illustrations. Tables of numerical data are relatively awkward and laborious to handle. Moreover, arithmetical examples may lead to generalizations which are correct only in special cases. As an example, John Stuart Mill argued, on the basis of a numerical illustration that a certain type of agricultural improvement (one that raised the marginal productivity curve of capital by a fixed percentage) always led to a fall of land rents. This was wrong: it is easy to set up a numerical example where an improvement of this type will increase land rents.[1] Finally, particular numerical examples may raise theoretical difficulties which are essentially irrelevant or unimportant, and thus unnecessarily complicate the theory. Here Böhm-Bawerk provides an example: he established the clumsy and misleading theory of "marginal pairs" of buyers and sellers to circumvent difficulties arising out of his choice of indivisible commodities (horses) to illustrate the theory of values.[2]

---

[1] See John Stuart Mill, *Principles of Political Economy,* Ashley edition (New York: Longmans, Green, 1929), pp. 717–18. The error is discussed by A. Marshall, *Principles of Economics,* (London: Macmillan, 1922), pp. 836–37.

[2] See Eugen von Böhm-Bawerk, *Positive Theory of Capital* (New York: Stechert, 1930), Bk. IV, Ch. 3. The theory is appraised by F. Y. Edgeworth, *Papers Relating to Political Economy* (London: Macmillan, 1925), Vol. I, 37–39. He characteristically observes that Böhm-Bawerk is "riding a one-horse illustration to death." Mill also supplies an example of this point; see J. Viner, *Studies in the Theory of International Trade* (New York: Harper, 1937), p. 541.

As a result of these weighty objections, the arithmetical method has yielded much ground to graphical analysis, and symbolic mathematical analysis (the infinitesimal calculus in particular) has increased in popularity. The preference for geometrical analysis is largely justified: graphs are relatively easy to handle, and yet they are adequate to derive very general theorems.

Economic quantities are generally treated as infinitely divisible, and economic relationships as continuously variable. Thus we assume that butter can take on *any* price (varying even by an infinitesimal fraction of a cent per pound) and that no matter how small the decrease in price, there will be some resulting increase in the quantity demanded. These assumptions are adopted in part for convenience—the analysis of discrete variation is more complicated than that of continuous variation.[3] But the chief defense is that the economic system displays great ingenuity in circumventing lumpiness of quantities because someone can usually gain by contriving divisibility.

Most of the necessary apparatus will be developed in this appendix; the nature of indifference curves is taken up at the appropriate points in Chapter 4. The important relations between total, average, and marginal quantities will be taken up twice, first with discrete numerical illustrations and then with continuous curves. The same propositions are true in both cases, but they are more difficult to prove in the latter case. Thereafter the relation between these quantities and the concept of elasticity will be developed.[4]

TOTAL, AVERAGE, AND MARGINAL QUANTITIES: THE DISCRETE CASE

The present discussion will center about the important relationships between a total quantity, an average quantity, and a marginal quantity. This exposition will be presented in terms of specific problems—for example, the product secured by cultivating land with increasing intensiveness—but every conclusion here established will

[3] For example, with continuous variation we can say that the price will be such that the quantity supplied *equals* the quantity demanded. With discrete variation, we must say: the price will lie between the highest price at which the quantity demanded exceeds the quantity supplied and the lowest price at which the quantity supplied exceeds the quantity demanded.

[4] See mathematical notes 1 and 2 in Appendix B.

be equally applicable to any other quantitative problem which involves these types of quantities.

Table A–1 is the basis for the immediate discussion: it presents the product (in bushels) secured by cultivating a hypothetical farm with a variable amount of labor. The definitions now to be given are illustrated from Table A–1.

Table A–1

UNITS OF LABOR	TOTAL PRODUCT (*bushels*)	AVERAGE PRODUCT (*bushels*)	MARGINAL PRODUCT (*bushels*)
0	0	0	0
1	5	5	5
2	13	$6\frac{1}{2}$	8
3	23	$7\frac{2}{3}$	10
4	38	$9\frac{1}{2}$	15
5	50	10	12
6	60	10	10
7	68	$9\frac{5}{7}$	8
8	75	$9\frac{3}{8}$	7
9	81	9	6
10	86	$8\frac{3}{5}$	5
11	90	$8\frac{2}{11}$	4

1. *Total Product.* The total product of a given number of units of labor, when applied to this hypothetical farm, is obviously the number of bushels of product secured by the assistance of that quantity of labor. The second column of Table A–1 gives the various total products.

2. *Average Product.* The average product of n units of labor is the total product of n units divided by n. The third column of Table A–1 gives the average products.

3. *Marginal Product.* The basic definition of marginal product is

$$\frac{\text{change in total product}}{\text{corresponding change in quantity of labor}}.$$

As a special case of this definition, we may define the marginal product of n units of labor as the increase in total product which results from increasing the quantity of labor from $(n-1)$ units to *n* units. Restating this second definition: marginal product is the amount added to total product by the addition of one more unit of labor.[5] The last column of Table A–1 gives the marginal products.

> *Proposition 1:* The sum of the first *n* marginal products is equal to the total product of *n* units of labor.

This proposition follows directly from the definition of the marginal product of labor, for

marginal product of 1 unit = amount added by first unit

marginal product of 2 units = amount added by second unit

marginal produce of 3 units = amount added by third unit

. . . . .

marginal product of *n* units = amount added by *n*th unit

If these marginal products (the left sides of these equations) are added, they equal the total product of *n* units of labor (the right sides of the equations). Table A–1 illustrates the proposition: the sum of the marginal products of the first six units of labor is $5 + 8 + 10 + 15 + 12 + 10 = 60$.

> *Proposition 2:* When the average product is increasing, marginal product is greater than average product.[6]

This proposition is illustrated in Table A–1, where average product is increasing up to the fifth unit of labor, and the marginal product is greater than the average product for the first five units of labor. (The equality of average and marginal product when one unit of labor is employed is due to the discrete nature of the data.)

---

[5] A common definition of *marginal product* is that it is the amount added to total product by the *last* unit of labor. Two implications of such a statement are undesirable: (1) It is the task of economics to discover which is the last unit; this is not known until the end of the analysis. (2) This definition may suggest that the "last" unit of labor differs from the preceding units either in its nature or its duties. But all units of labor are assumed to be homogeneous: all are equally efficient, and all do equally important things. It is for that reason that the text speaks of the marginal produce of n units, not the marginal produce of the nth unit.

[6] Note that it is not said that the marginal product increases when the average increases, for this is not necessarily true.

Proposition 3: When average product is decreasing, marginal product is less than average product.

This proposition is also illustrated in Table A–1, where average product declines after the sixth unit of labor is applied, and marginal product is less than average product.

Proposition 4: When average product is at a maximum, marginal product equals average product.

This is a corollary of Propositions 2 and 3, for if average product is at a maximum, at that point it is neither increasing nor decreasing, and therefore marginal product is neither greater than nor less than average product. This point is illustrated in Table A–1 at six units of labor. (In the table, average product has two maximums of 10; this again is due to the discrete nature of the data.)

Proposition 5: The addition of a fixed sum to all the total products will have no effect on the marginal products.

In order to verify this proposition, the reader can add, say, 10 bushels to each of the total products in the second column of Table A–1. It is obvious that the difference between any two total products (that is, the marginal product) will not be affected.

TOTAL, AVERAGE, AND MARGINAL QUANTITIES: THE CONTINUOUS CASE

If the variable quantity of labor is measured along the horizontal axis (or axis of abscissas) and the total product is measured along the vertical axis (or axis of ordinates), it is possible to represent the data in Table A–1 by rectangles such as those in Figure A-1. The area of each rectangle corresponding to the excess product over the preceding total product is indicated in Figure A-1; these areas are by definition the marginal products. They are plotted separately in Figure A-2.

Proposition 1: The area under the marginal product curve up to any point is equal to the height of the total product curve at that point.

The area enclosed by n rectangles in Figure A-2 is equal to the area of the nth rectangle in Figure A-1; this is true by construction.

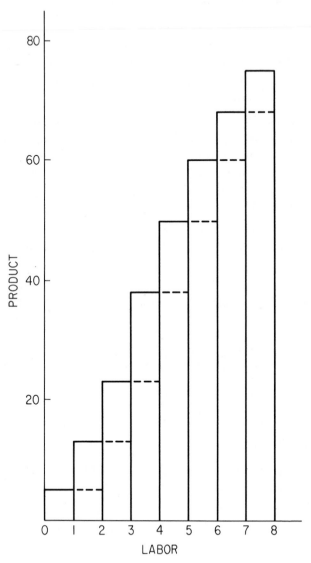

Figure A-1

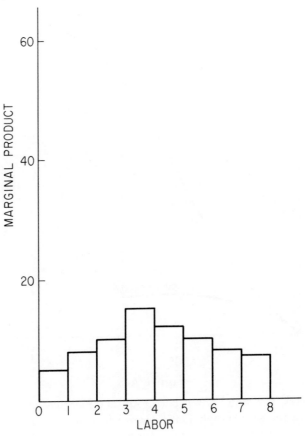

Figure A-2

If these rectangles are sufficiently narrow (that is, if the units of labor are made small enough), continuous curves are approximated. Such curves are shown in Figure A-3, where at any quantity (A) of labor, the area under the marginal product curve ($0BA$) is equal to the height of the total product curve (AC). Figures **A-1** and **A-2** suggest that this is true; it cannot be proved by elementary methods.

It should be noticed that the dimensions of total and marginal (and average) quantities are not the same. The dimension of total product is (say) bushels, those of marginal and average product

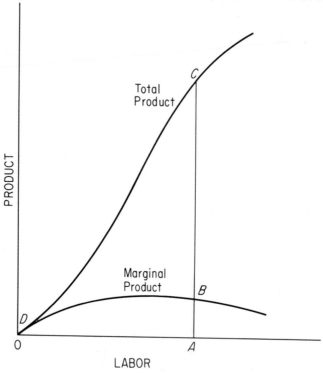

Figure A-3

are bushels per man.[7] Often both total and marginal quantities are drawn in the same graph (as in those which follow), and although this practice is convenient it is also loose: the vertical scale represents different things for the two curves. To convert the average or marginal *rates* into a total quantity, it is necessary to multiply by the variable factor: this is why a given total product can be represented in a graph by both the height of one curve and the area under another.[8]

[7] Both may be per year, but the time dimension is common to all and does not present any difficulties here.

[8] This is also why the marginal product curve can lie above the total product curve. An arithmetical example may be helpful:

LABOR	TOTAL PRODUCT	MARGINAL PRODUCT PER UNIT OF LABOR
0.	0	—
0.25	1.0	4.0
0.50	2.1	4.4
0.75	3.3	4.8
1.00	4.6	5.2
1.25	6.0	5.6

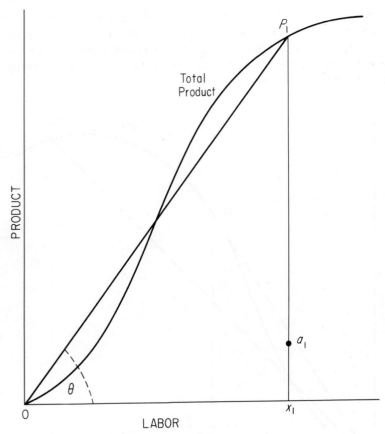

Figure A-4

In order to prove the next four propositions, it is necessary to explain the derivation of the average and marginal product curves from the total product curve. The average product is derived in Figure A-4. For any quantity of labor (x_1), there is a corresponding total product (P_1). Average product is the latter divided by the former, or P_1/x_1. This ratio can be computed by measuring P_1 and x_1; it is found to be x_1a_1.

This example emphasizes the fact that the size of the marginal product depends upon the size of the increments of labor; just as the inclination of a hill depends upon the particular points on its side that we compare. As the increments approach zero, the marginal product approaches a limiting value, and this limiting value is "the" marginal product drawn in the graphs for the continuous case.

Average product is computed for three different quantities of labor in Figure A-5; x_1a_1, x_2a_2, and x_3a_3 are these average products. If enough of these average products are computed, we can connect the points a_1, a_2, a_3, and so on, by a continuous average product curve, as is done in Figure A-5.

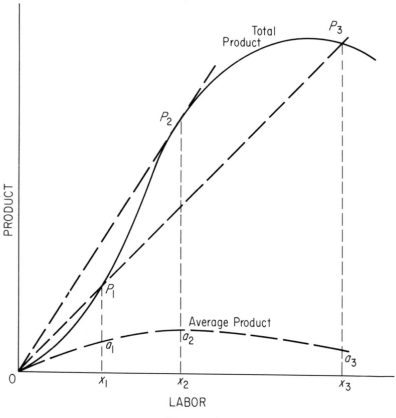

Figure A-5

The line drawn from the origin to the total product curve forms an angle θ at the origin (see Figure A-4). The size of this angle can be measured by P_1/x_1, or conversely P_1/x_1 can be measured by θ; the two increase and decrease together.[9] This relationship is useful; it is possible to determine whether the average product increases or decreases between two quantities of labor (x_1 and x_2,

---

[9] This amounts only to the trigonometrical definition, $\tan \theta = P_1/x_1$.

for instance) merely by ascertaining whether the angle formed by OP_1 is larger or smaller than the angle formed by OP_2. It is now possible to discover where average product reaches a maximum; x_2 in Figure A-5 yields the maximum average product, since no other line can be drawn from the total product curve to the origin to form a larger angle. This particular point (P_2) can be described more generally; average product is at a maximum at that quantity of labor where a straight line from the origin touches (or is tangent to) the total product curve.

The final task is the derivation of the marginal product curve from the total product curve. It is desirable to use the broad definition of the marginal product: marginal product is the change (increase) in total product divided by the change (increase) in the quantity of labor which brought it about.[10] In Figure A-6(a) the

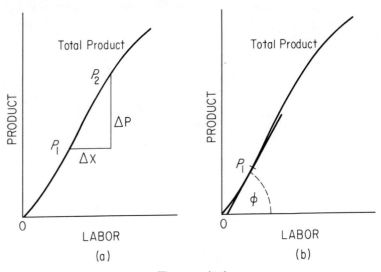

Figure A-6

increase of labor is labeled Δx (where Δx means a small amount of x), and the resulting increase of product is labeled ΔP (where ΔP is the corresponding small increase of P). The marginal product is then $\Delta P / \Delta x$.

As the increment of labor is made smaller and smaller, P_2 ap-

[10] Marginal product is properly defined in terms of change rather than increase, since the total product may decrease when the quantity of labor increases, in which case the marginal product is negative.

proaches P_1—see Figure A-6(a)—and the line joining them becomes the tangent of the total product curve at P_1—see Figure A-6(b). It was observed in connection with the discussion of the average product curve that θ is a measure of P_1/x_1; similarly, ϕ is a measure of $\Delta P/\Delta x$. We have reached the conclusion: marginal product is equal to the slope of the total product curve, and the marginal product will increase (or decrease) with the increase (or decrease) of the angle which the tangent to the total product curve forms with the horizontal axis.

Proposition 2: When the average product is increasing, marginal product is greater than average product.

This proposition is demonstrable for continuous curves by means of Figure A-7. Up to x_2 of labor, the average product of labor is increasing. At any point x_1 in this region erect a perpendicular line

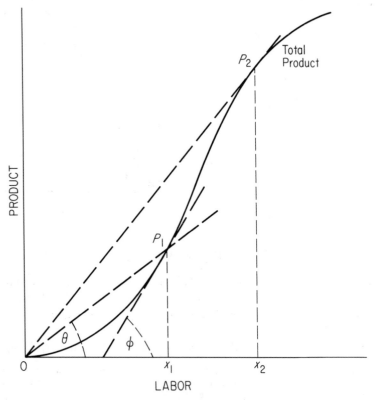

Figure A-7

to P_1. Then the average product is measured by θ, where θ is the angle formed by $0P_1$. The marginal product is measured by ϕ, where ϕ is the angle formed by the line tangent to the total product curve at P_1. Since ϕ is greater than θ up to x_2, marginal product is greater than average product up to x_2.

Proposition 3: When average product is decreasing, marginal product is less than average product.

Figure A-8 serves to prove this proposition. Beyond P_2 the average product is decreasing, and it is evident that in this region θ

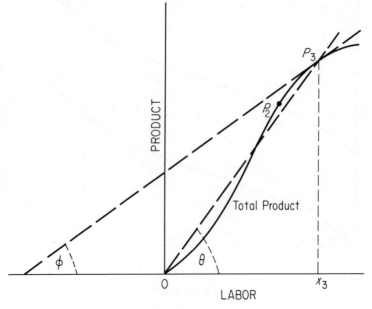

Figure A-8

is larger than ϕ. Therefore average product is greater than marginal product.[11]

Proposition 4: When average product is at a maximum, marginal product equals average product.

At the point where average product reaches a maximum, θ and ϕ coincide (see Figure A-5, for instance) and therefore average and marginal products are equal.

[11] If the total product is decreasing, marginal product becomes negative, and the proposition is still true.

Proposition 5: The addition of a fixed quantity to a total curve
will not affect its marginal curve.

For the demonstration of this proposition it is convenient to shift
to another example: total cost. In Figure A-9, *TVC* is total variable
cost, and *TC* is total cost; they differ by the constant amount of

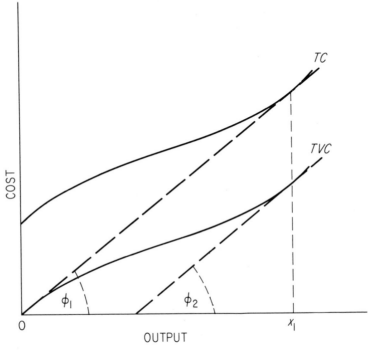

Figure A-9

total fixed cost. At every output the two curves are therefore equi-
distant, so their slopes are equal $(\phi_1 = \phi_2)$. Hence marginal cost
is the same for both curves.

THE CONCEPT OF ELASTICITY

The particular dimensions in which economic quantities are
quoted are arbitrary. It is permissible to say that sugar is 10 cents
a pound, or that it is one one-billionth of a billion dollars per 10
pounds. A wage rate may be per hour or per year (but we would

suspect deception if it were per three workers). This may seem triv-
ial and obvious, but it is easily forgotten. A dozen large books could
quickly be filled with quotations to the effect that the prices of
various commodities are high or low. Often the reader can supply
the frame of reference, usually the price at some time in the past,
but often he cannot. Thus even the great Marshall made the meaningless statement, "The price of house-room . . . has never fallen
very low . . . ."[12] Nor would it be difficult to find many quotations
to the effect that the output of a commodity was small or large,
or that it was scarce or plentiful. All such statements involving
dimensions are meaningless without a frame of reference.

Nor are ratios free from this ambiguity. To say that labor is
scarce relative to land is equally meaningless: one may write the
ratio of 10 men to 5 acres as

$$\frac{20{,}000 \text{ man-hours}}{5 \text{ acres}} = 4000 \text{ man-hours per acre,}$$

or as

$$\frac{10 \text{ men}}{24{,}200 \text{ square yards}} = \frac{1}{2420} \text{ men per square yard.}$$

Again a frame of reference is necessary. Even pure ratios, like the
percentage of income spent on food, have no natural level, and to
refer to 20 per cent as low is arbitrary.

One natually objects to the implication that the frame of reference always be supplied. It seems enough to say, "The babysitter
wanted $10 an hour, which is a high wage" without adding "as
babysitters' wages used to go." But often the frame of reference
is not obvious: one is less likely to say "the wages of domestic
servants are extremely high" when she must add, "compared to
what they were when McKinley was President." Or that "there is
a shortage of housing" if one must add "not relative to the past,
but relative to the amount desired with postwar incomes at prewar
prices." I recommend specifying the frame of reference in all un-
obvious cases, in spite of the fact that the reader will no doubt
be able to find lapses in these pages; we are entitled to expect
each generation of economists to be more precise than their
predecessors.

[12] *Principles of Economics,* p. 107.

The notion of elasticity has been devised precisely with this problem of dimensions in mind and serves to avoid dimensional arbitrariness in a considerable range of problems. Consider the demand curve and schedule in Figure A-10 and Table A–2. The measurement of responsiveness of quantity to changes in price could be

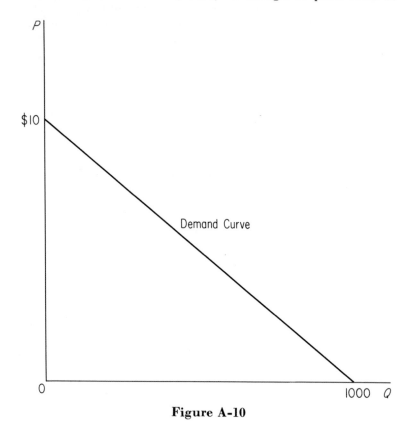

Figure A-10

measured by the slope of the demand curve: in this example a fall in price of $1 leads to an increase in quantity purchased of 100 units, so the

$$\text{slope} = \frac{\text{change in price}}{\text{change in quantity}} = -\frac{1}{100}.$$

By quoting the price in cents, however, we could make the slope = −1. The notion of elasticity, which was first popularized by

Table A–2

QUANTITY	PRICE
0	$10
100	9
200	8
300	7
400	6
500	5
600	4
700	3
800	2
900	1

Marshall, is independent of the units in which quantity and price are quoted.[13]

Elasticity at a Point

The fundamental definition of the elasticity of demand (the definition applies equally well to supply) is, if we denote elasticity by η,

$$\eta = \frac{\text{relative change in quantity}}{\text{corresponding relative change in price}},$$

when both of these changes are infinitesimally small. In symbols,

$$\eta = \frac{(\Delta q/q)}{(\Delta p/p)} = \frac{\Delta q}{\Delta p} \cdot \frac{p}{q},$$

where q = quantity, p = price, Δq = infinitesimal change in quantity, and Δp = infinitesimal change in price. This definition leads to a measure which is independent of the units in which quantities and prices are quoted. If we change price quotations from dollars to cents, both the price (p) and the change in price (Δp) are increased a hundredfold $(100\Delta p/100p)$, and of course the 100's cancel out, leaving the elasticity unchanged. Since the elasticity is an abstract number (having no dimensions), the elasticities of demand for various commodities can be compared. The reason for defining the elasticity in terms of infinitesimal changes of prices and quantities will be explained later.

[13] *Ibid.*, pp. 102–3*n*, 839–40.

Measurement of Elasticity at a Point

If a demand curve is known, the elasticity may be computed either symbolically or geometrically; the latter method will be used in the text.[14] The problem is to measure the elasticity of the demand

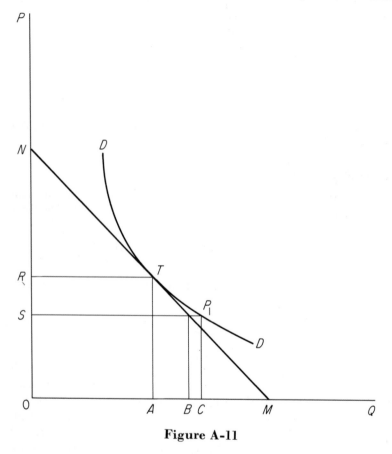

Figure A-11

curve, DD, in Figure A-11, at point T. First draw a line NM which touches (is tangent to) DD at T. If the price falls from OR to OS, the quantity increases from OA to OC. But if the price change is very small (that is, if P_1 is very close to T), OB will be approxi-

---

[14] See mathematical note 3 in Appendix B.

mately equal to $0C$. Turning now to our formula,

$$\eta = \frac{(\Delta q/q)}{(\Delta p/p)} = \frac{(AB/0A)}{(RS/0R)} = \frac{AB}{RS} \cdot \frac{0R}{0A}.$$

But by a well-known theorem on similar right triangles, $AB/RS = AM/R0$, so

$$\eta = \frac{AM}{R0} \cdot \frac{0R}{0A} = \frac{AM}{A0},$$

whence, finally, since $AM/A0 = TM/TN$,

$$\eta = \frac{TM}{TN}.$$

This is the measure of the elasticity of a demand curve at point T.

In the case of a demand curve, quantity increases when price decreases, and vice versa; so the changes are of opposite sign. The elasticity of demand is therefore negative. If the elasticity is -1, it is called *unitary* elasticity. If the elasticity is numerically greater than -1, for instance -2, the demand is called *elastic*. If the elasticity is numerically less than -1, for instance $-\frac{1}{2}$, the demand is *inelastic*.

Arc Elasticity

Until now the discussion of elasticity has been restricted to elasticity at a point; this limits the applicability of the concept to continuous curves and mathematical functions. But frequently data are secured for only a few prices and quantities. For example, it may be observed that when $5 is the price, 200 units of a commodity are purchased, and when $4 is the price, 300 units are purchased. What is the elasticity in this case?

The answer is that there is no single elasticity. The reason is explicable by means of Figure A-12. Points P_1 and P_2 are the two given sets of prices and quantities. It is clear that there are an infinite number of different curves on which these two points may lie, and these curves in general have different elasticities at P_1 and P_2.

Nevertheless, an approximation to the true point elasticity can be secured even in this case. The following tests are open: (1) trace the behavior of total receipts; (2) draw a freehand curve through

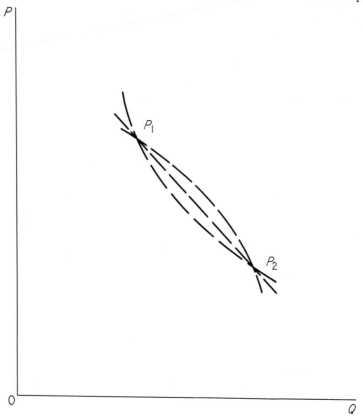

Figure A-12

the points or fit a curve by appropriate statistical methods, and then use the geometrical method; or finally, (3) define an arc elasticity to meet the problem.[15] A simple arc elasticity formula, equivalent to passing a line through the points and finding the point elasticity midway between the points, is as follows:

$$\eta = \frac{(q_0 - q_1)/(q_0 + q_1)}{(p_0 - p_1)/(p_0 + p_1)}$$

$$= \frac{q_0 - q_1}{q_0 + q_1} \cdot \frac{p_0 + p_1}{p_0 - p_1}.$$

[15] Only one such definition is given here; for a comprehensive treatment see R. G. D. Allen, "The Concept of Arc Elasticity of Demand," *Review of Economic Studies,* **1** (1934), 226–29.

where q_0, p_0 is one quantity and price, and q_1, p_1 is a second quantity and price. This measure is more accurate, the closer q_0 is to q_1. Applying it to our example:

$$\eta = \frac{(200 - 300)/(200 + 300)}{(5 - 4)/(5 + 4)} = \frac{-\frac{1}{5}}{\frac{1}{9}} = -1.8.$$

RELATIONS BETWEEN ELASTICITY AND TOTAL AND MARGINAL QUANTITIES

If the demand curve has an elasticity of unity at all points, the proportional changes in quantity and price are numerically equal and opposite in sign and exactly offset one another. Total receipts (quantity times price) therefore remain unchanged when price changes; this case is illustrated in Figure A-13A. The reader can

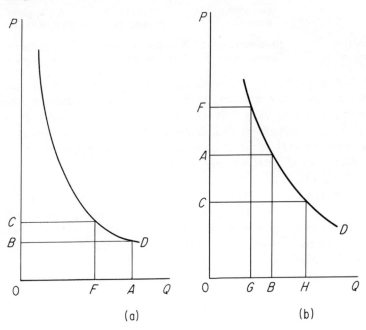

(a)   (b)

Figure A-13

readily verify for himself (by using the geometrical test) that the demand curve has an elasticity of unity at all points. At price $0B$, quantity $0A$ is taken, and total receipts are $0B \times 0A$. At price $0C$, quantity is $0F$, and total receipts are $0C \times 0F$ ($= 0B \times 0A$).

If the demand curve is inelastic, that is, elasticity is numerically less than unity, the relative change in quantity will be less than the relative change in price from which the quantity change results. This holds true of the demand curve in Figure A-13B, as can be verified by the geometrical test. In this case, if price falls from $0A$ to $0C$, total receipts fall from $0A \times 0B$ to $0C \times 0H$. If price rises from $0A$ to $0F$, total receipts rise from $0A \times 0B$ to $0F \times 0G$. If the demand curve is elastic, these conclusions are reversed. The relations are summarized in Table A–3.

Marginal revenue may be defined as the change in total revenue divided by the corresponding change in output. If output increases

Table A–3

	INELASTIC DEMAND	UNITARY ELASTICITY	ELASTIC DEMAND
Price rise	Receipts rise	Receipts unchanged	Receipts fall
Price fall	Receipts fall	Receipts unchanged	Receipts rise

by only one unit, then the resulting change of total revenue is marginal revenue. The relations between total and marginal revenue are identical with those between total and marginal product. It follows immediately from this definition that, given an increase in the quantity, (1) if total revenue increases, marginal revenue is positive; (2) if total revenue is unchanged, marginal revenue is zero; and (3) if total revenue decreases, marginal revenue is negative. On the basis of these relationships and by reference to Table A–3, it is possible to derive the following relationships, given a fall in price and increase in quantity: (1) if marginal revenue is positive, demand is elastic; (2) if marginal revenue is zero, demand has unit elasticity; and (3) if marginal revenue is negative, demand is inelastic.

As a matter of fact, the relationship between elasticity and marginal revenue is more precise. It can be shown that

$$\text{marginal revenue} = p(1 + 1/\eta).$$

The proof is based on Figure A-14, in which NM represents a straight line demand curve.[16] Select a point R on NM. Then desig-

---

[16] It is shown in mathematical note 1 in Appendix B that the formula holds also for nonlinear curves.

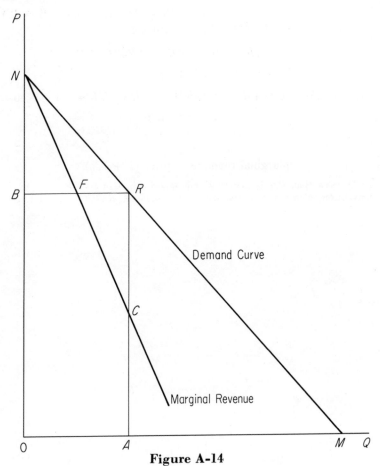

Figure A-14

nate the marginal revenue corresponding to output $0A$ by AC (which is still to be determined). The proof of the formula follows in two steps:

1. AC is determined by the fact that $BF = FR$. For total revenue = output times price, or $BRA0$, and total revenue also = the sum of the marginal receipts, or $NCA0$ (by Proposition 1). But if $BRA0 = NCA0$, then right triangles NFB and FRC are of equal area. Since angle NFB = angle RFC, therefore $BF = FR$.

2. Marginal revenue = $p(1 + 1/\eta)$, or $AC = AR(1 + 1/\eta)$. For

$AC = AR - CR$, and since $BN/BR = AR/AM$ and $CR = BN$, therefore $CR = (AR/AM)BR$. Substituting

$$AC = AR - CR = AR - AR(BR/AM)$$
$$= AR(1 - BR/AM).$$

But $BR/AM = 0A/AM = NR/RM = -RN/RM = -1/\eta,$[17] so

$$AC = AR(1 + 1/\eta)$$

or

$$\text{marginal revenue} = \text{price } (1 + 1/\eta).$$

[17] Observe that RN is negative and opposite in sign to NR. It is by this convention as to sign that the elasticity of demand, RM/RN, is negative.

appendix B

Mathematical Notes

1. (p. 314) The relationships between total (T), average (A), and marginal (M) quantities are as follows:

   (a) The discontinuous case. Let T be a function of X, so $T/X = A$, and $\Delta T / \Delta X = M$. If A is increasing,

   $$\frac{T + \Delta T}{X + \Delta X} - \frac{T}{X} > 0,$$

   $$X(T + \Delta T) > (X + \Delta X)T,$$

   $$\frac{\Delta T}{\Delta X} > \frac{T}{X}.$$

   M is also larger than the larger A (at rate $X + \Delta X$), for let

   $$\frac{\Delta T}{\Delta X} = \frac{kT}{X}, \qquad (k > 1)$$

   $$\frac{\Delta T}{\Delta X} = \frac{kT + \Delta T}{X + \Delta X} > \frac{T + \Delta T}{X + \Delta X}.$$

   Hence $M > A$ when A is increasing. Similarly, $M < A$ when A is decreasing, and $M = A$ when A is constant. Of course the sum of the M equals T, that is, $\Sigma M \Delta X = T$.

   (b) The continuous case. If the average is increasing,

   $$\frac{d(T/X)}{dX} > 0,$$

   $$\frac{XT' - T'}{X^2} > 0,$$

   $$T' > T/X = A.$$

The sum of the M equals T, for

$$\int T'dX = T.$$

Furthermore,

$$M = \frac{d(AX)}{dX} = A + X\frac{dA}{dX},$$

and the elasticity of X with respect to A (see Note 3) is

$$\eta_{XA} = \frac{dX}{dA} \cdot \frac{A}{X},$$

$$M = A\left(1 + \frac{1}{\eta}\right).$$

2. (p. 314) Students are often worried because propositions true of a continuous function do not hold precisely for (what appears to be) the same function when its independent variable takes on only discrete values. The simple answer is that the two functions are different even though they appear identical: the permissible values of the independent variable are part of the definition of a function. For example, consider the cost function, $C = a + bq + cq^2$, where q is output.

(a) If q is a continuous variable, marginal cost is

$$\frac{dC}{dq} = b + 2cq. \tag{1}$$

(b) If output varies only by increments of h, marginal cost is

$$\frac{C_{q+h} - C_q}{h} = \frac{a + b(q + h) + c(q + h)^2 - a - bq - cq^2}{h},$$

$$= b + 2cq + hc. \tag{2}$$

There is no basis for saying that one of these formulas for marginal cost is superior to the other; each pertains to a different function. One can say that (2) approaches (1) as h approaches zero, and that (1) is easier to manipulate than (2).

Part of the difficulty stems also from a lack of precision. It is noticed, for example, that in an arithmetical table, average cost will have one or two minimum points, and that marginal cost does not equal minimum average cost at its single minimum point (if there is only one) or at both of its minimum points (if there are two). But if there is a single minimum, say at q_0, then average cost is falling to q_0, and marginal cost must be less than average cost at q_0, and at the next output, $q_0 + h$, average cost is rising so marginal cost must be greater than average cost. If there are two minimum points, average cost falls to the first minimum, so marginal cost must be less than average cost at this minimum.

3. (p. 330) The elasticity of y with respect to x is

$$\eta_{yx} = \frac{dy}{dx} \cdot \frac{x}{y}.$$

If the elasticity is a constant, η, then

$$\frac{dy}{dx} \cdot \frac{x}{y} = \eta,$$

$$\int \frac{dy}{y} = \eta \int \frac{dx}{x},$$

$$\log y = \eta \log x + \log c,$$

$$y = cx^\eta.$$

Since the elasticity of y with respect to x is

$$\eta_{yx} = \frac{d(\log y)}{d(\log x)},$$

it is natural, although hardly inevitable, to take as the measure of arc elasticity,

$$\frac{\log y_0 - \log y_1}{\log x_0 - \log x_1} = \frac{\log (y_0/y_1)}{\log (x_0/x_1)},$$

where x_0, y_0, and x_1, y_1 are two pairs of observations. This formula fits a constant elasticity curve to the points, for if

$$y_0 x_0{}^\eta = k, \qquad y_1 x_1{}^\eta = k,$$

then

$$\log \frac{y_0}{y_1} = -\eta \log \frac{x_0}{x_1}.$$

The slope of the line connecting the two observed points is

$$\frac{y_0 - y_1}{x_0 - x_1},$$

and the coordinates of the point midway between the points are

$$\frac{y_0 + y_1}{2}, \qquad \frac{x_0 + x_1}{2},$$

so the arc formula given in the text represents the point elasticity at the midpoint of a straight line connecting the observed points.

4. (p. 42) We use two families. Let their demand functions be

$$q_1 = f(p_1), \qquad q_2 = g(p_2).$$

Then aggregate demand is $Q = q_1 + q_2$, and its price elasticity is

$$\eta_{Qp} = \frac{dQ}{dp} \cdot \frac{p}{Q} = (f' + g') \frac{p}{Q}$$

$$= \frac{q_1}{Q} \eta_1 + \frac{q_2}{Q} \eta_2,$$

where η_1 and η_2 are the individuals' demand elasticities. If individual 2 is at a distance t (measured in terms of the cost of transporting one unit of the commodity), his demand curve at the market is $f(p + t)$, and the market demand elasticity will generally depend upon t.

5. (p. 42) The demonstration will be given for two families, with the respective income functions,

$$e_1 = f(m_1), \qquad e_2 = g(m_2),$$

where e is the expenditure on a commodity and m is money income. Let $E = e_1 + e_2$, and $M = m_1 + m_2$. The market income elasticity is

$$\eta_{EM} = \frac{dE}{dM} \cdot \frac{M}{E}$$

$$= \frac{M d(e_1 + e_2)}{E d(m_1 + m_2)}.$$

If each family receives the same relative increase of income,

$$\frac{dm_1}{m_1} = \frac{dm_2}{m_2} \quad \text{or} \quad \frac{dm_1}{dm_2} = \frac{m_1}{m_2}.$$

Using this relation, we find that

$$\frac{d(e_1 + e_2)}{d(m_1 + m_2)} = \frac{de_1}{dm_1} \cdot \frac{m_1}{M} + \frac{de_2}{dm_2} \cdot \frac{m_2}{M},$$

$$= \frac{e_1}{M} \eta_1 + \frac{e_2}{M} \eta_2,$$

where η_1 and η_2 are the individual families' income elasticities. Substituting into the definition of the aggregate income elasticity,

$$\eta_{EM} = \frac{e_1}{E} \eta_1 + \frac{e_2}{E} \eta_2.$$

6. (p. 52) The relationship between the marginal rate of substitution and marginal utility is as follows. Let $U = \phi(x,y)$ be the utility function, so ϕ_x is the marginal utility of X. The equation of the indifference curves is $U = $ constant, whence $\phi_x \, dx + \phi_y \, dy = 0$, or

$$S_{yx} = -\frac{dy}{dx} = \frac{\phi_x}{\phi_y}.$$

Diminishing marginal utility ($\phi_{xx} < 0$, $\phi_{yy} < 0$) is not identical with convex indifference curves. The condition of convexity is

$$\frac{d(S_{yx})}{dx} < 0,$$

or

$$\frac{d(\phi_x/\phi_y)}{dx} = \frac{\phi_y \phi_{xx} + \phi_y \phi_{xy} \dfrac{dy}{dx} - \phi_x \phi_{xy} - \phi_x \phi_{yy} \dfrac{dy}{dx}}{\phi_y{}^2} < 0,$$

$$= \frac{\phi_y{}^2 \phi_{xx} - 2\phi_x \phi_y \phi_{xy} + \phi_x{}^2 \phi_{yy}}{\phi_y{}^3} < 0.$$

Hence diminishing marginal utility does not imply convexity, for ϕ_{xy} may be negative (once a favorite definition of a relationship of substitution between x and y), nor does convexity imply diminishing marginal utility, for ϕ_{xy} may be positive.

7. (p. 90) Let the output of r firms be Q, and that of the $(r + 1)$st firm q. The market demand curve will be

$$Q + q = \mathfrak{F}(p),$$

so

$$\frac{dq}{dp} = \mathfrak{F}'(p) - \frac{dQ}{dp},$$

and

$$\frac{dq}{dp} \cdot \frac{p}{q} = \frac{p\mathfrak{F}'(p)}{Q + q} \cdot \frac{Q + q}{q} - \frac{dQ}{dp} \cdot \frac{p}{Q} \cdot \frac{Q}{q},$$

or

$$\eta_{qp} = \frac{Q + q}{q}\, \eta_{Q+q,p} - \frac{Q}{q}\, \eta_{Qp},$$

where the first elasticity is that of demand for the output of the $(r + 1)$st firm, the second is the market price elasticity, and the third is the elasticity of supply of the r firms. If we take $Q = rq$,

$$\eta_{qp} = (r + 1)\eta_{Q+q,p} - r\eta_{Qp}.$$

8. (p. 116) If $P = f(A,B)$ is the production function, the increment of product resulting from an increment of each input is

$$\Delta P = f(A + \Delta A, B + \Delta B) - f(A, B).$$

In a Taylor expansion,

$$\Delta P = \Delta A\, \frac{\partial f}{\partial A} + \Delta B\, \frac{\partial f}{\partial B}$$
$$+ \frac{1}{2}\left\{ (\Delta A)^2\, \frac{\partial^2 f}{\partial A^2} + 2(\Delta A) \cdot (\Delta B)\, \frac{\partial^2 f}{\partial A\, \partial B} \right.$$
$$\left. + (\Delta B)^2\, \frac{\partial^2 f}{\partial B^2} \right\} + \cdots .$$

We define the marginal product of A as $\partial f/\partial A$. If ΔA and ΔB are sufficiently small, then

$$dP = \frac{\partial f}{\partial A}\, dA + \frac{\partial f}{\partial B}\, dB,$$

approximately, and the effect of variation in B on the marginal product of A,

$$\frac{\partial^2 f}{\partial A\, \partial B}\, dB,$$

is of negligible magnitude.

9. (p. 126) Constant returns to scale implies a homogeneous production function of the first degree. On this assumption,

$$P = \phi(A,B),$$

and

$$mP = \phi(mA,mB),$$

and by Euler's theorem,

$$P \equiv A\phi_a + B\phi_b.$$

Then if one average product, say that of A, is increasing, we know that

$$\phi_a > P/A,$$

or

$$A\phi_a > P,$$

so necessarily ϕ_b is negative. If there is increasing returns to scale but still homogeneity, so

$$m^k P = \phi(mA,mB), \qquad k > 1$$

then

$$kP \equiv A\phi_a + B\phi_b,$$

and a rising average product of one productive service no longer implies necessarily that the marginal product of the other service is negative.

10. (p. 198) The income and substitution effects can be written as

$$\frac{\partial x_1}{\partial p_1} = \left(\frac{\partial x_1}{\partial p_1}\right)_{u=\text{constant}} - x_1\left(\frac{\partial x_1}{\partial M}\right)_{p=\text{constant}},$$

where M is money income. The first term on the right is the movement along an indifference curve and the second term is the income effect. One may also write the Slutsky equation as

$$\frac{\partial x_2}{\partial p_1} + x_1\frac{\partial x_2}{\partial M} = \frac{\partial x_1}{\partial p_2} + x_2\frac{\partial x_1}{\partial M},$$

If this is converted into elasticities, we get

$$\frac{x_2}{p_1}\eta_{21} + \frac{x_1 x_2}{M}\eta_{2M} = \frac{x_1}{p_2}\eta_{12} + \frac{x_1 x_2}{M}\eta_{1M}.$$

Then, if we may assume either negligible income elasticities or, what is more probable in this context, that the terms involving income elasticities are approximately equal, we get

$$x_2 p_2 \eta_{21} = x_1 p_1 \eta_{12}.$$

[See H. Schultz, *Theory and Measurement of Demand* (Chicago: University of Chicago Press, 1938), Ch. 1, and J. M. Henderson and R. E. Quandt, *Microeconomic Theory* (New York: McGraw-Hill, 1958), Ch. 2.]

11. (p. 227) Let the excess of aggregate profits above the competitive level be π_t in period t, for an entrant of given size. If he enters and thereafter shares in the increase in demand, which grows at the rate θ, let us assume that profits also grow at this rate, so

$$\pi_t = \pi_0 e^{\theta t}.$$

If the interest rate is ρ, the present value of aggregate excess profits are

$$V = \pi_0 \int_0^\infty e^{\theta t} e^{-\rho t} \, dt,$$

$$= \frac{\pi_0}{\rho - \theta},$$

if $\theta < \rho$. (If $\theta \geq \rho$, the present value is infinite, and no positive current profit rate will discourage entry.) The elasticity of V with respect to π_0 is $+1$, whereas the elasticity of V with respect to θ is

$$\frac{dV}{d\theta} \cdot \frac{\theta}{V} = \frac{\theta}{\rho - \theta},$$

which is greater than unity if $\theta > \rho/2$. If π declines over time, as one would normally expect, its relative importance becomes all the smaller.

12. (p. 229) Let the industry demand be $p = f(q)$ or $q = g(p)$, and the cost function of each duopolist, $\phi(q_i)$.

    (a) *The Cournot solution*. The profits of a duopolist are

$$\pi_i = p q_i - \phi(q_i) = q_i f(q_i + q_j) - \phi(q_i).$$

For this to be a maximum,

$$\frac{d\pi_i}{dq_i} = f + q_i f' \left(1 + \frac{dq_j}{dq_i} \right) - \phi'(q_i) = 0.$$

Cournot assumed that $dq_j/dq_i = 0$, so

$$p + q_i \cdot \frac{dp}{dq} = \phi'(q_i).$$

This is sometimes called i's reaction curve: it indicates the value of q_i which will maximize π_i for a given q_j. Solving the two duopolists' reaction curves simultaneously yields the solution. (b) *The Bertrand solution.* Suppose the two duopolists are selling at the same price, p; then the profits of duopolist i are

$$\frac{pg(p)}{2} - \phi\left(\frac{g(p)}{2}\right).$$

Should he cut his price by some small amount δ, his profits become

$$(p - \delta)g(p - \delta) - \phi[g(p - \delta)].$$

It is commonly stated that this process of price cutting continues until price reaches marginal cost. Test this statement arithmetically or algebraically for the case where marginal cost is positively sloping.

(c) *The Edgeworth solution.* Edgeworth assumed that no buyer would deal with both sellers. It would seem more reasonable to assume that each buyer purchases in the same proportions from each seller. This is equivalent to assuming that some sort of arbitrage leads to a single price. Then the demand curve of all buyers is

$$q = g\left(\frac{q_1 p_1 + q_2 p_2}{q_1 + q_2}\right).$$

For price reductions, the Bertrand theory holds. For price increases, a duopolist has the above demand curve *minus* the quantity the rival will supply at the price he is currently quoting (that is, the quantity such that his marginal cost equals this price).

13. (p. 240) Let $x = \phi(a,b)$ be the production function, so the profits of the firm are

$$\pi = p_x \phi(a,b) - ap_a - bp_b.$$

The necessary conditions for maximum profits are

$$p_x \phi_a = p_a,$$
$$p_x \phi_b = p_b.$$

The sufficient conditions for a maximum are $\phi_{aa} < 0$, $\phi_{bb} < 0$, and $\phi_{aa}\phi_{bb} > \phi_{ab}^2$. Differentiate the necessary conditions with respect to p_a, holding p_b and p_x constant, to get:

$$p_x\left(\phi_{aa}\frac{\partial a}{\partial p_a} + \phi_{ab}\frac{\partial b}{\partial p_a}\right) = 1,$$

$$p_x\left(\phi_{ab}\frac{\partial a}{\partial p_a} + \phi_{bb}\frac{\partial b}{\partial p_a}\right) = 0,$$

whence

$$\frac{\partial a}{\partial p_a} = \frac{\phi_{bb}}{p_x(\phi_{aa}\phi_{bb} - \phi_{ab}^2)}.$$

From the sufficient conditions it follows that the slope of the demand curve for the productive service is negative. The value of the marginal product of A is $p_a = p_x\phi_a$, and if we differentiate this expression with respect to p_a, holding b and p_x constant, we get

$$\frac{\partial a}{\partial p_a} = \frac{1}{p_x\phi_{aa}}.$$

This slope is smaller in numerical value than that of the demand curve of the productive service. Note that both slopes are taken with respect to the price axis.

[For a comprehensive analysis of the demand for a factor of production, see J. L. Mosak, "Interrelations of Production, Price, and Derived Demand," *Journal of Political Economy*, **46** (1938), 761–87.]

14. (p. 242) J. R. Hicks presented the formula for derived demand in his *The Theory of Wages* (London: Macmillan 1935), p. 242. On the assumption of constant returns to scale and competition, it becomes

$$\eta_{ap_a} = -\frac{\sigma(\eta_{bp_b} - \eta_{xp_x}) - k\eta_{bp_b}(\eta_{xp_x} + \sigma)}{\eta_{bp_b} - \eta_{xp_x} + k(\eta_{xp_x} + \sigma)}$$

where

$\eta_{ap_a} =$ the demand elasticity for productive service a,

$\eta_{bp_b} =$ the supply elasticity of productive service b,

$\eta_{xp_x} =$ the demand elasticity for the product,

$\sigma =$ elasticity of substitution, taken positively—that is,

$$= \frac{d(a/b)}{a/b} \Big/ \frac{d(p_b/p_a)}{p_a/p_b}$$

$k = ap_a/qp_x.$

The rules are obtained by differentiating partially with respect to these variables. Note that, unlike Hicks' original version, η_{ap_a} and η_{xp_x} are given the conventional definitions which make them negative.

15. (p. 293) Let the cumulative percentage of recipients with incomes less than m_i be p_i, and let their cumulative percentage of aggregate income be q_i. Then the Lorenz curve has the equation, $q_i = f(p_i)$. If the incomes are reported in classes, let r_i be the percentage of recipients in income class i (whose maximum income is m_i). Then the area under the Lorenz curve is the sum of the areas of the polygons:

$$\frac{0 + q_1}{2}\, r_1,$$

$$\frac{q_1 + q_2}{2}\, r_2,$$

$$\cdot \quad \cdot \quad \cdot$$

$$\frac{q_n + q_{n-1}}{2}\, r_n,$$

or

$$\tfrac{1}{2}\Sigma(q_i + q_{i-1})r_i.$$

The manipulation of Lorenz curves may be illustrated for the simplest form of distribution, the so-called rectangular distribution where the N income recipients are equally spaced between incomes a and b. Then

$$p_i = \frac{1}{N} \int_a^t \frac{N}{b-a}\, dx = \frac{t-a}{b-a},$$

$$q_i = \frac{\displaystyle\int_a^t \frac{N}{b-a}\, x dx}{\displaystyle\int_a^b \frac{N}{b-a}\, x dx} = \frac{t^2 - a^2}{b^2 - a^2}.$$

Eliminating the parameter t, we obtain the equation of the Lorenz curve,

$$q_i = \frac{p_i^2(b-a) + 2ap_i}{b+a}.$$

The area under the Lorenz curve is

$$\int_0^1 q_i dp = \frac{b + 2a}{3(b + a)}.$$

The area under the line of equality is $\frac{1}{2}$, so the index of inequality is

$$\frac{\frac{1}{2} - \frac{b + 2a}{3(b + a)}}{1/2} = \frac{b - a}{3(b + a)}.$$

If $a = 0$, the index is $\frac{1}{3}$. The student may wish to show that the slope of the Lorenz curve is $+1$ at the mean income.

Index

Ability, and earnings, 291 f.
Adaptability, 129 f.
Advertising, 200 ff.
Agricultural protection, 187 ff.
Alchian, A., 73n, 83, 172, 174
Allen, R. G. D., 65n, 332n
Allocation of resources, 14 ff.
Alternative cost, 105 ff.
Arc elasticity, 331, 339
Archimedes, 308n
Average cost, shiftiness of, 140

Bailey, Martin, 279n
Bain, J. S., 228
Balance of processes, 161
Barnett, H. J., 255
Barriers to entry, 220 ff.
Baumol, W. J., 154n
Becker, G., 263n, 267n, 273n
Bertrand, J., 229, 345
Böhm-Bawerk, Eugen von, 313n
Bronfenbrenner, M., 242n, 246
Bruford, W. H., 9n

Budget line, 53 ff.
Bury, J. B., 19

Capacity, 156 f.
Capital
  definition, 275
  and investment, 284 f.
Cartel, 230 ff.
Christmas fund, 57 f.
Coase, Ronald, 111n, 119, 171n,
  174
Cobb-Douglas function, 151
Coefficient of variation, 294
Competition, 87 ff.
Competitive equilibrium, 176 f.
Complements, 31
Composition of output, 12 ff.
Conscription, 106
Constant returns to scale, 149 ff.
Consumer
  behavior, 21 ff.
  sovereignty, 14
Consumer's surplus, 78 ff.